BVDDHAM SARANAM
GACCHĀMI,
DHAMMAM SARANAM
GACCHĀMI,
SANGHAM SARANAM
GACCHĀMI.

THE GOSPEL
OF BUDDHA

COMPILED FROM ANCIENT RECORDS

BY

PAUL CARUS

ILLUSTRATED

BY

O. KOPETZKY

CHICAGO AND LONDON

THE OPEN COURT PUBLISHING COMPANY

1915

PREFACE.

THIS booklet needs no preface for those who are familiar with the sacred books of Buddhism, which have been made accessible to the Western world by the indefatigable zeal and industry of scholars like Beal, Bigandet, Bühler, Burnouf, Childers, Alexander Csoma, Rhys Davids, Dutoit, Eitel, Fausböll, Foucaux, Francke, Edmund Hardy, Spence Hardy, Hodgson, Charles R. Lanman, F. Max Müller, Karl Eugen Neumann, Oldenberg, Pischel, Schiefner, Senart, Seidenstücker, Bhikkhu Nyānatiloka, D. M. Strong, Henry Clarke Warren, Wassiljew, Weber, Windisch, Winternitz &c. To those not familiar with the subject it may be stated that the bulk of its contents is derived from the old Buddhist canon. Many passages, and indeed the most important ones, are literally copied in translations from the original texts. Some are rendered rather freely in order to make them intelligible to the present generation; others have been rearranged; and still others are abbreviated. Besides the three introductory and the three concluding chapters there are only a few purely original additions, which, however, are neither mere literary embellishments nor deviations from Buddhist doctrines. Wherever the compiler has admitted modernization he has done so with due consideration and always in the spirit of a legitimate development. Additions and modifications contain nothing but ideas for which prototypes can be found somewhere among the traditions of Buddhism, and have been introduced as elucidations of its main principles.

The best evidence that this book characterizes the spirit of Buddhism correctly can be found in the welcome it has received throughout the entire Buddhist world. It has even been officially introduced in Buddhist schools and temples of Japan and Ceylon. Soon after the appearance of the first edition of 1894 the Right Rev. Shaku Soyen, a prominent Buddhist abbot of Kamakura, Japan, had a Japanese translation made by Teitaro Suzuki, and soon afterwards a Chinese version was made by Mr. Ohara of Otzu, the talented editor of a Buddhist periodical, who in the meantime has unfortunately met with a premature death. In 1895 the Open Court Publishing Company brought out a German edition by E. F. L. Gauss, and Dr. L. de Milloué, the curator of the Musée Guimet, of Paris, followed with a French translation. Dr. Federigo Rodriguez has translated the book into Spanish and Felix Orth into Dutch. The privilege of translating the book into Russian, Czechic, Italian, also into Siamese and other Oriental tongues has been granted, but of these latter the publishers have received only a version in the Urdu language, a dialect of eastern India.

Inasmuch as twelve editions of the *Gospel of Buddha* have been exhausted and the plates are worn out, the publishers have decided to bring out an *édition de luxe* and have engaged Miss Olga Kopetzky, of Munich, to supply illustrations. The artist has undertaken the task methodically and with great zeal. She has studied in the Ajanta caves the Buddhist paintings and sculptures and other monuments of Gandhāra. Thus the drawings faithfully reflect the spirit of the classical period of Buddhist art.

For those who want to trace the Buddhism of this book to its fountainhead, a table of reference has been added, which indicates as briefly as possible the main sources of the various chapters and points out the parallelisms with Western thought, especially in the Christian Gospels.

*　　　*　　　*

Buddhism, like Christianity, is split up into innumerable sects, and these sects not infrequently cling to their sectarian tenets as being the main and most indispensable features of their religion. The present book follows none of the sectarian doctrines, but takes an ideal position upon which all true Buddhists may stand as upon common ground. Thus the arrangement into a harmonious and systematic form is the main original feature of this Gospel of Buddha. Considering the bulk of the various details of the Buddhist canon, however, it must be regarded as a mere compilation, and the aim of the compiler has been to treat his material in about the same way as he thinks that the author of the Fourth Gospel of the New Testament utilized the accounts of the life of Jesus of Nazareth. He has ventured to present the data of the Buddha's life in the light of their religio-philosophical importance; he has cut out most of their apocryphal adornments, especially those in which the Northern traditions abound, yet he did not deem it wise to shrink from preserving the marvellous that appears in the old records, whenever its moral seemed to justify its mention; he only pruned away the exuberance of wonder which delights in relating the most incredible things, apparently put on to impress while in fact they can only tire. Miracles have ceased to be a religious test; yet the belief in the miraculous powers of the Master still bears witness to the holy awe of the first disciples and reflects their religious enthusiasm.

Lest the fundamental idea of the Buddha's doctrines be misunderstood, the reader is warned to take the term "self" in the sense in which the Buddha uses it. The "self" of man translates the word *ātman* which can be and has been understood, even in the Buddhist canon, in a sense to which the Buddha would never have made any objection. The Buddha denies the existence of a "self" as it was commonly understood in his time; he does not deny man's mentality, his spiritual constitution, the importance of his personality, in a word, his soul. But he does deny the mysterious ego-entity, the *ātman*, in the sense of a kind of soul-monad which by some schools was supposed to reside behind or within man's bodily and psychical activity as a distinct being, a kind of thing-in-itself, and a metaphysical agent assumed to be the soul.

Buddhism is monistic. It claims that man's soul does not consist of two things, of an *ātman* (self) and of a *manas* (mind or thoughts), but that there is one reality, our thoughts, our mind or *manas*, and this *manas* constitutes the soul. Man's thoughts, if anything, are his self, and there is no *ātman*, no additional and separate "self" besides. Accordingly, the translation of *ātman* by "soul", which would imply that the Buddha denied the existence of the soul, is extremely misleading.

Representative Buddhists, of different schools and of various countries, acknowledge the correctness of the view here taken, and we emphasize especially the assent of Southern Buddhists because they have preserved the tradition most faithfully and are very punctilious in the statement of doctrinal points.

"*The Buddhist*, the Organ of the Southern Church of Buddhism," writes in a review of *The Gospel of Buddha*:

"The eminent feature of the work is its grasp of the difficult subject and the clear enunciation of the doctrine of the most puzzling problem of *ātman*, as taught in Buddhism. So far as we have examined the question of *ātman* ourselves from the works of the Southern canon, the view taken by Dr. Paul Carus is accurate, and we venture to think that it is not opposed to the doctrine of Northern Buddhism."

This *ātman*-superstition, so common not only in India, but all over the world, corresponds to man's habitual egotism in practical life. Both are illusions growing out of the same root, which is the vanity of worldliness, inducing man to believe that the purpose of his life lies in his self. The Buddha proposes to cut off entirely all thought of self, so that it will no longer bear fruit. Thus Nirvāna is an ideal state, in which man's soul, after being cleansed from all selfishness, hatred and lust, has become a habitation of the truth, teaching him to distrust the allurements of pleasure and to confine all his energies to attending to the duties of life.

The Buddha's doctrine is not negativism. An investigation of the nature of man's soul shows that, while there is no ātman or ego-entity, the very being of man consists in his karma, his deeds, and his karma remains untouched by death and continues to live. Thus, by denying the existence of that which appears to be our soul and for the destruction of which in death we tremble, the Buddha actually opens (as he expresses it himself) the door of immortality to mankind; and here lies the corner-stone of his ethics and also of the comfort as well as the enthusiasm which his religion imparts. Any one who does not see the positive aspect of Buddhism, will be unable to understand how it could exercise such a powerful influence upon millions and millions of people.

The present volume is not designed to contribute to the solution of historical problems. The compiler has studied his subject as well as he could under the circumstances, but he does not intend here to offer a scientific production. Nor is this book an attempt at popularizing the Buddhist religious writings, nor at presenting them in a poetic shape. If this *Gospel of Buddha* helps people to comprehend Buddhism better, and if in its simple style it impresses the reader with the poetic grandeur of the Buddha's personality, these effects must be counted as incidental; its main purpose lies deeper still. The present book has been written to set the reader thinking on the religious problems of to-day. It sketches the picture of a religious leader of the remote past with the view of making it bear upon the living present and become a factor in the formation of the future.

*   *   *

It is a remarkable fact that the two greatest religions of the world, Christianity and Buddhism, present so many striking coincidences in the philosophical basis as well as in the ethical applications of their faith, while their modes of systematizing them in dogmas are radically different; and it is difficult to understand why these agreements should have caused animosity, instead of creating sentiments of friendship and good-will. Why should not Christians say with Prof. F. Max Müller: "If I do find in certain Buddhist works doctrines identically the same as in Christianity, so far from being frightened, I feel delighted, for surely truth is not the less true because it is believed by the majority of the human race."

The main trouble arises from a wrong conception of Christianity. There are many Christians who assume that Christianity alone is in the possession of truth and that man could not, in the natural way of his moral evolution, have obtained that nobler conception of life which enjoins the practice of a universal good-will towards both friends and enemies. This narrow view of Christianity is refuted by the mere existence of Buddhism.

Must we add that the lamentable exclusiveness that prevails in many Christian churches, is not based upon Scriptural teachings, but upon a wrong metaphysics?

All the essential moral truths of Christianity, especially the principle of a universal love, of the eradication of hatred, are in our opinion deeply rooted in the nature of things, and do not, as is often assumed, stand in contradiction to the cosmic order of the world. Further, some doctrines of the constitution of existence have been formulated by the church in certain symbols, and since these symbols contain contradictions and come in conflict with science, the educated classes are estranged from religion. Now, Buddhism is a religion which knows of no supernatural revelation, and proclaims doctrines that require no other argument than the "come and see." The Buddha bases his religion solely upon man's knowledge of the nature of things, upon provable truth. Thus, we trust that a comparison of Christianity with Buddhism will be a great help to distinguish in both religions the essential from the accidental, the eternal from the transient, the truth from the allegory in which it has found its symbolic expression. We are anxious to press the necessity of discriminating between the symbol and its meaning, between dogma and religion, between metaphysical theories and statements of fact, between man-made formulas and eternal truth. And this is the spirit in which we offer this book to the public, cherishing the hope that it will help to develop in Christianity not less than in Buddhism the cosmic religion of truth.

The strength as well as the weakness of original Buddhism lies in its philosophical character, which enabled a thinker, but not the masses, to understand the dispensation of the moral law that pervades the world. As such, the original Buddhism has been called by Buddhists the little vessel of salvation, or Hīnayāna; for it is comparable to a small boat on which a man may cross the stream of worldliness, so as to reach the shore of Nirvāna. Following the spirit of a missionary propaganda, so natural to religious men who are earnest in their convictions, later Buddhists popularized the Buddha's doctrines and made them accessible to the multitudes. It is true that they admitted many mythical and even fantastic notions, but they succeeded nevertheless in bringing its moral truths home to the people who could but incompletely grasp the philosophical meaning of the Buddha's religion. They constructed, as they called it, a large vessel of salvation, the Mahāyāna, in which the multitudes would find room and could be safely carried over. Although the Mahāyāna unquestionably has its shortcomings, it must not be condemned offhand, for it serves its purpose. Without regarding it as the final stage of the religious development of the nations among which it prevails, we must concede that it resulted from an adaptation to their condition and has accomplished much to educate them. The Mahāyāna is a step forward in so far as it changes a philosophy into a religion, and attempts to preach doctrines that were negatively expressed, in positive propositions.

Far from rejecting the religious zeal which gave rise to the Mahāyāna in Buddhism, we can still less join those who denounce Christianity on account of its dogmatology and mythological ingredients. Christianity has certainly had and still has a great mission in the evolution of mankind. It has succeeded in imbuing with the religion of charity and mercy the most powerful nations of the world, to whose spiritual needs it is especially adapted. It ex tends the blessings of universal good-will with the least possible amount of antagonism to the natural selfishness that is so strongly developed in the Western races. Christianity is *the religion of love made easy*. This is its advantage, which, however, is not without its drawbacks. Christianity teaches charity without dispelling the ego-illusion; and in this sense it surpasses even the Mahāyāna: it is still more adapted to the needs of multitudes than a large vessel fitted to carry over those who embark on it: it is comparable to a grand bridge, a Mahāsetu, on which a child who has no comprehension as yet of the nature of self can cross the stream of self-hood and worldly vanity.

A comparison of the many striking agreements between Christianity and Buddhism may prove fatal to sectarian conceptions of either religion, but will in the end help to mature our insight into the true significance of both. It will bring out a nobler faith which aspires to be the cosmic religion of universal truth.

Let us hope that this Gospel of Buddha will serve both Buddhists and Christians as a help to penetrate further into the spirit of their faith, so as to see its full height, length and breadth.

Above any Hīnayāna, Mahāyāna, and Mahāsetu is the Religion of Truth.

PAUL CARUS.

PRONUNCIATION.

Pronounce:

a as the Italian and German short *a*.

ā as *a* in f*a*ther.

e as *e* in *e*ight.

i as *i* in h*i*t.

ī as *i* in mach*i*ne.

o as *o* in h*o*me.

u as *oo* in good.

ū as *u* in r*u*mor.

ai as in *eye*.

au as *ow* in h*ow*.

ñ as *ny*.

jñ as *dny*.

ññ as *n-ny*.

ch as *ch* in *ch*urch.

cch as *ch-ch* in ri*ch* *ch*ance.

Note that *o* and *e* are always long.

s, j, y, and other letters, as usual in English words.

Double consonants are pronounced as two distinct sounds, e. g., *ka'm-ma*, not *kă'ma*.

The h after *p*, *b*, *k*, *g*, *t*, *d* is audible as in du*b* *h*im, be*g* *h*er, bric*k* *h*ouse, an*t* *h*ill. Pronounce Tat-hāgata, not Ta-thāgata.

To the average European it is difficult to catch, let alone to imitate, the difference of sound between dotted and non-dotted letters. All those who are desirous for information on this point must consult Sanskrit and Pāli grammars.

Lest the reader be unnecessarily bewildered with foreign-looking dots and signs, which after all are no help to him, all dotted t, d, m, n, and italicized *t*, *d*, *m*, *n* have been replaced in the text of the book by t, d, m, n, ñ, ññ, dotted ṛ and italicized *s* have been transcribed by ny, nny, ri, and sh, while the Glossary preserves the more exact transcription.

We did not follow the spelling of the *Sacred Books of the East*, where it must be misleading to the uninitiated, especially when they write italicized *K* to denote spelling of the English sound ch, and italicized *g* to denote j. Thus we write "rājā," not "rā*g*ā," and "Chunda," not "*K*unda."

TABLE OF CONTENTS.

INTRODUCTION.

PRINCE SIDDHATTHA BECOMES BUDDHA.

THE FOUNDATION OF THE KINGDOM OF RIGHTEOUSNESS.

CONSOLIDATION OF THE BUDDHA'S RELIGION.

THE TEACHER.

PARABLES AND STORIES.

THE LAST DAYS.

CONCLUSION.

„The Gospel of Buddha"
illustrated
by
O. Kopetzky.

INTRODUCTION.

I.

REJOICE!

REJOICE at the glad tidings! The Buddha, our Lord, has found the root of all evil; he has shown us the way of salvation.   1

The Buddha dispels the illusions of our mind and redeems us from the terror of death.   2

The Buddha, our Lord, brings comfort to the weary and sorrow-laden; he restores peace to those who are broken down under the burden of life. He gives courage to the weak when they would fain give up self-reliance and hope.   3

Ye that suffer from the tribulations of life, ye that have to struggle and endure, ye that yearn for a life of truth, rejoice at the glad tidings!   4

There is balm for the wounded, and there is bread for the hungry. There is water for the thirsty, and there is hope for the despairing. There is light for those in darkness, and there is inexhaustible blessing for the upright. 5

Heal your wounds, ye wounded, and eat your fill, ye hungry. Rest, ye weary, and ye who are thirsty quench your thirst. Look up to the light, ye that sit in darkness; be full of good cheer, ye that are forlorn. 6

Trust in truth, ye that love the truth, for the kingdom of righteousness is founded upon earth. The darkness of error is dispelled by the light of truth. We can see our way and take firm and certain steps. 7

The Buddha, our Lord, has revealed the truth. 8

The truth cures our diseases and redeems us from perdition; the truth strengthens us in life and in death; the truth alone can conquer the evils of error. 9

Rejoice at the glad tidings! 10

II.

SAMSĀRA AND NIRVĀNA.

Look about and contemplate life! 1

Everything is transient and nothing endures. There is birth and death, growth and decay; there is combination and separation. 2

The glory of the world is like a flower: it stands in full bloom in the morning and fades in the heat of the day. 3

Wherever you look, there is a rushing and a struggling, and an eager pursuit of pleasure. There is a panic flight from pain and death, and hot are the flames of burning desires. The world is vanity fair, full of changes and transformations. All is Samsāra. 4

Is there nothing permanent in the world? Is there in the universal turmoil no resting-place where our troubled heart can find peace? Is there nothing everlasting? 5

Oh, that we could have cessation of anxiety, that our burning desires would be extinguished! When shall the mind become tranquil and composed?   6

The Buddha, our Lord, was grieved at the ills of life. He saw the vanity of worldly happiness and sought salvation in the one thing that will not fade or perish, but will abide for ever and ever.   7

Ye who long for life, know that immortality is hidden in transiency. Ye who wish for happiness without the sting of regret, lead a life of righteousness. Ye who yearn for riches, receive treasures that are eternal. Truth is wealth, and a life of truth is happiness.   8

All compounds will be dissolved again, but the verities which determine all combinations and separations as laws of nature endure for ever and aye. Bodies fall to dust, but the truths of the mind will not be destroyed.   9

Truth knows neither birth nor death; it has no beginning and no end. Welcome the truth. The truth is the immortal part of mind.   10

Establish the truth in your mind, for the truth is the image of the eternal; it portrays the immutable; it reveals the everlasting; the truth gives unto mortals the boon of immortality.   11

The Buddha has proclaimed the truth; let the truth of the Buddha dwell in your hearts. Extinguish in yourselves every desire that antagonizes the Buddha, and in the perfection of your spiritual growth you will become like unto him.   12

That of your heart which cannot or will not develop into Buddha must perish, for it is mere illusion and unreal; it is the source of your error; it is the cause of your misery.   13

You attain to immortality by filling your minds with truth. Therefore, become like unto vessels fit to receive the Master's words. Cleanse yourselves of evil and sanctify your lives. There is no other way of reaching truth.   14

Learn to distinguish between Self and Truth. Self is the cause of selfishness and the source of evil; truth cleaves to no self; it is universal and leads to justice and righteousness. 15

Self, that which seems to those who love their self as their being, is not the eternal, the everlasting, the imperishable. Seek not self, but seek the truth. 16

If we liberate our souls from our petty selves, wish no ill to others, and become clear as a crystal diamond reflecting the light of truth, what a radiant picture will appear in us mirroring things as they are, without the admixture of burning desires, without the distortion of erroneous illusion, without the agitation of clinging and unrest. 17

Yet ye love self and will not abandon self-love. So be it, but then, verily, ye should learn to distinguish between the false self and the true self. The ego with all its egotism is the false self. It is an unreal illusion and a perishable combination. He only who identifies his self with the truth will attain Nirvāna; and he who has entered Nirvāna has attained Buddhahood; he has acquired the highest good; he has become eternal and immortal. 18

All compound things shall be dissolved again, worlds will break to pieces and our individualities will be scattered; but the words of the Buddha will remain for ever. 19

The extinction of self is salvation; the annihilation of self is the condition of enlightenment; the blotting out of self is Nirvāna. Happy is he who has ceased to live for pleasure and rests in the truth. Verily his composure and tranquillity of mind are the highest bliss. 20

Let us take our refuge in the Buddha, for he has found the everlasting in the transient. Let us take our refuge in that which is the immutable in the changes of existence. Let us take our refuge in the truth that is established through the enlightenment of the Buddha. Let us take our refuge in the community of those who seek the truth and endeavor to live in the truth. 21

4

TRUTH THE SAVIOUR.

The things of the world and its inhabitants are subject to change. They are combinations of elements that existed before, and all living creatures are what their past actions made them; for the law of cause and effect is uniform and without exception. 1

But in the changing things there is a constancy of law, and when the law is seen there is truth. The truth lies hidden in Samsāra as the permanent in its changes. 2

Truth desires to appear; truth longs to become conscious; truth strives to know itself. 3

There is truth in the stone, for the stone is here; and no power in the world, no god, no man, no demon, can destroy its existence. But the stone has no consciousness. 4

There is truth in the plant and its life can expand; the plant grows and blossoms and bears fruit. Its beauty is marvellous, but it has no consciousness. 5

There is truth in the animal; it moves about and perceives its surroundings; it distinguishes and learns to choose. There is consciousness, but it is not yet the consciousness of Truth. It is a consciousness of self only. 6

The consciousness of self dims the eyes of the mind and hides the truth. It is the origin of error, it is the source of illusion, it is the germ of evil. 7

Self begets selfishness. There is no evil but what flows from self. There is no wrong but what is done by the assertion of self. 8

Self is the beginning of all hatred, of iniquity and slander, of impudence and indecency, of theft and robbery, of oppression and bloodshed. Self is Māra, the tempter, the evildoer, the creator of mischief. 9

Self entices with pleasures. Self promises a fairy's paradise. Self is the veil of Māyā, the enchanter. But the pleasures of self are unreal, its paradisian labyrinth is the road to misery, and its fading beauty kindles the flames of desires that never can be satisfied. 10

Who shall deliver us from the power of self? Who shall save us from misery? Who shall restore us to a life of blessedness? 11

There is misery in the world of Samsāra; there is much misery and pain. But greater than all the misery is the bliss of truth. Truth gives peace to the yearning mind; it conquers error; it quenches the flames of desires; it leads to Nirvāna. 12

Blessed is he who has found the peace of Nirvāna. He is at rest in the struggles and tribulations of life; he is above all changes; he is above birth and death; he remains unaffected by the evils of life. 13

Blessed is he who has found enlightenment. He conquers, although he may be wounded; he is glorious and happy, although he may suffer; he is strong, although he may break down under the burden of his work; he is immortal, although he may die. The essence of his being is purity and goodness. 14

Blessed is he who has attained the sacred state of Buddhahood, for he is fit to work out the salvation of his fellow-beings. The truth has taken its abode in him. Perfect wisdom illumines his understanding, and righteousness ensouls the purpose of all his actions. 15

The truth is a living power for good, indestructible and invincible! Work the truth out in your mind, and spread it among mankind, for truth alone is the saviour from evil and misery. The Buddha has found the truth and the truth has been proclaimed by the Buddha! Blessed be the Buddha! 16

PRINCE SIDDHATTHA
BECOMES BUDDHA.

IV.

THE BODHISATTA'S BIRTH.

THERE was in Kapilavatthu a Sakya king, strong of purpose and reverenced by all men, a descendant of the Okkākas, who call themselves Gotama, and his name was Suddhodana or Pure-Rice.

His wife Māya-devī was beautiful as the water-lily and pure in mind as the

I

lotus. As the Queen of Heaven, she lived on earth, untainted by desire, and immaculate. 2

The king, her husband, honored her in her holiness, and the spirit of truth, glorious and strong in his wisdom like unto a white elephant, descended upon her. 3

When she knew that the hour of motherhood was near, she asked the king to send her home to her parents; and Suddhodana, anxious about his wife and the child she would bear him, willingly granted her request. 4

At Lumbinī there is a beautiful grove, and when Māyādevī passed through it the trees were one mass of fragrant flowers and many birds were warbling in their branches. The Queen, wishing to stroll through the shady walks, left her golden palanquin, and, when she reached the giant Sāla tree in the midst of the grove, felt that her hour had come. She took hold of a branch. Her attendants hung a curtain about her and retired. When the pain of travail came upon her, four pure-minded angels of the great Brahmā held out a golden net to receive the babe, who came forth from her right side like the rising sun bright and perfect. 5

The Brahma-angels took the child and placing him before the mother said: "Rejoice, O queen, a mighty son has been born unto thee." 6

At her couch stood an aged woman imploring the heavens to bless the child. 7

All the worlds were flooded with light. The blind received their sight by longing to see the coming glory of the Lord; the deaf and dumb spoke with one another of the good omens indicating the birth of the Buddha to be. The crooked became straight; the lame walked. All prisoners were freed from their chains and the fires of all the hells were extinguished. 8

No clouds gathered in the skies and the polluted streams became clear, whilst celestial music rang through the air and the angels rejoiced with gladness. With no selfish or partial joy but for the sake of the law they rejoiced, for creation engulfed in the ocean of pain was now to obtain release.   9

The cries of beasts were hushed; all malevolent beings received a loving heart, and peace reigned on earth. Māra, the evil one, alone was grieved and rejoiced not.   10

The Nāga kings, earnestly desiring to show their reverence for the most excellent law, as they had paid honor to former Buddhas, now went to greet the Bodhisatta. They scattered before him mandāra flowers, rejoicing with heartfelt joy to pay their religious homage.   11

The royal father, pondering the meaning of these signs, was now full of joy and now sore distressed.   12

The queen mother, beholding her child and the commotion which his birth created, felt in her timorous heart the pangs of doubt.   13

Now the rewas at that time in a grove near Lumbinī Asita, a rishi, leading the life of a hermit. He was a Brahman of dignified mien, famed not only for wisdom and scholarship, but also for his skill in the interpretation of signs. And the king invited him to see the royal babe.   14

The seer, beholding the prince, wept and sighed deeply. And when the king saw the tears of Asita he became alarmed and asked: "Why has the sight of my son caused thee grief and pain?"   15

But Asita's heart rejoiced, and, knowing the king's mind to be perplexed, he addressed him, saying: 16

"The king, like the moon when full, should feel great joy, for he has begotten a wondrously noble son.   17

"I do not worship Brahmā, but I worship this child; and the gods in the temples will descend from their places of honor to adore him.   18

"Banish all anxiety and doubt. The spiritual omens manifested indicate that the child now born will bring deliverance to the whole world.   19

"Recollecting that I myself am old, on that account I could not hold my tears; for now my end is coming on and I shall not see the glory of this babe. For this son of thine will rule the world.   20

"The wheel of empire will come to him. He will either be a king of kings to govern all the lands of the earth, or verily will become a Buddha. He is born for the sake of everything that lives.   21

"His pure teaching will be like the shore that receives the shipwrecked. His power of meditation will be like a cool lake; and all creatures parched with the drought of lust may freely drink thereof.   22

"On the fire of covetousness he will cause the cloud of his mercy to rise, so that the rain of the law may extinguish it. The heavy gates of despondency will he open, and give deliverance to all creatures ensnared in the self-entwined meshes of folly and ignorance.   23

"The king of the law has come forth to rescue from bondage all the poor, the miserable, the helpless."   24

When the royal parents heard Asita's words they rejoiced in their hearts and named their new-born infant Siddhattha, that is, "he who has accomplished his purpose."   25

And the queen said to her sister, Pajāpatī: "A mother who has borne a future Buddha will never give birth to another child. I shall soon leave this world, my husband, the king, and Siddhattha, my child. When I am gone, be thou a mother to him."   26

And Pajāpatī wept and promised.   27

When the queen had departed from the living, Pajāpatī took the boy Siddhattha and reared him. And as the light of the moon increases little by little, so the royal child grew from day to day in mind and in body; and truthfulness and love resided in his heart.   28

When a year had passed Suddhodana the king made Pajāpatī his queen and there was never a better stepmother than she.   29

V.

THE TIES OF LIFE.

When Siddhattha had grown to youth, his father desired to see him married, and he sent to all his kinsfolk, commanding them to bring their princesses that the prince might select one of them as his wife.   1

But the kinsfolk replied and said: "The prince is young and delicate; nor has he learned any of the sciences. He would not be able to maintain our daughter, and should there be war he would be unable to cope with the enemy." 2

The prince was not boisterous, but pensive in his nature. He loved to stay under the great jambu-tree in the garden of his father, and, observing the ways of the world, gave himself up to meditation.   3

And the prince said to his father: "Invite our kinsfolk that they may see me and put my strength to the test." And his father did as his son bade him.   4

When the kinsfolk came, and the people of the city Kapilavatthu had assembled to test the prowess and scholarship of the prince, he proved himself manly in all the exercises both of the body and of the mind, and there was no rival among the youths and men of India who could surpass him in any test, bodily or mental.   5

He replied to all the questions of the sages; but when he questioned them, even the wisest among them were silenced.   6

Then Siddhattha chose himself a wife. He selected Yasodharā, his cousin, the gentle daughter of the king of Koli. And Yasodharā was betrothed to the prince.   7

In their wedlock was born a son whom they named Rā-hula which means "fetter" or "tie", and King Suddhodana, glad that an heir was born to his son, said: 8

"The prince having begotten a son, will love him as I love the prince. This will be a strong tie to bind Sid-dhattha's heart to the interests of the world, and the king-dom of the Sakyas will remain under the sceptre of my descendants."   9

With no selfish aim, but regarding his child and the people at large, Siddhattha, the prince, attended to his re-ligious duties, bathing his body in the holy Ganges and cleansing his heart in the waters of the law. Even as men desire to give happiness to their children, so did he long to give peace to the world.   10

VI.

THE THREE WOES.

The palace which the king had given to the prince was resplendent with all the luxuries of India; for the king was anxious to see his son happy.   1

All sorrowful sights, all misery, and all knowledge of misery were kept away from Siddhattha, for the king de-sired that no troubles should come nigh him; he should not know that there was evil in the world.   2

But as the chained elephant longs for the wilds of the jungles, so the prince was eager to see the world, and he asked his father, the king, for permission to do so.   3

And Suddhodana ordered a jewel-fronted chariot with four stately horses to be held ready, and commanded the roads to be adorned where his son would pass.   4

The houses of the city were decorated with curtains and banners, and spectators arranged themselves on either side, eagerly gazing at the heir to the throne. Thus Siddhattha rode with Channa, his charioteer, through the streets of the city, and into a country watered by rivulets and covered with pleasant trees.   5

There by the wayside they met an old man with bent frame, wrinkled face and sorrowful brow, and the prince asked the charioteer: "Who is this? His head is white, his eyes are bleared, and his body is withered. He can barely support himself on his staff."   6

The charioteer, much embarrassed, hardly dared speak the truth. He said: "These are the symptoms of old age. This same man was once a suckling child, and as a youth full of sportive life; but now, as years have passed away, his beauty is gone and the strength of his life is wasted." 7

Siddhattha was greatly affected by the words of the charioteer, and he sighed because of the pain of old age. "What joy or pleasure can men take," he thought to himself, "when they know they must soon wither and pine away!" 8

And lo! while they were passing on, a sick man appeared on the way-side, gasping for breath, his body disfigured, convulsed and groaning with pain.   9

The prince asked his charioteer: "What kind of man is this?" And the charioteer replied and said: "This man is sick. The four elements of his body are confused and out of order. We are all subject to such conditions: the poor and the rich, the ignorant and the wise, all creatures that have bodies, are liable to the same calamity."   10

And Siddhattha was still more moved. All pleasures appeared stale to him, and he loathed the joys of life.   11

The charioteer sped the horses on to escape the dreary sight, when suddenly they were stopped in their fiery course.   12

Four persons passed by, carrying a corpse; and the prince, shuddering at the sight of a lifeless body, asked the charioteer: "What is this they carry? There are streamers and flower garlands; but the men that follow are overwhelmed with grief!"   13

The charioteer replied: "This is a dead man: his body is stark; his life is gone; his thoughts are still; his family and the friends who loved him now carry the corpse to the grave."   14

And the prince was full of awe and terror: "Is this the only dead man," he asked, "or does the world contain other instances?"   15

With a heavy heart the charioteer replied: "All over the world it is the same. He who begins life must end it. There is no escape from death."   16

With bated breath and stammering accents the prince exclaimed: "O worldly men! How fatal is your delusion! Inevitably your body will crumble to dust, yet carelessly, unheedingly, ye live on."   17

The charioteer observing the deep impression these sad sights had made on the prince, turned his horses and drove back to the city.   18

When they passed by the palaces of the nobility, Kisā Gotamī, a young princess and niece of the king, saw Siddhattha in his manliness and beauty, and, observing the thoughtfulness of his countenance, said: "Happy the father that begot thee, happy the mother that nursed thee, happy the wife that calls husband this lord so glorious."   19

The prince hearing this greeting, said: "Happy are they that have found deliverance. Longing for peace of mind, I shall seek the bliss of Nirvāna."   20

Then asked Kisā Gotamī: "How is Nirvāna attained?" The prince paused, and to him whose mind was estranged from wrong the answer came: "When the fire of lust is gone out, then Nirvāna is gained; when the fires of hatred and delusion are gone out, then Nirvāna is gained; when the troubles of mind, arising from blind credulity, and all other evils have ceased, then Nirvāna is gained!" Siddhattha

Ò. KOPETZKY

handed her his precious pearl necklace as a reward for the instruction she had given him, and having returned home looked with disdain upon the treasures of his palace. 21

His wife welcomed him and entreated him to tell her the cause of his grief. He said: "I see everywhere the impression of change; therefore, my heart is heavy. Men grow old, sicken, and die. That is enough to take away the zest of life." 22

The king, his father, hearing that the prince had become estranged from pleasure, was greatly overcome with sorrow and like a sword it pierced his heart. 23

VII.

THE BODHISATTA'S RENUNCIATION.

It was night. The prince found no rest on his soft pillow; he arose and went out into the garden. "Alas!" he cried, "all the world is full of darkness and ignorance; there is no one who knows how to cure the ills of existence." And he groaned with pain. 1

Siddhattha sat down beneath the great jambu-tree and gave himself to thought, pondering on life and death and the evils of decay. Concentrating his mind he became free from confusion. All low desires vanished from his heart and perfect tranquillity came over him. 2

In this state of ecstasy he saw with his mental eye all the misery and sorrow of the world; he saw the pains of pleasure and the inevitable certainty of death that hovers over every being; yet men are not awakened to the truth. And a deep compassion seized his heart. 3

While the prince was pondering on the problem of evil, he beheld with his mind's eye under the jambu-tree a lofty figure endowed with majesty, calm and dignified. "Whence comest thou, and who mayst thou be?" asked the prince. 4

In reply the vision said: "I am a samana. Troubled at the thought of old age, disease, and death I have left my home to seek the path of salvation. All things hasten to decay; only the truth abideth forever. Everything changes, and there is no permanency; yet the words of the Buddhas are immutable. I long for the happiness that does not decay; the treasure that will never perish; the life that knows of no beginning and no end. Therefore, I have destroyed all worldly thought. I have retired into an unfrequented dell to live in solitude; and, begging for food, I devote myself to the one thing needful." 5

Siddhattha asked: "Can peace be gained in this world of unrest? I am struck with the emptiness of pleasure and have become disgusted with lust. All oppresses me, and existence itself seems intolerable." 6

The samana replied: "Where heat is, there is also a possibility of cold; creatures subject to pain possess the faculty of pleasure; the origin of evil indicates that good can be developed. For these things are correlatives. Thus where there is much suffering, there will be much bliss, if thou but open thine eyes to behold it. Just as a man who has fallen into a heap of filth ought to seek the great pond of water covered with lotuses, which is near by: even so seek thou for the great deathless lake of Nirvāna to wash off the defilement of wrong. If the lake is not sought, it is not the fault of the lake. Even so when there is a blessed road leading the man held fast by wrong to the salvation of Nirvāna, if the road is not walked upon, it is not the fault of the road, but of the person. And when a man who is oppressed with sickness, there being a physician who can heal him, does not avail himself of the physician's help, that is not the fault of the physician. Even so when a man oppressed by the malady of wrong-doing does not seek the spiritual guide of enlightenment, that is no fault of the evil-destroying guide." 7

The prince listened to the noble words of his visitor and said: "Thou bringest good tidings, for now I know that my purpose will be accomplished. My father advises me to enjoy life and to undertake worldly duties, such as will bring honor to me and to our house. He tells me that I am too young still, that my pulse beats too full to lead a religious life." 8

The venerable figure shook his head and replied: "Thou shouldst know that for seeking a religious life no time can be inopportune." 9

A thrill of joy passed through Siddhattha's heart. "Now is the time to seek religion," he said; "now is the time to sever all ties that would prevent me from attaining perfect enlightenment; now is the time to wander into homelessness and, leading a mendicant's life, to find the path of deliverance." 10

The celestial messenger heard the resolution of Siddhattha with approval. 11

"Now, indeed," he added, "is the time to seek religion. Go, Siddhattha, and accomplish thy purpose. For thou art Bodhisatta, the Buddha-elect; thou art destined to enlighten the world. 12

"Thou art the Tathāgata, the great master, for thou wilt fulfil all righteousness and be Dharmarāja, the king of truth. Thou art Bhagavat, the Blessed One, for thou art called upon to become the saviour and redeemer of the world. 13

"Fulfil thou the perfection of truth. Though the thunderbolt descend upon thy head, yield thou never to the allurements that beguile men from the path of truth. As the sun at all seasons pursues his own course, nor ever goes on another, even so if thou forsake not the straight path of righteousness, thou shalt become a Buddha. 14

"Persevere in thy quest and thou shalt find what thou seekest. Pursue thy aim unswervingly and thou shalt gain the prize. Struggle earnestly and thou shalt conquer. The benediction of all deities, of all saints, of all that seek light is upon thee, and heavenly wisdom guides thy steps. Thou shalt be the Buddha, our Master, and our Lord; thou shalt enlighten the world and save mankind from perdition." 15

Having thus spoken, the vision vanished, and Siddhattha's heart was filled with peace. He said to himself: 16

"I have awakened to the truth and I am resolved to accomplish my purpose. I will sever all the ties that bind me to the world, and I will go out from my home to seek the way of salvation. 17

"The Buddhas are beings whose words cannot fail: there is no departure from truth in their speech. 18

"For as the fall of a stone thrown into the air, as the death of a mortal, as the sunrise at dawn, as the lion's roar when he leaves his lair, as the delivery of a woman with child, as all these things are sure and certain—even so the word of the Buddhas is sure and cannot fail. 19

"Verily I shall become a Buddha." 20

The prince returned to the bedroom of his wife to take a last farewell glance at those whom he dearly loved above all the treasures of the earth. He longed to take the infant once more into his arms and kiss him with a parting kiss. But the child lay in the arms of his mother, and the prince could not lift him without awakening both. 21

There Siddhattha stood gazing at his beautiful wife and his beloved son, and his heart grieved. The pain of parting overcame him powerfully. Although his mind was determined, so that nothing, be it good or evil, could shake his resolution, the tears flowed freely from his eyes, and it was beyond his power to check their stream. But the

O. Kopetzky.

prince tore himself away with a manly heart, suppressing his feelings but not extinguishing his memory.   22

The Bodhisatta mounted his noble steed Kanthaka, and when he left the palace, Māra stood in the gate and stopped him: "Depart not, O my Lord," exclaimed Māra. "In seven days from now the wheel of empire will appear, and will make thee sovereign over the four continents and the two thousand adjacent islands. Therefore, stay, my Lord."   23

The Bodhisatta replied: "Well do I know that the wheel of empire will appear to me; but it is not sovereignty that I desire. I will become a Buddha and make all the world shout for joy."   24

Thus Siddhattha, the prince, renounced power and worldly pleasures, gave up his kingdom, severed all ties, and went into homelessness. He rode out into the silent night, accompanied only by his faithful charioteer Channa.   25

Darkness lay upon the earth, but the stars shone brightly in the heavens.   26

VIII.

KING BIMBISĀRA.

Siddhattha had cut his waving hair and had exchanged his royal robe for a mean dress of the color of the ground. Having sent home Channa, the charioteer, together with the noble steed Kanthaka, to king Suddhodana to bear him the message that the prince had left the world, the Bodhisatta walked along on the highroad with a beggar's bowl in his hand.   I

Yet the majesty of his mind was ill-concealed under the poverty of his appearance. His erect gait betrayed his royal birth and his eyes beamed with a fervid zeal for truth.

The beauty of his youth was transfigured by holiness and surrounded his head like a halo. 2

All the people who saw this unusual sight gazed at him in wonder. Those who were in haste arrested their steps and looked back; and there was no one who did not pay him homage. 3

Having entered the city of Rājagaha, the prince went from house to house silently waiting till the poeple offered him food. Wherever the Blessed One came, the people gave him what they had; they bowed before him in humility and were filled with gratitude because he condescended to approach their homes. 4

Old and young people were moved and said: "This is a noble muni! His approach is bliss. What a great joy for us!" 5

And king Bimbisāra, noticing the commotion in the city, inquired the cause of it, and when he learned the news sent one of his attendants to observe the stranger. 6

Having heard that the muni must be a Sakya and of noble family, and that he had retired to the bank of a flowing river in the woods to eat the food in his bowl, the king was moved in his heart; he donned his royal robe, placed his golden crown upon his head and went out in the company of aged and wise counselors to meet his mysterious guest. 7

The king found the muni of the Sakya race seated under a tree. Contemplating the composure of his face and the gentleness of his deportment, Bimbisāra greeted him reverently and said: 8

"O samana, thy hands are fit to grasp the reins of an empire and should not hold a beggar's bowl. I am sorry to see thee wasting thy youth. Believing that thou art of royal descent, I invite thee to join me in the government of my country and share my royal power. Desire for power is becoming to the noble-minded, and wealth should not be despised. To grow rich and lose religion is not true gain. But he who possesses all three, power, wealth, and religion, enjoying them in discretion and with wisdom, him I call a great master." 9

The great Sakyamuni lifted his eyes and replied: 10 "Thou art known, O king, to be liberal and religious, and thy words are prudent. A kind man who makes good use of wealth is rightly said to possess a great treasure; but the miser who hoards up his riches will have no profit. 11

"Charity is rich in returns; charity is the greatest wealth, for though it scatters, it brings no repentance. 12

"I have severed all ties because I seek deliverance. How is it possible for me to return to the world? He who seeks religious truth, which is the highest treasure of all, must leave behind all that can concern him or draw away his attention, and must be bent upon that one goal alone. He must free his soul from covetousness and lust, and also from the desire for power. 13

"Indulge in lust but a little, and lust like a child will grow. Wield worldly power and you will be burdened with cares. 14

"Better than sovereignty over the earth, better than living in heaven, better than lordship over all the worlds, is the fruit of holiness. 15

"The Bodhisatta has recognized the illusory nature of wealth and will not take poison as food. 16

"Will a fish that has been baited still covet the hook, or an escaped bird love the net? 17

"Would a rabbit rescued from the serpent's mouth go back to be devoured? Would a man who has burnt his hand with a torch take up the torch after he had dropped it to the earth? Would a blind man who has recovered his sight desire to spoil his eyes again? 18

"The sick man suffering from fever seeks for a cooling medicine. Shall we advise him to drink that which will increase the fever? Shall we quench a fire by heaping fuel upon it? 19

"I pray thee, pity me not. Rather pity those who are burdened with the cares of royalty and the worry of great riches. They enjoy them in fear and trembling, for they are constantly threatened with a loss of those boons on whose possession their hearts are set, and when they die they cannot take along either their gold or the kingly diadem. 20

"My heart hankers after no vulgar profit, so I have put away my royal inheritance and prefer to be free from the burdens of life. 21

"Therefore, try not to entangle me in new relationships and duties, nor hinder me from completing the work I have begun. 22

"I regret to leave thee. But I will go to the sages who can teach me religion and so find the path on which we can escape evil. 23

"May thy country enjoy peace and prosperity, and may wisdom be shed upon thy rule like the brightness of the noon-day sun. May thy royal power be strong and may righteousness be the sceptre in thine hand." 24

The king, clasping his hands with reverence, bowed down before Sakyamuni and said: "Mayest thou obtain that which thou seekest, and when thou hast obtained it, come back, I pray thee, and receive me as thy disciple." 25

The Bodhisatta parted from the king in friendship and goodwill, and purposed in his heart to grant his request. 26

IX

THE BODHISATTA'S SEARCH.

Alāra and Uddaka were renowned as teachers among the Brahmans, and there was no one in those days who surpassed them in learning and philosophical knowledge.　　　　　　　　　　　　　　　　　　　　　1

The Bodhisatta went to them and sat at their feet. He listened to their doctrines of the ātman or self, which is the ego of the mind and the doer of all doings. He learned their views of the transmigration of souls and of the law of karma; how the souls of bad men had to suffer by being reborn in men of low caste, in animals, or in hell, while those who purified themselves by libations, by sacrifices, and by self-mortification would become kings, or Brahmans, or devas, so as to rise higher and higher in the grades of existence. He studied their incantations and offerings and the methods by which they attained deliverance of the ego from material existence in states of ecstasy.　　　　　　　　　　　　　　　　　　　　　2

Alāra said: "What is that self which perceives the actions of the five roots of mind, touch, smell, taste, sight, and hearing? What is that which is active in the two ways of motion, in the hands and in the feet? The problem of the soul appears in the expressions 'I say,' 'I know and perceive,' 'I come,' and 'I go' or 'I will stay here.' Thy soul is not thy body; it is not thy eye, not thy ear, not thy nose, not thy tongue, nor is it thy mind. The I is the one who feels the touch in thy body. The I is the smeller in the nose, the taster in the tongue, the seer in the eye, the hearer in the ear, and the thinker in the mind. The I moves thy hands and thy feet. The I is thy soul. Doubt in the existence of the soul is irreligious, and without discerning this truth there is no way of salvation. Deep speculation will easily involve the mind; it leads to confusion and unbelief; but a purification of the soul leads to the way of escape. True deliverance is reached by removing from the crowd and leading a hermit's life, depending entirely on alms for food. Putting away all desire and clearly recognizing the non-existence of matter, we reach a state of perfect emptiness. Here we find the condition of immaterial life. As the muñja grass when freed from its horny case, as a sword when drawn from its scabbard, or as the wild bird escaped from its prison, so the ego, liberating itself from all limitations, finds perfect release. This is true deliverance, but those only who will have deep faith will learn." 3

The Bodhisatta found no satisfaction in these teachings. He replied: "People are in bondage, because they have not yet removed the idea of the ego. 4

"The thing and its quality are different in our thought, but not in reality. Heat is different from fire in our thought, but you cannot remove heat from fire in reality. You say that you can remove the qualities and leave the thing, but if you think your theory to the end, you will find that this is not so. 5

"Is not man an organism of many aggregates? Are we not composed of various attributes? Man consists of the material form, of sensation, of thought, of dispositions, and, lastly, of understanding. That which men call the ego when they say '*I* am' is not an entity behind the attributes; it originates by their co-operation. There is mind; there is sensation and thought, and there is truth; and truth is mind when it walks in the path of righteousness. But there is no separate ego-soul outside or behind the thought of man. He who believes that the ego is a distinct being has no correct conception of things. The very search for the ātman is wrong; it is a wrong start and it will lead you in a false direction. 6

"How much confusion of thought comes from our interest in self, and from our vanity when thinking 'I am so great,' or 'I have done this wonderful deed?' The thought of thine ego stands between thy rational nature and truth; banish it, and then wilt thou see things as they are. He who thinks correctly will rid himself of ignorance and acquire wisdom. The ideas 'I am' and 'I shall be' or 'I shall not be' do not occur to a clear thinker. 7

"Moreover, if our ego remains, how can we attain true deliverance? If the ego is to be reborn in any of the three worlds, be it in hell, upon earth, or be it even in heaven, we shall meet again and again the same inevitable doom of sorrow. We shall remain chained to the wheel of individuality and shall be implicated in egotism and wrong. 8

"All combination is subject to separation, and we cannot escape birth, disease, old age, and death. Is this a final escape?" 9

Said Uddaka: "Consider the unity of things. Things are not their parts, yet they exist. The members and organs of thy body are not thine ego, but thine ego possesses all these parts. What, for instance, is the Ganges? Is the sand the Ganges? Is the water the Ganges? Is the hither bank the Ganges? Is the farther bank the Ganges? The Ganges is a mighty river and it possesses all these several qualities. Exactly so is our ego". 10

But the Bodhisatta replied: "Not so, sir! If we except the water, the sand, the hither bank and the farther bank, where can we find any Ganges? In the same way I observe the activities of man in their harmonious union, but there is no ground for an ego outside its parts." 11

The Brahman sage, however, insisted on the existence of the ego, saying: "The ego is the doer of our deeds. How can there be karma without a self as its performer? Do we not see around us the effects of karma? What makes men different in character, station, possessions, and fate? It is their karma, and karma includes merit and demerit. The transmigration of the soul is subject to its karma. We inherit from former existences the evil effects of our evil deeds and the good effects of our good deeds. If that were not so, how could we be different?" 12

The Tathāgata meditated deeply on the problems of transmigration and karma, and found the truth that lies in them. 13

"The doctrine of karma," he said, "is undeniable, but thy theory of the ego has no foundation. 14

"Like everything else in nature, the life of man is subject to the law of cause and effect. The present reaps what the past has sown, and the future is the product of the present. But there is no evidence of the existence of an immutable ego-being, of a self which remains the same and migrates from body to body. There is rebirth but no transmigration. 15

"Is not this individuality of mine a combination, material as well as mental? Is it not made up of qualities that sprang into being by a gradual evolution? The five roots of sense-perception in this organism have come from ancestors who performed these functions. The ideas which I think, came to me partly from others who thought them, and partly they rise from combinations of the ideas in my own mind. Those who have used the same sense-organs, and have thought the same ideas before I was composed into this individuality of mine are my previous existences; they are my ancestors as much as the *I* of yesterday is the father of the *I* of to-day, and the karma of my past deeds conditions the fate of my present existence. 16

"Supposing there were an ātman that performs the actions of the senses, then if the door of sight were torn down and the eye plucked out, that ātman would be able to peep through the larger aperture and see the forms of its surroundings better and more clearly than before. It would be able to hear sounds better if the ears were torn away; smell better if the nose were cut off; taste better if the tongue were pulled out; and feel better if the body were destroyed.   17

"I observe the preservation and transmission of character; I perceive the truth of karma, but see no ātman whom your doctrine makes the doer of your deeds. There is rebirth without the transmigration of a self. For this ātman, this self, this ego in the '*I* say' and in the '*I* will' is an illusion. If this self were a reality, how could there be an escape from selfhood? The terror of hell would be infinite, and no release could be granted. The evils of existence would not be due to our ignorance and wrong-doing, but would constitute the very nature of our being."   18

And the Bodhisatta went to the priests officiating in the temples. But the gentle mind of the Sakyamuni was offended at the unnecessary cruelty performed on the altars of the gods. He said: 19

"Ignorance only can make these men prepare festivals and hold vast meetings for sacrifices. Far better to revere the truth than try to appease the gods by shedding blood.   20

"What love can a man possess who believes that the destruction of life will atone for evil deeds? Can a new wrong expiate old wrongs? And can the slaughter of an innocent victim blot out the evil deeds of mankind? This is practising religion by the neglect of moral conduct.   21

"Purify your hearts and cease to kill; that is true religion.   22

"Rituals have no efficacy; prayers are vain repetitions; and incantations have no saving power. But to abandon covetousness and lust, to become free from evil passions, and to give up all hatred and ill-will, that is the right sacrifice and the true worship."   23

X.

URUVELĀ, THE PLACE OF MORTIFICATION.

The Bodhisatta went in search of a better system and came to a settlement of five bhikkhus in the jungle of Uruvelā; and when the Blessed One saw the life of those five men, virtuously keeping in check their senses, subduing their passions, and practising austere self-discipline, he admired their earnestness and joined their company. 1

With holy zeal and a strong heart, the Sakyamuni gave himself up to meditative thought and rigorous mortification of the body. Whereas the five bhikkhus were severe, the Sakyamuni was severer still, and they revered him, their junior, as their master. 2

So the Bodhisatta continued for six years patiently torturing himself and suppressing the wants of nature. He trained his body and exercised his mind in the modes of the most rigorous ascetic life. At last, he ate each day one hemp-grain only, seeking to cross the ocean of birth and death and to arrive at the shore of deliverance. 3

And when the Bodhisatta was ahungered, lo! Māra, the Evil One, approached him and said: "Thou art emaciated from fasts, and death is near. What good is thy exertion? Deign to live, and thou wilt be able to do good works." But the Sakyamuni made reply: "O thou friend of the indolent, thou wicked one; for what purpose hast thou come? Let the flesh waste away, if but the mind becomes more tranquil and attention more steadfast. What is life in this world? Death in battle is better to me than that I should live defeated." 4

And Māra withdrew, saying: "For seven years I have followed the Blessed One step by step, but I have found no fault in the Tathāgata". 5

The Bodhisatta was shrunken and attenuated, and his body was like a withered branch; but the fame of his holiness spread in the surrounding countries, and people came from great distances to see him and receive his blessing. 6

However, the Holy One was not satisfied. Seeking true wisdom he did not find it, and he came to the conclusion that mortification would not extinguish desire nor afford enlightenment in ecstatic contemplation. 7

Seated beneath a jambu-tree, he considered the state of his mind and the fruits of his mortification. His body had become weaker, nor had his fasts advanced him in his search for salvation, and therefore when he saw that it was not the right path, he proposed to abandon it. 8

He went to bathe in the Nerañjara river, but when he strove to leave the water he could not rise on account of his weakness. Then espying the branch of a tree and taking hold of it, he raised himself and left the stream. But while returning to his abode, he staggered and fell to the ground, and the five bhikkhus thought he was dead. 9

There was a chief herdsman living near the grove whose eldest daughter was called Nandā; and Nandā happened to pass by the spot where the Blessed One had swooned, and bowing down before him she offered him rice-milk and he accepted the gift. When he had partaken of the rice-milk all his limbs were refreshed, his mind became clear again, and he was strong to receive the highest enlightenment. 10

After this occurrence, the Bodhisatta again took some food. His disciples, having witnessed the scene of Nandā and observing the change in his mode of living, were filled with suspicion. They were convinced that Siddhattha's religious zeal was flagging and that he whom they had hitherto revered as their Master had become oblivious of his high purpose. 11

When the Bodhisatta saw the bhikkhus turning away from him, he felt sorry for their lack of confidence, and was aware of the loneliness in which he lived. 12

Suppressing his grief he wandered on alone, and his disciples said, "Siddhattha leaves us to seek a more pleasant abode." 13

XI.

MĀRA THE EVIL ONE.

The Holy One directed his steps to that blessed Bodhitree beneath whose shade he was to accomplish his search. 1

As he walked, the earth shook and a brilliant light transfigured the world. 2

When he sat down the heavens resounded with joy and all living beings were filled with good cheer. 3

Māra alone, lord of the five desires, bringer of death and enemy of truth, was grieved and rejoiced not. With his three daughters, Tanhā, Ragā and Arati, the tempters, and with his host of evil demons, he went to the place where the great samana sat. But Sakyamuni heeded him not. 4

Māra uttered fear-inspiring threats and raised a whirlwind so that the skies were darkened and the ocean roared and trembled. But the Blessed One under the Bodhitree remained calm and feared not. The Enlightened One knew that no harm could befall him. 5

The three daughters of Māra tempted the Bodhisatta, but he paid no attention to them, and when Māra saw that he could kindle no desire in the heart of the victorious samana, he ordered all the evil spirits at his command to attack him and overawe the great muni. 6

But the Blessed One watched them as one would watch the harmless games of children. All the fierce hatred of the evil spirits was of no avail. The flames of hell became

O. KOPETZKY.

wholesome breezes of perfume, and the angry thunderbolts were changed into lotus-blossoms.   7

When Māra saw this, he fled away with his army from the Bodhi-tree, whilst from above a rain of heavenly flowers fell, and voices of good spirits were heard: 8

"Behold the great muni! his heart unmoved by hatred. The wicked Māra's host 'gainst him did not prevail. Pure is he and wise, loving and full of mercy.   9

"As the rays of the sun drown the darkness of the world, so he who perseveres in his search will find the truth and the truth will enlighten him."   10

XII.

ENLIGHTENMENT.

The Bodhisatta, having put Māra to flight, gave himself up to meditation. All the miseries of the world, the evils produced by evil deeds and the sufferings arising therefrom, passed before his mental eye, and he thought: 1

"Surely if living creatures saw the results of all their evil deeds, they would turn away from them in disgust. But selfhood blinds them, and they cling to their obnoxious desires.   2

"They crave pleasure for themselves and they cause pain to others; when death destroys their individuality, they find no peace; their thirst for existence abides and their selfhood reappears in new births.   3

"Thus they continue to move in the coil and can find no escape from the hell of their own making. And how empty are their pleasures, how vain are their endeavors! Hollow like the plantain-tree and without contents like the bubble.   4

"The world is full of evil and sorrow, because it is full of lust. Men go astray because they think that delusion is better than truth. Rather than truth they follow error, which is pleasant to look at in the beginning but in the end causes anxiety, tribulation, and misery."   5

And the Bodhisatta began to expound the Dharma. The Dharma is the truth. The Dharma is the sacred law. The Dharma is religion. The Dharma alone can deliver us from error, from wrong and from sorrow.   6

Pondering on the origin of birth and death, the Enlightened One recognized that ignorance was the root of all evil; and these are the links in the development of life, called the twelve nidānas: 7

In the beginning there is existence blind and without knowledge; and in this sea of ignorance there are stirrings formative and organizing. From stirrings, formative and organizing, rises awareness or feelings. Feelings beget organisms that live as individual beings. These organisms develop the six fields, that is, the five senses and the mind. The six fields come in contact with things. Contact begets sensation. Sensation creates the thirst of individualized being. The thirst of being creates a cleaving to things. The cleaving produces the growth and continuation of selfhood. Selfhood continues in renewed births. The renewed births of selfhood are the cause of suffering, old age, sickness, and death. They produce lamentation, anxiety, and despair.   8

The cause of all sorrow lies at the very beginning; it is hidden in the ignorance from which life grows. Remove ignorance and you will destroy the wrong appetences that rise from ignorance; destroy these appetences and you will wipe out the wrong perception that rises from them. Destroy wrong perception and there is an end of errors in individualized beings. Destroy the errors in individualized beings and the illusions of the six fields will disappear.

Destroy illusions and the contact with things will cease to beget misconception. Destroy misconception and you do away with thirst. Destroy thirst and you will be free of all morbid cleaving. Remove the cleaving and you destroy the selfishness of selfhood. If the selfishness of selfhood is destroyed you will be above birth, old age, disease, and death, and you will escape all suffering.   9

The Enlightened One saw the four noble truths which point out the path that leads to Nirvāna or the extinction of self: 10

The first noble truth is the existence of sorrow.   11

The second noble truth is the cause of suffering.   12

The third noble truth is the cessation of sorrow.   13

The fourth noble truth is the eightfold path that leads to the cessation of sorrow.   14

This is the Dharma. This is the truth. This is religion. And the Enlightened One uttered this stanza: 15

> "Through many births I sought in vain
> The Builder of this House of Pain.
> Now, Builder, thee I plainly see!
> This is the last abode for me.
> Thy gable's yoke and rafters broke,
> My heart has peace. All lust will cease."   16

There is self and there is truth. Where self is, truth is not. Where truth is, self is not. Self is the fleeting error of samsāra; it is individual separateness and that egotism which begets envy and hatred. Self is the yearning for pleasure and the lust after vanity. Truth is the correct comprehension of things; it is the permanent and everlasting, the real in all existence, the bliss of righteousness.   17

The existence of self is an illusion, and there is no wrong in this world, no vice, no evil, except what flows from the assertion of self.   18

The attainment of truth is possible only when self is recognized as an illusion. Righteousness can be practised only when we have freed our mind from passions of egotism. Perfect peace can dwell only where all vanity has disappeared.   19

Blessed is he who has understood the Dharma. Blessed is he who does no harm to his fellow-beings. Blessed is he who overcomes wrong and is free from passion. To the highest bliss has he attained who has conquered all selfishness and vanity. He has become the Buddha, the Perfect One, the Blessed One, the Holy One.   20

XIII.

THE FIRST CONVERTS.

The Blessed One tarried in solitude seven times seven days, enjoying the bliss of emancipation.   1

At that time Tapussa and Bhallika, two merchants, came traveling on the road near by, and when they saw the great samana, majestic and full of peace, they approached him respectfully and offered him rice cakes and honey. 2

This was the first food that the Enlightened One ate after he attained Buddhahood.   3

And the Buddha addressed them and pointed out to them the way of salvation. The two merchants, conceiving in their minds the holiness of the conqueror of Māra, bowed down in reverence and said: "We take our refuge, Lord, in the Blessed One and in the Dharma."   4

Tapussa and Bhallika were the first that became followers of the Buddha and they were lay disciples.   5

XIV.

BRAHMĀS REQUEST.

The Blessed One having attained Buddhahood while resting under the shepherd's Nigrodha tree on the banks of the river Nerañjarā, pronounced this solemn utterance: 1

"How blest in happy solitude
Is he who hears of truth the call!
How blest to be both kind and good,
To practice self-restraint to all!
How blest from passion to be free,
All sensuous joys to let pass by!
Yet highest bliss enjoyeth he
Who quits the pride of 'I am I.' 2

"I have recognized the deepest truth, which is sublime and peace-giving, but difficult to understand; for most men move in a sphere of worldly interests and find their delight in worldly desires. 3

"The worldling will not understand the doctrine, for to him there is happiness in selfhood only, and the bliss that lies in a complete surrender to truth is unintelligible to him. 4

"He will call resignation what to the enlightened mind is the purest joy. He will see annihilation where the perfected one finds immortality. He will regard as death what the conqueror of self knows to be life everlasting. 5

"The truth remains hidden from him who is in the bondage of hate and desire. Nirvāna remains incomprehensible and mysterious to the vulgar whose minds are beclouded with worldly interests. Should I preach the doctrine and mankind not comprehend it, it would bring me only fatigue and trouble." 6

Māra, the Evil One, on hearing the words of the Blessed Buddha, approached and said: "Be greeted, thou Holy One.

Thou hast attained the highest bliss and it is time for thee to enter into the final Nirvāna." 7

Then Brahmā Sahampati descended from the heavens and, having worshipped the Blessed One, said: 8

"Alas! the world must perish, should the Holy One, the Tathāgata, decide not to teach the Dharma. 9

"Be merciful to those that struggle; have compassion upon the sufferers; pity the creatures who are hopelessly entangled in the snares of sorrow. 10

"There are some beings that are almost free from the dust of worldliness. If they hear not the doctrine preached, they will be lost. But if they hear it, they will believe and be saved." 11

The Blessed One, full of compassion, looked with the eye of a Buddha upon all sentient creatures, and he saw among them beings whose minds were but scarcely covered by the dust of worldliness, who were of good disposition and easy to instruct. He saw some who were conscious of the dangers of lust and wrong doing. 12

And the Blessed One said to Brahmā Sahampati: "Wide open be the door of immortality to all who have ears to hear. May they receive the Dharma with faith." 13

And the Blessed One turned to Māra, saying: "I shall not pass into the final Nirvāna, O Evil One, until there be not only brethren and sisters of an Order, but also lay-disciples of both sexes, who shall have become true hearers, wise, well trained, ready and learned, versed in the scriptures, fulfilling all the greater and lesser duties, correct in life, walking according to the precepts—until they, having thus themselves learned the doctrine, shall be able to give information to others concerning it, preach it, make it known, establish it, open it, minutely explain it, and make it clear —until they, when others start vain doctrines, shall be able to vanquish and refute them, and so to spread the wonder-working truth abroad. I shall not die until the pure religion of truth shall have become successful, prosperous, wide-spread, and popular in all its full extent—until, in a word, it shall have been well proclaimed among men!"   14

Then Brahmā Sahampati understood that the Blessed One had granted his request and would preach the doctrine.   15

THE FOUNDATION OF THE KINGDOM OF RIGHTEOUSNESS.

XV.

UPAKA.

NOW the Blessed One thought: "To whom shall I preach the doctrine first? My old teachers are dead. They would have received the good news with joy. But my five disciples are still alive. I shall go to them, and to them shall I first proclaim the gospel of deliverance."   1

At that time the five bhikkhus dwelt in the Deer Park at Benares, and the Blessed

One rose and journeyed to their abode, not thinking of their unkindness in having left him at a time when he was most in need of their sympathy and help, but mindful only of the services which they had ministered unto him, and pitying them for the austerities which they practised in vain. 2

Upaka, a young Brahman and a Jain, a former acquaintance of Siddhattha, saw the Blessed One while he journeyed to Benares, and, amazed at the majesty and sublime joyfulness of his appearance, said: "Thy countenance, friend, is serene; thine eyes are bright and indicate purity and blessedness." 3

The holy Buddha replied: "I have obtained deliverance by the extinction of self. My body is chastened, my mind is free from desire, and the deepest truth has taken abode in my heart. I have obtained Nirvāna, and this is the reason that my countenance is serene and my eyes are bright. I now desire to found the kingdom of truth upon earth, to give light to those who are enshrouded in darkness and to open the gate of deathlessness." 4

Upaka replied: "Thou professest then, friend, to be Jina, the conqueror of the world, the absolute one and the holy one." 5

The Blessed One said: "Jinas are all those who have conquered self and the passions of self, those alone are victors who control their minds and abstain from evil. Therefore, Upaka, I am the Jina." 6

Upaka shook his head. "Venerable Gotama," he said, "thy way lies yonder," and taking another road, he went away. 7

XVI

THE SERMON AT BENARES.

On seeing their old teacher approach, the five bhikkhus agreed among themselves not to salute him, nor to address him as a master, but by his name only. "For," so they said, "he has broken his vow and has abandoned holiness. He is no bhikkhu but Gotama, and Gotama has become a man who lives in abundance and indulges in the pleasures of worldliness." 1

But when the Blessed One approached in a dignified manner, they involuntarily rose from their seats and greeted him in spite of their resolution. Still they called him by his name and addressed him as "friend Gotama." 2

When they had thus received the Blessed One, he said: "Do not call the Tathāgata by his name nor address him as 'friend,' for he is the Buddha, the Holy One. The Buddha looks with a kind heart equally on all living beings, and they therefore call him 'Father.' To disrespect a father is wrong; to despise him, is wicked. 3

"The Tathāgata," the Buddha continued, "does not seek salvation in austerities, but neither does he for that reason indulge in worldly pleasures, nor live in abundance. The Tathāgata has found the middle path 4

"There are two extremes, O bhikkhus, which the man who has given up the world ought not to follow—the habitual practice, on the one hand, of self-indulgence which is unworthy, vain and fit only for the worldly-minded—and the habitual practice, on the other hand, of self-mortification, which is painful, useless and unprofitable. 5

"Neither abstinence from fish or flesh, nor going naked, nor shaving the head, nor wearing matted hair, nor dressing in a rough garment, nor covering oneself with dirt, nor sacrificing to Agni, will cleanse a man who is not free from delusions. 6

"Reading the Vedas, making offerings to priests, or sacrifices to the gods, self-mortification by heat or cold, and many such penances performed for the sake of immortality, these do not cleanse the man who is not free from delusions. 7

"Anger, drunkenness, obstinacy, bigotry, deception, envy, self-praise, disparaging others, superciliousness and evil intentions constitute uncleanness; not verily the eating of flesh. 8

"A middle path, O bhikkhus, avoiding the two extremes, has been discovered by the Tathāgata—a path which opens the eyes, and bestows understanding, which leads to peace of mind, to the higher wisdom, to full enlightenment, to Nirvāna! 9

"What is that middle path, O bhikkhus, avoiding these two extremes, discovered by the Tathāgata—that path which opens the eyes, and bestows understanding, which leads to peace of mind, to the higher wisdom, to full enlightenment, to Nirvāna? 10

"Let me teach you, O bhikkhus, the middle path, which keeps aloof from both extremes. By suffering, the emaciated devotee produces confusion and sickly thoughts in his mind. Mortification is not conducive even to worldly knowledge; how much less to a triumph over the senses! 11

"He who fills his lamp with water will not dispel the darkness, and he who tries to light a fire with rotten wood will fail. And how can any one be free from self by leading a wretched life, if he does not succeed in quenching the fires of lust, if he still hankers after either worldly or heavenly pleasures. But he in whom self has become extinct is free from lust; he will desire neither worldly nor heavenly pleasures, and the satisfaction of his natural wants will not defile him. However, let him be moderate, let him eat and drink according to the needs of the body. 12

"Sensuality is enervating; the self-indulgent man is a slave to his passions, and pleasure-seeking is degrading and vulgar. 13

"But to satisfy the necessities of life is not evil. To keep the body in good health is a duty, for otherwise we shall not be able to trim the lamp of wisdom, and keep our mind strong and clear. Water surrounds the lotus-flower, but does not wet its petals. 14

"This is the middle path, O bhikkhus, that keeps aloof from both extremes." 15

And the Blessed One spoke kindly to his disciples, pitying them for their errors, and pointing out the uselessness of their endeavors, and the ice of ill-will that chilled their hearts melted away under the gentle warmth of the Master's persuasion. 16

Now the Blessed One set the wheel of the most excellent law rolling, and he began to preach to the five bhikkhus, opening to them the gate of immortality, and showing them the bliss of Nirvāna. 17

The Buddha said: 18

"The spokes of the wheel are the rules of pure conduct: justice is the uniformity of their length; wisdom is the tire; modesty and thoughtfulness are the hub in which the immovable axle of truth is fixed. 19

"He who recognizes the existence of suffering, its cause, its remedy, and its cessation has fathomed the four noble truths. He will walk in the right path. 20

"Right views will be the torch to light his way. Right aspirations will be his guide. Right speech will be his dwelling-place on the road. His gait will be straight, for it is right behavior. His refreshments will be the right way of earning his livelihood. Right efforts will be his steps: right thoughts his breath; and right contemplation will give him the peace that follows in his footprints. 21

"Now, this, O bhikkhus, is the noble truth concerning suffering: 22

"Birth is attended with pain, decay is painful, disease is painful, death is painful. Union with the unpleasant is painful, painful is separation from the pleasant; and any craving that is unsatisfied, that too is painful. In brief, bodily conditions which spring from attachment are painful.   23

"This, then, O bhikkhus, is the noble truth concerning suffering.   24

"Now this, O bhikkhus, is the noble truth concerning the origin of suffering: 25

"Verily, it is that craving which causes the renewal of existence, accompanied by sensual delight, seeking satisfaction now here, now there, the craving for the gratification of the passions, the craving for a future life, and the craving for happiness in this life.   26

"This, then, O bhikkhus, is the noble truth concerning the origin of suffering.   27

"Now this, O bhikkhus, is the noble truth concerning the destruction of suffering: 28

"Verily, it is the destruction, in which no passion remains, of this very thirst; it is the laying aside of, the being free from, the dwelling no longer upon this thirst.   29

"This, then, O bhikkhus, is the noble truth concerning the destruction of suffering.   30

"Now this, O bhikkhus, is the noble truth concerning the way which leads to the destruction of sorrow. Verily! it is this noble eightfold path; that is to say: 31

"Right views; right aspirations; right speech; right behavior; right livelihood; right effort; right thoughts; and right contemplation.   32

"This, then, O bhikkhus, is the noble truth concerning the destruction of sorrow.   33

O. KOPETZKY.

"By the practice of lovingkindness I have attained liberation of heart, and thus I am assured that I shall never return in renewed births. I have even now attained Nirvāna." 34

And when the Blessed One had thus set the royal chariot-wheel of truth rolling onward, a rapture thrilled through all the universes. 35

The devas left their heavenly abodes to listen to the sweetness of the truth; the saints that had parted from life crowded around the great teacher to receive the glad tidings; even the animals of the earth felt the bliss that rested upon the words of the Tathāgata: and all the creatures of the host of sentient beings, gods, men, and beasts, hearing the message of deliverance, received and understood it in their own language. 36

And when the doctrine was propounded, the venerable Kondañña, the oldest one among the five bhikkhus, discerned the truth with his mental eye, and he said: "Truly, O Buddha, our Lord, thou hast found the truth!" Then the other bhikkhus too, joined him and exclaimed: "Truly, thou art the Buddha, thou hast found the truth." 37

And the devas and saints and all the good spirits of the departed generations that had listened to the sermon of the Tathāgata, joyfully received the doctrine and shouted: "Truly, the Blessed One has founded the kingdom of righteousness. The Blessed One has moved the earth; he has set the wheel of Truth rolling, which by no one in the universe, be he god or man, can ever be turned back. The kingdom of Truth will be preached upon earth; it will spread; and righteousness, good-will, and peace will reign among mankind." 38

XVII

THE SANGHA.

Having pointed out to the five bhikkhus the truth, the Buddha said: 1

"A man that stands alone, having decided to obey the truth, may be weak and slip back into his old ways. Therefore, stand ye together, assist one another, and strengthen one another's efforts. 2

"Be like unto brothers; one in love, one in holiness, and one in your zeal for the truth. 3

"Spread the truth and preach the doctrine in all quarters of the world, so that in the end all living creatures will be citizens of the kingdom of righteousness. 4

"This is the holy brotherhood; this is the church, the congregation of the saints of the Buddha; this is the Sangha that establishes a communion among all those who have taken their refuge in the Buddha." 5

And Kondañña was the first disciple of the Buddha who had thoroughly grasped the doctrine of the Holy One, and the Tathāgata looking into his heart said: "Truly, Kondañña has understood the truth." Hence the venerable Kondañña received the name "Aññāta-Kondañña," that is, "Kondañña who has understood the doctrine." 6

Then the venerable Kondañña spoke to the Buddha and said: "Lord, let us receive the ordination from the Blessed One." 7

And the Buddha said: "Come, O bhikkhus! Well taught is the doctrine. Lead a holy life for the extinction of suffering." 8

Then Kondañña and the other bhikkhus uttered three times these solemn vows: 9

"To the Buddha will I look in faith: He, the Perfect One, is holy and supreme. The Buddha conveys to us instruction, wisdom, and salvation; he is the Blessed One, who knows the law of being; he is the Lord of the world, who yoketh men like oxen, the Teacher of gods and men, the Exalted Buddha. Therefore, to the Buddha will I look in faith. 10

"To the doctrine will I look in faith: well-preached is the doctrine by the Exalted One. The doctrine has been revealed so as to become visible; the doctrine is above time and space. The doctrine is not based upon hearsay, it means 'Come and see'; the doctrine leads to welfare; the doctrine is recognized by the wise in their own hearts. Therefore to the doctrine will I look in faith. 11

"To the community will I look in faith; the community of the Buddha's disciples instructs us how to lead a life of righteousness; the community of the Buddha's disciples teaches us how to exercise honesty and justice; the community of the Buddha's disciples shows us how to practise the truth. They form a brotherhood in kindness and charity, and their saints are worthy of reverence. The community of the Buddha's disciples is founded as a holy brotherhood in which men bind themselves together to teach the behests of rectitude and to do good. Therefore, to the community will I look in faith." 12

And the gospel of the Blessed One increased from day to day, and many people came to hear him and to accept the ordination to lead thenceforth a holy life for the sake of the extinction of suffering. 13

And the Blessed One seeing that it was impossible to attend to all who wanted to hear the truth and receive the ordination, sent out from the number of his disciples such as were to preach the Dharma and said unto them: 14

"The Dharma and the Vinaya proclaimed by the Tathāgata shine forth when they are displayed, and not when they are concealed. But let not this doctrine, so full of truth and so excellent, fall into the hands of those unworthy of it, where it would be despised and contemned, treated shamefully, ridiculed and censured.   15

"I now grant you, O bhikkhus, this permission. Confer henceforth in the different countries the ordination upon those who are eager to receive it, when you find them worthy.   16

"Go ye now, O bhikkhus, for the benefit of the many, for the welfare of mankind, out of compassion for the world. Preach the doctrine which is glorious in the beginning, glorious in the middle, and glorious in the end, in the spirit as well as in the letter. There are beings whose eyes are scarcely covered with dust, but if the doctrine is not preached to them they cannot attain salvation. Proclaim to them a life of holiness. They will understand the doctrine and accept it."   17

And it became an established custom that the bhikkhus went out preaching while the weather was good, but in the rainy season they came together again and joined their master, to listen to the exhortations of the Tathāgata.   18

XVIII.

YASA, THE YOUTH OF BENARES.

At that time there was in Benares a noble youth, Yasa by name, the son of a wealthy merchant. Troubled in his mind about the sorrows of the world, he secretly rose up in the night and stole away to the Blessed One.   1

The Blessed One saw Yasa, the noble youth, coming from afar. And Yasa approached and exclaimed: "Alas, what distress! What tribulations!"   2

The Blessed One said to Yasa: "Here is no distress; here are no tribulations. Come to me and I will teach you the truth, and the truth will dispel your sorrows."   3

And when Yasa, the noble youth, heard that there were neither distress, nor tribulations, nor sorrows, his heart was comforted. He went into the place where the Blessed One was, and sat down near him. 4

Then the Blessed One preached about charity and morality. He explained the vanity of the thought "I am"; the dangers of desire, and the necessity of avoiding the evils of life in order to walk on the path of deliverance. 5

Instead of disgust with the world, Yasa felt the cooling stream of holy wisdom, and, having obtained the pure and spotless eye of truth, he looked at his person, richly adorned with pearls and precious stones, and his heart was filled with shame. 6

The Tathāgata, knowing his inward thoughts, said: 7

"Though a person be ornamented with jewels, the heart may have conquered the senses. The outward form does not constitute religion or affect the mind. Thus the body of a samana may wear an ascetic's garb while his mind is immersed in worldliness. 8

"A man that dwells in lonely woods and yet covets worldly vanities, is a worldling, while the man in worldly garments may let his heart soar high to heavenly thoughts. 9

"There is no distinction between the layman and the hermit, if but both have banished the thought of self." 10

Seeing that Yasa was ready to enter upon the path, the Blessed One said to him: "Follow me!" And Yasa joined the brotherhood, and having put on a bhikkhu's robe, received the ordination. 11

While the Blessed One and Yasa were discussing the doctrine, Yasa's father passed by in search of his son; and in passing he asked the Blessed One: "Pray, Lord, hast thou seen Yasa, my son?" 12

And the Buddha said to Yasa's father: "Come in, sir, thou wilt find thy son"; and Yasa's father became full of joy and he entered. He sat down near his son, but his eyes were holden and he knew him not; and the Lord began to preach. And Yasa's father, understanding the doctrine of the Blessed One, said: 13

"Glorious is the truth, O Lord! The Buddha, the Holy One, our Master, sets up what has been overturned; he reveals what has been hidden; he points out the way to the wanderer who has gone astray; he lights a lamp in the darkness so that all who have eyes to see can discern the things that surround them. I take refuge in the Buddha, our Lord: I take refuge in the doctrine revealed by him: I take refuge in the brotherhood which he has founded. May the Blessed One receive me from this day forth while my life lasts as a lay disciple who has taken refuge in him." 14

Yasa's father was the first lay-member who became the first lay disciple of the Buddha by pronouncing the three-fold formula of refuge. 15

When the wealthy merchant had taken refuge in the Buddha, his eyes were opened and he saw his son sitting at his side in a bhikkhu's robe. "My son, Yasa," he said, "thy mother is absorbed in lamentation and grief. Return home and restore thy mother to life." 16

Then Yasa looked at the Blessed One, and the Blessed One said: "Should Yasa return to the world and enjoy the pleasures of a worldly life as he did before?" 17

And Yasa's father replied: "If Yasa, my son, finds it a gain to stay with thee, let him stay. He has become delivered from the bondage of worldliness." 18

When the Blessed One had cheered their hearts with words of truth and righteousness, Yasa's father said: "May the Blessed One, O Lord, consent to take his meal with me together with Yasa as his attendant?" 19

The Blessed One, having donned his robes, took his alms-bowl and went with Yasa to the house of the rich merchant. When they had arrived there, the mother and also the former wife of Yasa saluted the Blessed One and sat down near him. 20

Then the Blessed One preached, and the women having understood his doctrine, exclaimed: "Glorious is the truth, O Lord! We take refuge in the Buddha, our Lord. We take refuge in the doctrine revealed by him. We take refuge in the brotherhood which has been founded by him. May the Blessed One receive us from this day forth while our life lasts as lay disciples who have taken refuge in him." 21

The mother and the wife of Yasa, the noble youth of Benares, were the first women who became lay disciples and took their refuge in the Buddha. 22

Now there were four friends of Yasa belonging to the wealthy families of Benares. Their names were Vimala, Subāhu, Puññaji, and Gavampati. 23

When Yasa's friends heard that Yasa had cut off his hair and put on bhikkhu robes to give up the world and go forth into homelessness, they thought: "Surely that cannot be a common doctrine, that must be a noble renunciation of the world, if Yasa, whom we know to be good and wise, has shaved his hair and put on bhikkhu robes to give up the world and go forth into homelessness." 24

And they went to Yasa, and Yasa addressed the Blessed One, saying: "May the Blessed One administer exhortation and instruction to these four friends of mine." And the Blessed One preached to them, and Yasa's friends accepted the doctrine and took refuge in the Buddha, the Dharma, and the Sangha. 25

XIX.

KASSAPA.

At that time there lived in Uruvelā the Jatilas, Brahman hermits with matted hair, worshipping the fire and keeping a fire-dragon; and Kassapa was their chief.   1

Kassapa was renowned throughout all India, and his name was honored as one of the wisest men on earth and an authority on religion.   2

And the Blessed One went to Kassapa of Uruvelā, the Jatila, and said: "Let me stay a night in the room where you keep your sacred fire."   3

Kassapa, seeing the Blessed One in his majesty and beauty, thought to himself: "This is a great muni and a noble teacher. Should he stay over night in the room where the sacred fire is kept, the serpent will bite him and he will die." And he said: "I do not object to your staying over-night in the room where the sacred fire is kept, but the serpent lives there; he will kill you and I should be sorry to see you perish."   4

But the Buddha insisted and Kassapa admitted him to the room where the sacred fire was kept.   5

And the Blessed One sat down with his body erect, surrounding himself with watchfulness.   6

In the night the dragon came to the Buddha, belching forth in rage his fiery poison, and filling the air with burning vapor, but could do him no harm, and the fire consumed itself while the World-honored One remained composed. And the venomous fiend became very wroth so that he died in his anger.   7

When Kassapa saw the light shining forth from the room he said: "Alas, what misery! Truly, the countenance of Gotama the great Sakyamuni is beautiful, but the serpent will destroy him."   8

In the morning the Blessed One showed the dead body

of the fiend to Kassapa, saying: "His fire has been conquered by my fire." 9

And Kassapa thought to himself. "Sakyamuni is a great
samana and possesses high powers, but he is not holy
like me." 10

There was in those days a festival, and Kassapa thought:
"The people will come hither from all parts of the country
and will see the great Sakyamuni. When he speaks to
them, they will believe in him and abandon me." And he
grew envious. 11

When the day of the festival arrived, the Blessed One
retired and did not come to Kassapa. And Kassapa went
to the Buddha on the next morning and said: "Why did
the great Sakyamuni not come?" 12

The Tathāgata replied: "Didst thou not think, O Kassapa, that it would be better if I stayed away from the
festival?" 13

And Kassapa was astonished and thought: "Great is
Sakyamuni; he can read my most secret thoughts, but he
is not holy like me." 14

And the Blessed One addressed Kassapa and said:
"Thou seest the truth, but acceptest it not because of the
envy that dwells in thy heart. Is envy holiness? Envy is
the last remnant of self that has remained in thy mind.
Thou art not holy, Kassapa; thou hast not yet entered
the path." 15

And Kassapa gave up his resistance. His envy disap-
peared, and, bowing down before the Blessed One, he said:
"Lord, our Master, let me receive the ordination from the
Blessed One." 16

And the Blessed One said: "Thou, Kassapa, art chief
of the Jatilas. Go, then, first and inform them of thine
intention, and let them do as thou thinkest fit." 17

Then Kassapa went to the Jatilas and said: "I am anxious to lead a religious life under the direction of the

great Sakyamuni, who is the Enlightened One, the Buddha. Do as ye think best." 18

And the Jatilas replied: "We have conceived a profound affection for the great Sakyamuni, and if thou wilt join his brotherhood, we will do likewise." 19

The Jatilas of Uruvelā now flung their paraphernalia of fire-worship into the river and went to the Blessed One. 20

Nadī Kassapa and Gayā Kassapa, brothers of the great Uruvelā Kassapa, powerful men and chieftains among the people, were dwelling below on the stream, and when they saw the instruments used in fire-worship floating in the river, they said: "Something has happened to our brother." And they came with their folk to Uruvelā. Hearing what had happened, they, too, went to the Buddha. 21

The Blessed One, seeing that the Jatilas of Nadī and Gayā, who had practised severe austerities and worshipped fire, were now come to him, preached a sermon on fire, and said: 22

"Everything, O Jatilas, is burning. The eye is burning, all the senses are burning, thoughts are burning. They are burning with the fire of lust. There is anger, there is ignorance, there is hatred, and as long as the fire finds inflammable things upon which it can feed, so long will it burn, and there will be birth and death, decay, grief, lamentation, suffering, despair, and sorrow. Considering this, a disciple of the Dharma will see the four noble truths and walk in the eightfold path of holiness. He will become wary of his eye, wary of all his senses, wary of his thoughts. He will divest himself of passion and become free. He will be delivered from selfishness and attain the blessed state of Nirvāna." 23

And the Jatilas rejoiced and took refuge in the Buddha, the Dharma, and the Sangha. 24

XX

THE SERMON AT RĀJAGAHA.

And the Blessed One having dwelt some time in Uru-velā went forth to Rājagaha, accompanied by a great number of bhikkhus, many of whom had been Jatilas before; and the great Kassapa, chief of the Jatilas and formerly a fireworshipper, went with him.　　　　1

When the Magadha king, Seniya Bimbisāra, heard of the arrival of Gotama Sakyamuni, of whom the people said, "He is the Holy One, the blessed Buddha, guiding men as a driver curbs bullocks, the teacher of high and low," he went out surrounded with his counsellors and generals and came to the grove where the Blessed One was.　　　　2

There they saw the Blessed One in the company of Kassapa, the great religious teacher of the Jatilas, and they were astonished and thought: "Has the great Sakyamuni placed himself under the spiritual direction of Kassapa, or has Kassapa become a disciple of Gotama?"　　　　3

And the Tathāgata, reading the thoughts of the people, said to Kassapa: "What knowledge hast thou gained, O Kassapa, and what has induced thee to renounce the sacred fire and give up thine austere penances?"　　　　4

Kassapa said: "The profit I derived from adoring the fire was continuance in the wheel of individuality with all its sorrows and vanities. This service I have cast away, and instead of continuing penances and sacrifices I have gone in quest of the highest Nirvāna. Since I have seen the light of truth, I have abandoned worshipping the fire."　　　　5

The Buddha, perceiving that the whole assembly was ready as a vessel to receive the doctrine, spoke thus to Bimbisāra the king:　　　　6

"He who knows the nature of self and understands how the senses act, finds no room for selfishness, and thus he will attain peace unending. The world holds the thought of self, and from this arises false apprehension.   7

"Some say that the self endures after death, some say it perishes. Both are wrong and their error is most grievous.   8

"For if they say the self is perishable, the fruit they strive for will perish too, and at some time there will be no hereafter. Good and evil would be indifferent. This salvation from selfishness is without merit.   9

"When some, on the other hand, say the self will not perish, then in the midst of all life and death there is but one identity unborn and undying. If such is their self, then it is perfect and cannot be perfected by deeds. The lasting, imperishable self could never be changed. The self would be lord and master, and there would be no use in perfecting the perfect; moral aims and salvation would be unnecessary.   10

"But now we see the marks of joy and sorrow. Where is any constancy? If there is no permanent self that does our deeds, then there is no self; there is no actor behind our actions, no perceiver behind our perception, no lord behind our deeds.   11

"Now attend and listen: The senses meet the object and from their contact sensation is born. Thence results recollection. Thus, as the sun's power through a burning-glass causes fire to appear, so through the cognizance born of sense and object, the mind originates and with it the ego, the thought of self, whom some Brahman teachers call the lord. The shoot springs from the seed; the seed is not the shoot; both are not one and the same, but successive phases in a continuous growth. Such is the birth of animated life.   12

"Ye that are slaves of the self and toil in its service from morn until night, ye that live in constant fear of birth, old age, sickness, and death, receive the good tidings that your cruel master exists not.   13

"Self is an error, an illusion, a dream. Open your eyes and awaken. See things as they are and ye will be comforted. 14

"He who is awake will no longer be afraid of nightmares. He who has recognized the nature of the rope that seemed to be a serpent will cease to tremble. 15

"He who has found there is no self will let go all the lusts and desires of egotism. 16

"The cleaving to things, covetousness, and sensuality inherited from former existences, are the causes of the misery and vanity in the world. 17

"Surrender the grasping disposition of selfishness, and you will attain to that calm state of mind which conveys perfect peace, goodness, and wisdom." 18

And the Buddha breathed forth this solemn utterance: 19

"Do not deceive, do not despise
Each other, anywhere.
Do not be angry, nor should ye
Secret resentment bear;
For as a mother risks her life
And watches o'er her child,
So boundless be your love to all,
So tender, kind and mild. 20

"Yea, cherish good-will right and left,
All round, early and late,
And without hindrance, without stint,
From envy free and hate,
While standing, walking, sitting down,
Whate'er you have in mind,
The rule of life that's always best
Is to be loving-kind. 21

"Gifts are great, the founding of vihāras is meritorious, meditations and religious exercises pacify the heart, comprehension of the truth leads to Nirvāna, but greater than all is lovingkindness. As the light of the moon is sixteen times stronger than the light of all the stars, so lovingkindness is sixteen times more efficacious in liberating the heart than all other religious accomplishments taken together. 22

"This state of heart is the best in the world. Let a man remain steadfast in it while he is awake, whether he is standing, walking, sitting, or lying down." 23

When the Enlightened One had finished his sermon, the Magadha king said to the Blessed One: 24

"In former days, Lord, when I was a prince, I cherished five wishes. I wished: O, that I might be inaugurated as a king. This was my first wish, and it has been fulfilled. Further, I wished: Might the Holy Buddha, the Perfect One, appear on earth while I rule and might he come to my kingdom. This was my second wish and it is fulfilled now. Further I wished: Might I pay my respects to him. This was my third wish and it is fulfilled now. The fourth wish was: Might the Blessed One preach the doctrine to me, and this is fulfilled now. The greatest wish, however, was the fifth wish: Might I understand the doctrine of the Blessed One. And this wish is fulfilled too. 25

"Glorious Lord! Most glorious is the truth preached by the Tathāgata! Our Lord, the Buddha, sets up what has been overturned; he reveals what has been hidden; he points out the way to the wanderer who has gone astray; he lights a lamp in the darkness so that those who have eyes to see may see. 26

"I take my refuge in the Buddha. I take my refuge in the Dharma. I take my refuge in the Sangha." 27

The Tathāgata, by the exercise of his virtue and by wisdom, showed his unlimited spiritual power. He subdued and harmonized all minds. He made them see and accept the truth, and throughout the kingdom the seeds of virtue were sown. 28

XXI.

THE KING'S GIFT.

The king, having taken his refuge in the Buddha, invited the Tathāgata to his palace, saying: "Will the Blessed One consent to take his meal with me to-morrow together with the fraternity of bhikkhus?" 1

The next morning Seniya Bimbisāra, the king, announced to the Blessed One that it was time for taking food: "Thou art my most welcome guest, O Lord of the world, come; the meal is prepared." 2

And the Blessed One having donned his robes, took his alms-bowl and, together with a great number of bhikkhus, entered the city of Rājagaha. 3

Sakka, the king of the Devas, assuming the appearance of a young Brahman, walked in front, and said: 4

"He who teaches self-control with those who have learned self-control; the redeemer with those whom he has redeemed; the Blessed One with those to whom he has given peace, is entering Rājagaha! Hail to the Buddha, our Lord! Honor to his name and blessings to all who take refuge in him." And Sakka intoned this stanza: 5

"So blest is an age in which Buddhas arise,
So blest is the truth's proclamation.
So blest is the Sangha, concordant and wise,
So blest a devout congregation! 6

"And if by all the truth were known,
More seeds of kindness would be sown,
And richer crops of good deeds grown." 7

When the Blessed One had finished his meal, and had cleansed his bowl and his hands, the king sat down near him and thought: 8

"Where may I find a place for the Blessed One to live in, not too far from the town and not too near, suitable for going and coming, easily accessible to all people who want to see him, a place that is by day not too crowded and by night not exposed to noise, wholesome and well fitted for a retired life? There is my pleasure-garden, the bamboo grove Veluvana, fulfilling all these conditions. I shall offer it to the brotherhood whose head is the Buddha."   9

The king dedicated his garden to the brotherhood, saying: "May the Blessed One accept my gift."   10

Then the Blessed One, having silently shown his consent and having gladdened and edified the Magadha king by religious discourse, rose from his seat and went away.   11

XXII.

SĀRIPUTTA AND MOGGALLĀNA.

At that time Sāriputta and Moggallāna, two Brahmans and chiefs of the followers of Sañjaya, led a religious life. They had promised each other: "He who first attains Nirvāna shall tell the other one."   1

Sāriputta seeing the venerable Assaji begging for alms, modestly keeping his eyes to the ground and dignified in deportment,¹ exclaimed: "Truly this samana has entered the right path; I will ask him in whose name he has retired from the world and what doctrine he professes." Being addressed by Sāriputta, Assaji replied: "I am a follower of the Buddha, the Blessed One, but being a novice I can tell you the substance only of the doctrine."   2

Said Sāriputta: "Tell me, venerable monk, it is the substance I want." And Assaji recited the stanza: 3

"The Buddha did the cause unfold
Of all the things that spring from causes.
And further the great sage has told
How finally all passion pauses."   4

Having heard this stanza, Sāriputta obtained the pure and spotless eye of truth and said: "Now I see clearly, whatsoever is subject to origination is also subject to cessation. If this be the doctrine I have reached the state to enter Nirvāna which heretofore has remained hidden from me."   5

Sāriputta went to Moggallāna and told him, and both said: "We will go to the Blessed One, that he, the Blessed One, may be our teacher."   6

When the Buddha saw Sāriputta and Moggallāna coming from afar, he said to his disciples, "These two monks are highly auspicious."   7

When the two friends had taken refuge in the Buddha, the Dharma and the Sangha, the Holy One said to his other disciples: "Sāriputta, like the first-born son of a world-ruling monarch, is well able to assist the king as his chief follower to set the wheel of the law rolling."   8

And the people were annoyed. Seeing that many distinguished young men of the kingdom of Magadha led a religious life under the direction of the Blessed One, they became angry and murmured: "Gotama Sakyamuni induces fathers to leave their wives and causes families to become extinct."   9

When they saw the bhikkhus, they reviled them, saying: "The great Sakyamuni has come to Rājagaha subduing the minds of men. Who will be the next to be led astray by him?"   10

The bhikkhus told it to the Blessed One, and the Blessed One said: "This murmuring, O bhikkhus, will not last long. It will last seven days. If they revile you, O bhikkhus, answer them with these words: 11

" 'It is by preaching the truth that Tathāgatas lead men. Who will murmur at the wise? Who will blame the virtuous? Who will condemn self-control, righteousness, and kindness?' "   12

And the Blessed One proclaimed this verse:
"Commit no wrong but good deeds do
And let thy heart be pure.
All Buddhas teach this doctrine true
Which will for aye endure."   13

XXIII.

ANÂTHAPINDIKA.

At this time there was Anāthapindika, a man of unmeas-
ured wealth, visiting Rājagaha. Being of a charitable disposition, he was called "the supporter of orphans and the
friend of the poor."   1
Hearing that the Buddha had come into the world and
was stopping in the bamboo grove near the city, he set
out in the very night to meet the Blessed One.   2
And the Blessed One saw at once the sterling quality of
Anāthapindika's heart and greeted him with words of religious comfort. And they sat down together, and Anāthapindika listened to the sweetness of the truth preached
by the Blessed One. And the Buddha said: 3
"The restless, busy nature of the world, this, I declare,
is at the root of pain. Attain that composure of mind
which is resting in the peace of immortality. Self is but
a heap of composite qualities, and its world is empty like
a fantasy.   4
"Who is it that shapes our lives? Is it Īśvara, a personal creator? If Īśvara be the maker, all living things
should have silently to submit to their maker's power.
They would be like vessels formed by the potter's hand;
and if it were so, how would it be possible to practise
virtue? If the world had been made by Īśvara there should
be no such thing as sorrow, or calamity, or evil; for both

pure and impure deeds must come from him. If not, there would be another cause beside him, and he would not be self-existent. Thus, thou seest, the thought of Īśvara is overthrown. 5

"Again, it is said that the Absolute has created us. But that which is absolute cannot be a cause. All things around us come from a cause as the plant comes from the seed; but how can the Absolute be the cause of all things alike? If it pervades them, then, certainly, it does not make them. 6

"Again, it is said that Self is the maker. But if self is the maker, why did it not make things pleasing? The causes of sorrow and joy are real and objective. How can they have been made by self? 7

"Again, if we adopt the argument that there is no maker, our fate is such as it is, and there is no causation, what use would there be in shaping our lives and adjusting means to an end? 8

"Therefore, we argue that all things that exist are not without cause. However, neither Īśvara, nor the absolute, nor the self, nor causeless chance, is the maker, but our deeds produce results both good and evil according to the law of causation. 9

"Let us, then, abandon the heresy of worshipping Īśvara and of praying to him; let us no longer lose ourselves in vain speculations of profitless subtleties; let us surrender self and all selfishness, and as all things are fixed by causation, let us practise good so that good may result from our actions." 10

And Anāthapindika said: "I see that thou art the Buddha, the Blessed One, the Tathāgata, and I wish to open to thee my whole mind. Having listened to my words advise me what I shall do. 11

"My life is full of work, and having acquired great wealth, I am surrounded with cares. Yet I enjoy my work, and apply myself to it with all diligence. Many people are in my employ and depend upon the success of my enterprises. 12

"Now, I have heard thy disciples praise the bliss of the hermit and denounce the unrest of the world. 'The Holy One,' they say, 'has given up his kingdom and his inheritance, and has found the path of righteousness, thus setting an example to all the world how to attain Nirvāna.' 13

"My heart yearns to do what is right and to be a blessing unto my fellows. Let me then ask thee, Must I give up my wealth, my home, and my business enterprises, and, like thyself, go into homelessness in order to attain the bliss of a religious life?" 14

And the Buddha replied: "The bliss of a religious life is attainable by every one who walks in the noble eightfold path. He that cleaves to wealth had better cast it away than allow his heart to be poisoned by it; but he who does not cleave to wealth, and possessing riches, uses them rightly, will be a blessing unto his fellows. 15

"It is not life and wealth and power that enslave men, but the cleaving to life and wealth and power. 16

"The bhikkhu who retires from the world in order to lead a life of leisure will have no gain, for a life of indolence is an abomination, and lack of energy is to be despised. 17

"The Dharma of the Tathāgata does not require a man to go into homelessness or to resign the world, unless he feels called upon to do so; but the Dharma of the Tathāgata requires every man to free himself from the illusion of self, to cleanse his heart, to give up his thirst for pleasure and lead a life of righteousness. 18

"And whatever men do, whether they remain in the world as artisans, merchants, and officers of the king, or retire from the world and devote themselves to a life of religious meditation, let them put their whole heart into their task;

let them be diligent and energetic, and, if they are like the lotus, which, although it grows in the water, yet remains untouched by the water, if they struggle in life without cherishing envy or hatred, if they live in the world not a life of self but a life of truth, then surely joy, peace, and bliss will dwell in their minds." 19

XXIV.

THE SERMON ON CHARITY.

Anāthapindika rejoiced at the words of the Blessed One and said: "I dwell at Sāvatthi, the capital of Kosala, a land rich in produce and enjoying peace. Pasenadi is the king of the country, and his name is renowned among our own people and our neighbors. Now I wish to found there a vihāra which shall be a place of religious devotion for your brotherhood, and I pray you kindly to accept it." 1

The Buddha saw into the heart of the supporter of orphans; and knowing that unselfish charity was the moving cause of his offer, in acceptance of the gift, the Blessed One said: 2

"The charitable man is loved by all; his friendship is prized highly; in death his heart is at rest and full of joy, for he suffers not from repentance; he receives the opening flower of his reward and the fruit that ripens from it. 3

"Hard it is to understand: By giving away our food, we get more strength, by bestowing clothing on others, we gain more beauty; by donating abodes of purity and truth, we acquire great treasures. 4

"There is a proper time and a proper mode in charity just as the vigorous warrior goes to battle, so is the man; who is able to give. He is like an able warrior, a champion strong and wise in action. 5

"Loving and compassionate he gives with reverence and banishes all hatred, envy, and anger. 6

"The charitable man has found the path of salvation. He is like the man who plants a sapling, securing thereby the shade, the flowers, and the fruit in future years. Even so is the result of charity, even so is the joy of him who helps those that are in need of assistance; even so is the great Nirvāna. 7

"We reach the immortal path only by continuous acts of kindliness and we perfect our souls by compassion and charity." 8

Anāthapindika invited Sāriputta to accompany him on his return to Kosala and help him in selecting a pleasant site for the vihāra. 9

XXV.

JETAVANA.

Anāthapindika, the friend of the destitute and the supporter of orphans, having returned home, saw the garden of the heir-apparent, Jeta, with its green groves and limpid rivulets, and thought: "This is the place which will be most suitable as a vihāra for the brotherhood of the Blessed One." And he went to the prince and asked leave to buy the ground. 1

The prince was not inclined to sell the garden, for he valued it highly. He at first refused but said at last, "If thou canst cover it with gold, then, and for no other price, shalt thou have it." 2

Anāthapindika rejoiced and began to spread his gold; but Jeta said: "Spare thyself the trouble, for I will not sell." But Anāthapindika insisted. Thus they contended until they resorted to the magistrate. 3

Meanwhile the people began to talk of the unwonted proceeding, and the prince, hearing more of the details and knowing that Anāthapindika was not only very wealthy but also straightforward and sincere, inquired into his plans. On hearing the name of the Buddha, the prince became anxious to share in the foundation and he accepted only one-half of the gold, saying: "Yours is the land, but mine are the trees. I will give the trees as my share of this offering to the Buddha." 4

Then Anāthapindika took the land and Jeta the trees, and they placed them in trust of Sāriputta for the Buddha. 5

After the foundations were laid, they began to build the hall which rose loftily in due proportions according to the directions which the Buddha had suggested; and it was beautifully decorated with appropriate carvings. 6

This vihāra was called Jetavana, and the friend of the orphans invited the Lord to come to Sāvatthi and receive the donation. And the Blessed One left Kapilavatthu and came to Sāvatthi. 7

While the Blessed One was entering Jetavana, Anāthapindika scattered flowers and burned incense, and as a sign of the gift he poured water from a golden dragon decanter, saying, "This Jetavana vihāra I give for the use of the brotherhood throughout the world." 8

The Blessed One received the gift and replied: "May all evil influences be overcome; may the offering promote the kingdom of righteousness and be a permanent blessing to mankind in general, to the land of Kosala, and especially also to the giver." 9

Then the king Pasenadi, hearing that the Lord had come, went in his royal equipage to the Jetavana vihāra and saluted the Blessed One with clasped hands, saying: 10

"Blessed is my unworthy and obscure kingdom that it has met with so great a fortune. For how can calamities

and dangers befall it in the presence of the Lord of the
world, the Dharmarāja, the King of Truth.   11

"Now that I have seen thy sacred countenance, let me
partake of the refreshing waters of thy teachings.   12

"Worldly profit is fleeting and perishable, but religious
profit is eternal and inexhaustible. A worldly man, though
a king, is full of trouble, but even a common man who is
holy has peace of mind."   13

Knowing the tendency of the king's heart, weighed down
by avarice and love of pleasure, the Buddha seized the opportunity and said: 14

"Even those who, by their evil karma, have been born
in low degree, when they see a virtuous man, feel reverence
for him. How much more must an independent king, on
account of merits acquired in previous existences, when
meeting a Buddha, conceive reverence for him.   15

"And now as I briefly expound the law, let the Mahā-
rāja listen and weigh my words, and hold fast that which
I deliver!   16

"Our good or evil deeds follow us continually like shad-
ows.   17

"That which is most needed is a loving heart!   18

"Regard thy people as men do an only son. Do not oppress them, do not destroy them; keep in due check every
member of thy body, forsake unrighteous doctrine and walk
in the straight path. Exalt not thyself by trampling down
others, but comfort and befriend the suffering.   19

"Neither ponder on kingly dignity, nor listen to the
smooth words of flatterers.   20

"There is no profit in vexing oneself by austerities, but
meditate on the Buddha and weigh his righteous law.   21

"We are encompassed on all sides by the rocks of birth,
old age, disease, and death, and only by considering and
practising the true law can we escape from this sorrow-
piled mountain.   22

"What profit, then, in practising iniquity?   23

"All who are wise spurn the pleasures of the body. They loathe lust and seek to promote their spiritual existence.   24

"When a tree is burning with fierce flames, how can the birds congregate therein? Truth cannot dwell where passion lives. He who does not know this, though he be a learned man and be praised by others as a sage, is beclouded with ignorance.   25

"To him who has this knowledge true wisdom dawns, and he will beware of hankering after pleasure. To acquire this state of mind, wisdom is the one thing needful. To neglect wisdom will lead to failure in life.   26

"The teachings of all religions should center here, for without wisdom there is no reason.   27

"This truth is not for the hermit alone; it concerns every human being, priest and layman alike. There is no distinction between the monk who has taken the vows, and the man of the world living with his family. There are hermits who fall into perdition, and there are humble householders who mount to the rank of rishis.   28

"Hankering after pleasure is a danger common to all; it carries away the world. He who is involved in its eddies finds no escape. But wisdom is the handy boat, reflection is the rudder. The slogan of religion calls you to overcome the assaults of Māra, the enemy.   29

"Since it is impossible to escape the result of our deeds, let us practise good works.   30

"Let us guard our thoughts that we do no evil, for as we sow so shall we reap.   31

"There are ways from light into darkness and from darkness into light. There are ways, also, from the gloom into deeper darkness, and from the dawn into brighter light. The wise man will use the light he has to receive more light. He will constantly advance in the knowledge of truth.   32

"Exhibit true superiority by virtuous conduct and the exercise of reason; meditate deeply on the vanity of earthly things, and understand the fickleness of life.   33

"Elevate the mind, and seek sincere faith with firm purpose; transgress not the rules of kingly conduct, and let your happiness depend, not upon external things, but upon your own mind. Thus you will lay up a good name for distant ages and will secure the favor of the Tathāgata." 34

The king listened with reverence and remembered all the words of the Buddha in his heart.   35

XXVI.

THE THREE CHARACTERISTICS AND THE UNCREATE.

When the Buddha was staying at the Veluvana, the bamboo grove at Rājagaha, he addressed the brethren thus: 1

"Whether Buddhas arise, O priests, or whether Buddhas do not arise, it remains a fact and the fixed and necessary constitution of being that all conformations are transitory. This fact a Buddha discovers and masters, and when he has discovered and mastered it, he announces, teaches, publishes, proclaims, discloses, minutely explains and makes it clear that all conformations are transitory.   2

"Whether Buddhas arise, O priests, or whether Buddhas do not arise, it remains a fact and a fixed and necessary constitution of being, that all conformations are suffering. This fact a Buddha discovers and masters, and when he has discovered and mastered it, he announces, publishes, proclaims, discloses, minutely explains and makes it clear that all conformations are suffering.   3

"Whether Buddhas arise, O priests, or whether Buddhas do not arise, it remains a fact and a fixed and necessary constitution of being, that all conformations are lacking a self. This fact a Buddha discovers and masters, and when he has discovered and mastered it, he announces, teaches, publishes, proclaims, discloses, minutely explains and makes it clear that all conformations are lacking a self." 4

And on another occasion the Blessed One dwelt at Sāvatthī in the Jetavana, the garden of Anāthapindika. 5

At that time the Blessed One edified, aroused, quickened and gladdened the monks with a religious discourse on the subject of Nirvāna. And these monks grasping the meaning, thinking it out, and accepting with their hearts the whole doctrine, listened attentively. But there was one brother who had some doubt left in his heart. He arose and clasping his hands made the request: "May I be permitted to ask a question?" When permission was granted he spoke as follows: 6

"The Buddha teaches that all conformations are transient, that all conformations are subject to sorrow, that all conformations are lacking a self. How then can there be Nirvāna, a state of eternal bliss?" 7

And the Blessed One, in this connection, on that occasion, breathed forth this solemn utterance: 8

"There is, O monks, a state where there is neither earth, nor water, nor heat, nor air; neither infinity of space nor infinity of consciousness, nor nothingness, nor perception nor non-perception; neither this world nor that world, neither sun nor moon. It is the uncreate. 9

"That, O monks, I term neither coming nor going nor standing; neither death nor birth. It is without stability, without change; it is the eternal which never originates and never passes away. There is the end of sorrow. 10

"It is hard to realize the essential, the truth is not easily perceived; desire is mastered by him who knows, and to him who sees aright all things are naught. 11

"There is, O monks, an unborn, unoriginated, uncreated, unformed. Were there not, O monks, this unborn, unoriginated, uncreated, unformed, there would be no escape from the world of the born, originated, created, formed. 12

"Since, O monks, there is an unborn, unoriginated, uncreated, and unformed, therefore is there an escape from the born, originated, created, formed." 13

XXVII.

THE BUDDHA'S FATHER.

The Buddha's name became famous over all India and Suddhodana, his father, sent word to him saying: "I am growing old and wish to see my son before I die. Others have had the benefit of his doctrine, but not his father nor his relatives." 1

And the messenger said: "O world-honored Tathāgata, thy father looks for thy coming as the lily longs for the rising of the sun." 2

The Blessed One consented to the request of his father and set out on his journey to Kapilavatthu. Soon the tidings spread in the native country of the Buddha: "Prince Siddhattha, who wandered forth from home into homelessness to obtain enlightenment, having attained his purpose, is coming back." 3

Suddhodana went out with his relatives and ministers to meet the prince. When the king saw Siddhattha, his son, from afar, he was struck with his beauty and dignity, and he rejoiced in his heart, but his mouth found no words to utter. 4

This, indeed, was his son; these were the features of Siddhattha. How near was the great samana to his heart, and yet what a distance lay between them! That noble muni was no longer Siddhattha, his son; he was the Buddha, the Blessed One, the Holy One, Lord of truth, and teacher of mankind. 5

Suddhodana the king, considering the religious dignity of his son, descended from his chariot and after saluting his son said: "It is now seven years since I have seen thee. How I have longed for this moment!" 6

Then the Sakyamuni took a seat opposite his father, and the king gazed eagerly at his son. He longed to call him by his name, but he dared not. "Siddhattha," he exclaimed silently in his heart, "Siddhattha, come back to thine aged father and be his son again!" But seeing the determination of his son, he suppressed his sentiments, and desolation overcame him. 7

Thus the king sat face to face with his son, rejoicing in his sadness and sad in his rejoicing. Well might he be proud of his son, but his pride broke down at the idea that his great son would never be his heir. 8

"I would offer thee my kingdom," said the king, "but if I did, thou wouldst account it but as ashes." 9

And the Buddha said: "I know that the king's heart is full of love and that for his son's sake he feels deep grief. But let the ties of love that bind him to the son whom he lost embrace with equal kindness all his fellow-beings, and he will receive in his place a greater one than Siddhattha; he will receive the Buddha, the teacher of truth, the preacher of righteousness, and the peace of Nirvāna will enter into his heart." 10

Suddhodana trembled with joy when he heard the melodious words of his son, the Buddha, and clasping his hands, exclaimed with tears in his eyes: "Wonderful is this change! The overwhelming sorrow has passed away. At first my sorrowing heart was heavy, but now I reap the fruit of thy great renunciation. It was right that, moved by thy mighty sympathy, thou shouldst reject the pleasures of royal power and achieve thy noble purpose in religious devotion.

Now that thou hast found the path, thou canst preach the law of immortality to all the world that yearns for deliverance." 11

The king returned to the palace, while the Buddha remained in the grove before the city. 12

XXVIII.

YASODHARÁ.

On the next morning the Buddha took his bowl and set out to beg his food. 1

And the news spread abroad: "Prince Siddhattha is going from house to house to receive alms in the city where he used to ride in a chariot attended by his retinue. His robe is like a red clod, and he holds in his hand an earthen bowl." 2

On hearing the strange rumor, the king went forth in great haste and when he met his son he exclaimed: "Why dost thou thus disgrace me? Knowest thou not that I can easily supply thee and thy bhikkhus with food?" 3

And the Buddha replied: "It is the custom of my race." 4

But the king said: "How can this be? Thou art descended from kings, and not one of them ever begged for food." 5

"O great king," rejoined the Buddha, "thou and thy race may claim descent from kings; my descent is from the Buddhas of old. They, begging their food, lived on alms." 6

The king made no reply, and the Blessed One continued: "It is customary, O king, when one has found a hidden treasure, for him to make an offering of the most precious jewel to his father. Suffer me, therefore, to open this treasure of mine which is the Dharma, and accept from me this gem:" 7

And the Blessed One recited the following stanza:

"Rise from dreams and loiter not
Open to truth thy mind.
Practise righteousness and thou
Eternal bliss shalt find." 8

Then the king conducted the prince into the palace, and the ministers and all the members of the royal family greeted him with great reverence, but Yasodharā, the mother of Rāhula, did not make her appearance. The king sent for Yasodharā, but she replied: "Surely, if I am deserving of any regard, Siddhattha will come and see me." 9

The Blessed One, having greeted all his relatives and friends, asked: "Where is Yasodharā?" And on being informed that she had refused to come, he rose straightway and went to her apartments. 10

"I am free," the Blessed One said to his disciples, Sāriputta and Moggallāna, whom he had bidden to accompany him to the princess's chamber; "the princess, however, is not as yet free. Not having seen me for a long time, she is exceedingly sorrowful. Unless her grief be allowed its course her heart will cleave. Should she touch the Tathāgata, the Holy One, ye must not prevent her." 11

Yasodharā sat in her room, dressed in mean garments, and her hair cut. When Prince Siddhattha entered, she was, from the abundance of her affection, like an overflowing vessel, unable to contain her love. 12

Forgetting that the man whom she loved was the Buddha, the Lord of the world, the preacher of truth, she held him by his feet and wept bitterly. 13

Remembering, however, that Suddhodana was present, she felt ashamed, and rising, seated herself reverently at a little distance. 14

The king apologized for the princess, saying: "This arises from her deep affection, and is more than a temporary emotion. During the seven years that she has lost her husband, when she heard that Siddhattha had shaved his head, she did likewise; when she heard that he had left off the use of perfumes and ornaments, she also refused their use. Like her husband she had eaten at appointed times from an earthen bowl only. Like him she had renounced high beds with splendid coverings, and when other princes asked her in marriage, she replied that she was still his. Therefore, grant her forgiveness." 15

And the Blessed One spoke kindly to Yasodharā, telling of her great merits inherited from former lives. She had indeed been again and again of great assistance to him. Her purity, her gentleness, her devotion had been invaluable to the Bodhisatta when he aspired to attain enlightenment, the highest aim of mankind. And so holy had she been that she desired to become the wife of a Buddha. This, then, is her karma, and it is the result of great merits. Her grief has been unspeakable, but the consciousness of the glory that surrounds her spiritual inheritance increased by her noble attitude during her life, will be a balm that will miraculously transform all sorrows into heavenly joy. 16

XXIX.

RĀHULA.

Many people in Kapilavatthu believed in the Tathāgata and took refuge in his doctrine, among them Nanda, Siddhattha's halfbrother, the son of Pajāpatī; Devadatta, his cousin and brother-in-law; Upāli the barber; and Anuruddha the philosopher. Some years later Ānanda, another cousin of the Blessed One, also joined the Sangha. 1

Ānanda was a man after the heart of the Blessed One; he was his most beloved disciple, profound in comprehension and gentle in spirit. And Ānanda remained always near the Blessed Master of truth, until death parted them. 2

On the seventh day after the Buddha's arrival in Kapila-vatthu, Yasodharā dressed Rāhula, now seven years old, in all the splendor of a prince and said to him: 3

"This holy man, whose appearance is so glorious that he looks like the great Brahmā, is thy father. He possesses four great mines of wealth which I have not yet seen. Go to him and entreat him to put thee in possession of them, for the son ought to inherit the property of his father." 4

Rāhula replied: "I know of no father but the king. Who is my father?" 5

The princess took the boy in her arms and from the window she pointed out to him the Buddha, who happened to be near the palace, partaking of food. 6

Rāhula then went to the Buddha, and looking up into his face said without fear and with much affection: "My father!" 7

And standing near by him, he added: "O samana, even thy shadow is a place of bliss!" 8

When the Tathāgata had finished his repast, he gave blessings and went away from the palace, but Rāhula followed and asked his father for his inheritance. 9

No one prevented the boy, nor did the Blessed One himself. 10

Then the Blessed One turned to Sāriputta, saying: "My son asks for his inheritance. I cannot give him perishable treasures that will bring cares and sorrows, but I can give him the inheritance of a holy life, which is a treasure that will not perish." 11

Addressing Rāhula with earnestness, the Blessed One said: "Gold and silver and jewels are not in my possession. But if thou art willing to receive spiritual treasures, and art strong enough to carry them and to keep them, I shall give thee the four truths which will teach thee the eightfold path of righteousness. Dost thou desire to be admitted to the brotherhood of those who devote their life to the culture of the heart seeking for the highest bliss attainable?" 12

And Rāhula replied with firmness: "I do. I want to join the brotherhood of the Buddha." 13

When the king heard that Rāhula had joined the brotherhood of bhikkhus he was grieved. He had lost Siddhattha and Nanda, his sons, and Devadatta, his nephew. But now that his grandson had been taken from him, he went to the Blessed One and spoke to him. And the Blessed One promised that from that time forward he would not ordain any minor without the consent of his parents or guardians. 14

CONSOLIDATION
OF THE BUDDHA'S RELIGION.

XXX.

JĪVAKA, THE PHYSICIAN.

LONG before the Blessed One had attained enlightenment, self-mortification had been the custom among those who earnestly sought for salvation. Deliverance of the soul from all the necessities of life and finally from the body itself, they regarded as the aim of religion. Thus, they avoided everything that might be a luxury in food, shelter, and clothing, and lived like the beasts in the woods. Some went naked, while others wore the rags cast away upon cemeteries or dungheaps.

When the Blessed One retired from the world,

1

he recognized at once the error of the naked ascetics, and, considering the indecency of their habit, clad himself in cast-off rags. 2

Having attained enlightenment and rejected all unnecessary self-mortifications, the Blessed One and his bhikkhus continued for a long time to wear the cast-off rags of cemeteries and dung-heaps. 3

Then it happened that the bhikkhus were visited with diseases of all kinds, and the Blessed One permitted and explicitly ordered the use of medicines, and among them he even enjoined, whenever needed, the use of unguents. 4

One of the brethren suffered from a sore on his foot, and the Blessed One enjoined the bhikkhus to wear foot-coverings. 5

Now it happened that a disease befell the body of the Blessed One himself, and Ānanda went to Jīvaka, physician to Bimbisāra, the king. 6

And Jīvaka, a faithful believer in the Holy One, ministered unto the Blessed One with medicines and baths until the body of the Blessed One was completely restored. 7

At that time, Pajjota, king of Ujjenī, was suffering from jaundice, and Jīvaka, the physician to king Bimbisâra, was consulted. When king Pajjota had been restored to health, he sent to Jīvaka a suit of the most excellent cloth. And Jīvaka said to himself: "This suit is made of the best cloth, and nobody is worthy to receive it but the Blessed One, the perfect and holy Buddha, or the Magadha king, Senija Bimbisāra." 8

Then Jīvaka took that suit and went to the place where the Blessed One was; having approached him, and having respectfully saluted the Blessed One, he sat down near him and said: "Lord, I have a boon to ask of the Blessed One." 9

The Buddha replied: "The Tathāgatas, Jīvaka, do not grant boons before they know what they are." 10

Jīvaka said: "Lord, it is a proper and unobjectionable request."   11

"Speak, Jīvaka," said the Blessed One.   12

"Lord of the world, the Blessed One wears only robes made of rags taken from a dung-heap or a cemetery, and so also does the brotherhood of bhikkhus. Now, Lord, this suit has been sent to me by King Pajjota, which is the best and most excellent, and the finest and the most precious, and the noblest that can be found. Lord of the world, may the Blessed One accept from me this suit, and may he allow the brotherhood of bhikkhus to wear lay robes." 13

The Blessed One accepted the suit, and after having delivered a religious discourse, he addressed the bhikkhus thus: 14

"Henceforth ye shall be at liberty to wear either cast-off rags or lay robes. Whether ye are pleased with the one or with the other, I will approve of it."   15

When the people at Rājagaha heard, "The Blessed One has allowed the bhikkhus to wear lay robes," those who were willing to bestow gifts became glad. And in one day many thousands of robes were presented at Rājagaha to the bhikkhus.   16

XXXI.

THE BUDDHA'S PARENTS ATTAIN NIRVĀNA.

When Suddhodana had grown old, he fell sick and sent for his son to come and see him once more before he died; and the Blessed One came and stayed at the sick-bed, and Suddhodana, having attained perfect enlightenment, died in the arms of the Blessed One.   1

And it is said that the Blessed One, for the sake of preaching to his mother Māyā-devī, ascended to heaven and dwelt

with the devas. Having concluded his pious mission, he
returned to the earth and went about again, converting
those who listened to his teachings.   2

XXXII.

WOMEN ADMITTED TO THE SANGHA.

Yasodharā had three times requested of the Buddha that
she might be admitted to the Sangha, but her wish had not
been granted. Now Pajāpatī, the foster-mother of the
Blessed One, in the company of Yasodharā, and many other
women, went to the Tathāgata entreating him earnestly to
let them take the vows and be ordained as disciples.   1
And the Blessed One, foreseeing the danger that lurked
in admitting women to the Sangha, protested that while
the good religion ought surely to last a thousand years it
would, when women joined it, likely decay after five
hundred years; but observing the zeal of Pajāpatī and
Yasodharā for leading a religious life he could no longer
resist and assented to have them admitted as his disciples. 2
Then the venerable Ānanda addressed the Blessed One
thus: 3
"Are women competent, Venerable Lord, if they retire
from household life to the homeless state, under the doctrine
and discipline announced by the Tathāgata, to attain to the
fruit of conversion, to attain to a release from a wearisome
repetition of rebirths, to attain to saintship?"   4
And the Blessed One declared: "Women are competent,
Ānanda, if they retire from household life to the homeless
state, under the doctrine and discipline announced by the
Tathāgata, to attain to the fruit of conversion, to attain to
a release from a wearisome repetition of rebirths, to attain
to saintship.   5

"Consider, Ānanda, how great a benefactress Pajāpatī has been. She is the sister of the mother of the Blessed One, and as foster-mother and nurse, reared the Blessed One after the death of his mother. So, Ānanda, women may retire from household life to the homeless state, under the doctrine and discipline announced by the Tathāgata." 6

Pajāpatī was the first woman to become a disciple of the Buddha and to receive the ordination as a bhikkhunī. 7

XXXIII.

THE BHIKKHUS' CONDUCT TOWARD WOMEN.

The bhikkhus came to the Blessed One and asked him: 1

"O Tathāgata, our Lord and Master, what conduct toward women dost thou prescribe to the samanas who have left the world?" 2

And the Blessed One said: 3

"Guard against looking on a woman. 4

"If ye see a woman, let it be as though ye saw her not, and have no conversation with her. 5

"If, after all, ye must speak with her, let it be with a pure heart, and think to yourself, 'I as a samana will live in this sinful world as the spotless leaf of the lotus, unsoiled by the mud in which it grows.' 6

"If the woman be old, regard her as your mother, if young, as your sister, if very young, as your child. 7

"The samana who looks on a woman as a woman, or touches her as a woman, has broken his vow and is no longer a disciple of the Tathāgata. 8

"The power of lust is great with men, and is to be feared withal; take then the bow of earnest perseverance, and the sharp arrow-points of wisdom. 9

"Cover your heads with the helmet of right thought, and fight with fixed resolve against the five desires. 10

"Lust beclouds a man's heart, when it is confused with woman's beauty, and the mind is dazed. 11

"Better far with red-hot irons bore out both your eyes, than encourage in yourself sensual thoughts, or look upon a woman's form with lustful desires. 12

"Better fall into the fierce tiger's mouth, or under the sharp knife of the executioner, than dwell with a woman and excite in yourself lustful thoughts. 13

"A woman of the world is anxious to exhibit her form and shape, whether walking, standing, sitting, or sleeping. Even when represented as a picture, she desires to captivate with the charms of her beauty, and thus to rob men of their steadfast heart. 14

"How then ought ye to guard yourselves? 15

"By regarding her tears and her smiles as enemies, her stooping form, her hanging arms, and her disentangled hair as toils designed to entrap man's heart. 16

"Therefore, I say, restrain the heart, give it no unbridled license." 17

XXXIV.

VISĀKHĀ.

Visākhā, a wealthy woman in Sāvatthī who had many children and grandchildren, had given to the order the Pubbārāma or Eastern Garden, and was the first in Northern Kosala to become a matron of the lay sisters. 1

When the Blessed One stayed at Sāvatthī, Visākhā went up to the place where the Blessed One was, and tendered him an invitation to take his meal at her house, which the Blessed One accepted. 2

And a heavy rain fell during the night and the next morning; and the bhikkhus doffed their robes to keep them dry and let the rain fall upon their bodies. 3

When on the next day the Blessed One had finished
his meal, she took her seat at his side and spoke thus:
"Eight are the boons, Lord, which I beg of the Blessed
One."   4

Said the Blessed One: "The Tathāgatas, O Visākhā,
grant no boons until they know what they are."   5

Visākhā replied: "Befitting, Lord, and unobjectionable
are the boons I ask."   6

Having received permission to make known her requests,
Visākhā said: "I desire, Lord, through all my life long to
bestow robes for the rainy season on the Sangha, and
food for incoming bhikkhus, and food for outgoing bhikkhus, and food for the sick, and food for those who wait
upon the sick, and medicine for the sick, and a constant
supply of rice-milk for the Sangha, and bathing robes for
the bhikkhunīs, the sisters."   7

Said the Buddha: "But what circumstance is it, O Visākhā,
that thou hast in view in asking these eight boons of the
Tathāgata?"   8

And Visākhā replied: 9

"I gave command, Lord, to my maid-servant, saying, 'Go,
and announce to the brotherhood that the meal is ready.'
And the maid went, but when she came to the vihāra, she
observed that the bhikkhus had doffed their robes while it was
raining, and she thought: 'These are not bhikkhus, but naked
ascetics letting the rain fall on them.' So she returned to
me and reported accordingly, and I had to send her a
second time. Impure, Lord, is nakedness, and revolting.
It was this circumstance, Lord, that I had in view in
desiring to provide the Sangha my life long with special
garments for use in the rainy season.   10

"As to my second wish, Lord, an incoming bhikkhu,
not being able to take the direct roads, and not knowing
the places where food can be procured, comes on his way
tired out by seeking for alms. It was this circumstance,

Lord, that I had in view in desiring to provide the Sangha my life long with food for incoming bhikkhus.   11

"Thirdly, Lord, an outgoing bhikkhu, while seeking about for alms, may be left behind, or may arrive too late at the place whither he desires to go, and will set out on the road in weariness.   12

"Fourthly, Lord, if a sick bhikkhu does not obtain suitable food, his sickness may increase upon him, and he may die.   13

"Fifthly, Lord, a bhikkhu who is waiting upon the sick will lose his opportunity of going out to seek food for himself.   14

"Sixthly, Lord, if a sick bhikkhu does not obtain suitable medicines, his sickness may increase upon him, and he may die.   15

"Seventhly, Lord, I have heard that the Blessed One has praised rice-milk, because it gives readiness of mind, dispels hunger and thirst; it is wholesome for the healthy as nourishment, and for the sick as a medicine. Therefore I desire to provide the Sangha my life long with a constant supply of rice-milk.   16

"Finally, Lord, the bhikkhunīs are in the habit of bathing in the river Achiravatī with the courtesans, at the same landing-place, and naked. And the courtesans, Lord, ridicule the bhikkhunīs, saying, 'What is the good, ladies, of your maintaining chastity when you are young? When you are old, maintain chastity then; thus will you obtain both worldly pleasure and religious consolation.' Impure, Lord, is nakedness for a woman, disgusting, and revolting.   17

"These are the circumstances, Lord, that I had in view."   18

The Blessed One said: "But what was the advantage you had in view for yourself, O Visākhā, in asking the eight boons of the Tathāgatha?"   19

Visākhā replied: 20

"Bhikkhus who have spent the rainy seasons in various places will come, Lord, to Sāvatthī to visit the Blessed

One. And on coming to the Blessed One they will ask, saying: 'Such and such a bhikkhu, Lord, has died. What, now, is his destiny?' Then will the Blessed One explain that he has attained the fruits of conversion; that he has attained arahatship or has entered Nirvāna, as the case may be. 21

"And I, going up to them, will ask, 'Was that brother, Sirs, one of those who had formerly been at Sāvatthī?' If they reply to me, 'He has formerly been at Sāvatthī,' then shall I arrive at the conclusion, 'For a certainty did that brother enjoy either the robes for the rainy season, or the food for the incoming bhikkhus, or the food for the out-going bhikkhus, or the food for the sick, or the food for those that wait upon the sick, or the medicine for the sick, or the constant supply of rice-milk.' 22

"Then will gladness spring up within me; thus gladdened, joy will come to me; and so rejoicing all my mind will be at peace. Being thus at peace I shall experience a blissful feeling of content; and in that bliss my heart will be at rest. That will be to me an exercise of my moral sense, an exercise of my moral powers, an exercise of the seven kinds of wisdom! This, Lord, was the advantage I had in view for myself in asking those eight boons of the Blessed One." 23

The Blessed One said: "It is well, it is well, Visākhā. Thou hast done well in asking these eight boons of the Tathāgata with such advantages in view. Charity bestowed upon those who are worthy of it is like good seed sown on a good soil that yields an abundance of fruits. But alms given to those who are yet under the tyrannical yoke of the passions are like seed deposited in a bad soil. The passions of the receiver of the alms choke, as it were, the growth of merits." 24

And the Blessed One gave thanks to Visākhā in these verses: 25

"O noble woman of an upright life,
Disciple of the Blessed One, thou givest
Unstintedly in purity of heart.   26

"Thou spreadest joy, assuagest pain,
And verily thy gift will be a blessing
As well to many others as to thee."   27

XXXV.

THE UPOSATHA AND PÂTIMOKKHA.

When Seniya Bimbisāra, the king of Magadha, was advanced in years, he retired from the world and led a religious life. He observed that there were Brahmanical sects in Rājagaha keeping sacred certain days, and the people went to their meeting-houses and listened to their sermons.   1

Concerning the need of keeping regular days for retirement from worldly labors and religious instruction, the king went to the Blessed One and said: "The Parivrājaka, who belong to the Titthiya school, prosper and gain adherents because they keep the eighth day and also the fourteenth or fifteenth day of each half-month. Would it not be advisable for the reverend brethren of the Sangha also to assemble on days duly appointed for that purpose?"   2

And the Blessed One commanded the bhikkhus to assemble on the eighth day and also on the fourteenth or fifteenth day of each half-month, and to devote these days to religious exercises.   3

A bhikkhu duly appointed should address the congregation and expound the Dharma. He should exhort the people to walk in the eightfold path of righteousness; he should comfort them in the vicissitudes of life and gladden them with the bliss of the fruit of good deeds. Thus the brethren should keep the Uposatha. 4

Now the bhikkhus, in obedience to the rule laid down by the Blessed One, assembled in the vihāra on the day appointed, and the people went to hear the Dharma, but they were greatly disappointed, for the bhikkhus remained silent and delivered no discourse. 5

When the Blessed One heard of it, he ordered the bhikkhus to recite the Pātimokkha, which is a ceremony of disburdening the conscience; and he commanded them to make confession of their trespasses so as to receive the absolution of the order. 6

A fault, if there be one, should be confessed by the bhikkhu who remembers it and desires to be cleansed. For a fault, when confessed, shall be light on him. 7

And the Blessed One said: "The Pātimokkha must be recited in this way: 8

"Let a competent and venerable bhikkhu make the following proclamation to the Sangha: 'May the Sangha hear me! To-day is Uposatha, the eighth, or the fourteenth or fifteenth day of the half-month. If the Sangha is ready, let the Sangha hold the Uposatha service and recite the Pātimokkha. I will recite the Pātimokkha.' 9

"And the bhikkhus shall reply: 'We hear it well and we concentrate well our minds on it, all of us.' 10

"Then the officiating bhikkhu shall continue: 'Let him who has committed an offence, confess it; if there be no offence, let all remain silent; from your being silent I shall understand that the reverend brethren are free from offences. 11

"'As a single person who has been asked a question answers it, so also, if before an assembly like this a question is solemnly proclaimed three times, an answer is expected: if a bhikkhu, after a threefold proclamation, does not confess an existing offence which he remembers, he commits an intentional falsehood. 12

"'Now, reverend brethren, an intentional falsehood has been declared an impediment by the Blessed One. Therefore, if an offence has been committed by a bhikkhu who remembers it and desires to become pure, the offence should be confessed by the bhikkhu; and when it has been confessed, it is treated duly.'" 13

XXXVI.

THE SCHISM.

While the Blessed One dwelt at Kosambī, a certain bhikkhu was accused of having committed an offence, and, as he refused to acknowledge it, the brotherhood pronounced against him the sentence of expulsion. 1

Now, that bhikkhu was erudite. He knew the Dharma, had studied the rules of the order, and was wise, learned, intelligent, modest, conscientious, and ready to submit himself to discipline. And he went to his companions and friends among the bhikkhus, saying: "This is no offence, friends; this is no reason for a sentence of expulsion. I am not guilty. The verdict is unconstitutional and invalid. Therefore I consider myself still as a member of the order. May the venerable brethren assist me in maintaining my right." 2

Those who sided with the expelled brother went to the bhikkhus who had pronounced the sentence, saying: "This is no offence"; while the bhikkhus who had pronounced the sentence replied: "This is an offence." 3

Thus altercations and quarrels arose, and the Sangha was divided into two parties, reviling and slandering each other. 4

And all these happenings were reported to the Blessed One.
5

Then the Blessed One went to the place where the bhikkhus were who had pronounced the sentence of expulsion, and said to them: "Do not think, O bhikkhus, that you are to pronounce expulsion against a bhikkhu, whatever be the facts of the case, simply by saying: 'It occurs to us that it is so, and therefore we are pleased to proceed thus against our brother.' Let those bhikkhus who frivolously pronounce a sentence against a brother who knows the Dharma and the rules of the order, who is learned, wise, intelligent, modest, conscientious, and ready to submit himself to discipline, stand in awe of causing divisions. They must not pronounce a sentence of expulsion against a brother merely because he refuses to see his offence."
6

Then the Blessed One rose and went to the brethren who sided with the expelled brother and said to them: "Do not think, O bhikkhus, that if you have given offence you need not atone for it, thinking: 'We are without offence.' When a bhikkhu has committed an offence, which he considers no offence while the brotherhood consider him guilty, he should think: 'These brethren know the Dharma and the rules of the order; they are learned, wise, intelligent, modest, conscientious, and ready to submit themselves to discipline; it is impossible that they should on my account act with selfishness or in malice or in delusion or in fear.' Let him stand in awe of causing divisions, and rather acknowledge his offence on the authority of his brethren."
7

Both parties continued to keep Uposatha and perform official acts independently of one another; and when their doings were related to the Blessed One, he ruled that the keeping of Uposatha and the performance of official acts were lawful, unobjectionable, and valid for both parties.

For he said: "The bhikkhus who side with the expelled brother form a different communion from those who pronounced the sentence. There are venerable brethren in both parties. As they do not agree, let them keep Uposatha and perform official acts separately."　　　8

And the Blessed One reprimanded the quarrelsome bhikkhus saying to them:　　　9

"Loud is the voice which worldlings make; but how can they be blamed when divisions arise also in the Sangha? Hatred is not appeased in those who think: 'He has reviled me, he has wronged me, he has injured me.'　　　10

"For not by hatred is hatred appeased. Hatred is appeased by not-hatred. This is an eternal law.　　　11

"There are some who do not know the need of self-restraint; if they are quarrelsome we may excuse their behavior. But those who know better, should learn to live in concord.　　　12

"If a man finds a wise friend who lives righteously and is constant in his character, he may live with him, overcoming all dangers, happy and mindful.　　　13

"But if he finds not a friend who lives righteously and is constant in his character, let him rather walk alone, like a king who leaves his empire and the cares of government behind him to lead a life of retirement like a lonely elephant in the forest.　　　14

"With fools there is no companionship. Rather than to live with men who are selfish, vain, quarrelsome, and obstinate let a man walk alone."　　　15

And the Blessed One thought to himself: "It is no easy task to instruct these headstrong and infatuate fools." And he rose from his seat and went away.　　　16

XXXVII

THE RE-ESTABLISHMENT OF CONCORD.

Whilst the dispute between the parties was not yet settled, the Blessed One left Kosambī, and wandering from place to place he came at last to Sāvatthī.   1

And in the absence of the Blessed One the quarrels grew worse, so that the lay devotees of Kosambī became annoyed and they said: "These quarrelsome monks are a great nuisance and will bring upon us misfortunes. Worried by their altercations the Blessed One is gone, and has selected another abode for his residence. Let us, therefore, neither salute the bhikkhus nor support them. They are not worthy of wearing yellow robes, and must either propitiate the Blessed One, or return to the world."   2

And the bhikkhus of Kosambī, when no longer honored and no longer supported by the lay devotees, began to repent and said: "Let us go to the Blessed One and let him settle the question of our disagreement."   3

And both parties went to Sāvatthī to the Blessed One. And the venerable Sāriputta, having heard of their arrival, addressed the Blessed One and said: "These contentious, disputatious, and quarrelsome bhikkhus of Kosambī, the authors of dissensions, have come to Sāvatthī. How am I to behave, O Lord, toward those bhikkhus."   4

"Do not reprove them, Sāriputta," said the Blessed One, "for harsh words do not serve as a remedy and are pleasant to no one. Assign separate dwelling-places to each party and treat them with impartial justice. Listen with patience to both parties. He alone who weighs both sides is called a muni. When both parties have presented their case, let the Sangha come to an agreement and declare the re-establishment of concord."   5

And Pajāpatī, the matron, asked the Blessed One for advice, and the Blessed One said: "Let both parties enjoy the gifts of lay members, be they robes or food, as they may need, and let no one receive any noticeable preference over any other." 6

And the venerable Upāli, having approached the Blessed One, asked concerning the re-establishment of peace in the Sangha: "Would it be right, O Lord," said he, "that the Sangha, to avoid further disputations, should declare the restoration of concord without inquiring into the matter of the quarrel?" 7

And the Blessed One said: 8

"If the Sangha declares the re-establishment of concord without having inquired into the matter, the declaration is neither right nor lawful. 9

"There are two ways of re-establishing concord; one is in the letter, and the other one is in the spirit and in the letter. 10

"If the Sangha declares the re-establishment of concord without having inquired into the matter, the peace is concluded in the letter only. But if the Sangha, having inquired into the matter and having gone to the bottom of it, decides to declare the re-establishment of concord, the peace is concluded in the spirit and also in the letter. 11

"The concord re-established in the spirit and in the letter is alone right and lawful." 12

And the Blessed One addressed the bhikkhus and told them the story of Prince Dīghāvu, the Long-lived. He said: 13

"In former times, there lived at Benares a powerful king whose name was Brahmadatta of Kāsi; and he went to war against Dīghīti, the Long-suffering, a king of Kosala, for he thought, 'The kingdom of Kosala is small and Dīghīti will not be able to resist my armies.' 14

"And Dīghīti, seeing that resistance was impossible against the great host of the king of Kāsi, fled, leaving his little kingdom in the hands of Brahmadatta; and having wandered from place to place, he came at last to Benares, and lived there with his consort in a potter's dwelling outside the town.   15

"And the queen bore him a son and they called him Dīghāvu.   16

"When Dīghāvu had grown up, the king thought to himself: 'King Brahmadatta has done us great harm, and he is fearing our revenge; he will seek to kill us. Should he find us he will slay all three of us.' And he sent his son away, and Dīghāvu having received a good education from his father, applied himself diligently to learn all arts, becoming very skilful and wise.   17

"At that time the barber of king Dīghīti dwelt at Benares, and he saw the king, his former master, and, being of an avaricious nature, betrayed him to King Brahmadatta. 18

"When Brahmadatta, the king of Kāsi, heard that the fugitive king of Kosala and his queen, unknown and in disguise, were living a quiet life in a potter's dwelling, he ordered them to be bound and executed; and the sheriff to whom the order was given seized king Dīghīti and led him to the place of execution.   19

"While the captive king was being led through the streets of Benares he saw his son who had returned to visit his parents, and, careful not to betray the presence of his son, yet anxious to communicate to him his last advice, he cried: 'O Dīghāvu, my son! Be not far-sighted, be not near-sighted, for not by hatred is hatred appeased; hatred is appeased by not-hatred only.'   20

"The king and queen of Kosala were executed, but Dīghāvu their son bought strong wine and made the guards drunk. When the night arrived he laid the bodies of his parents upon a funeral pyre and burned them with all honors and religious rites.   21

"When king Brahmadatta heard of it, he became afraid, for he thought, 'Dīghāvu, the son of king Dīghīti, is a wise youth and he will take revenge for the death of his parents. If he espies a favorable opportunity, he will assassinate me.'   22

"Young Dīghāvu went to the forest and wept to his heart's content. Then he wiped his tears and returned to Benares. Hearing that assistants were wanted in the royal elephants' stable, he offered his services and was engaged by the master of the elephants.   23

"And it happened that the king heard a sweet voice ringing through the night and singing to the lute a beautiful song that gladdened his heart. And having inquired among his attendants who the singer might be, was told that the master of the elephants had in his service a young man of great accomplishments, and beloved by all his comrades. They said, 'He is wont to sing to the lute, and he must have been the singer that gladdened the heart of the king.'   24

"And the king summoned the young man before him and, being much pleased with Dīghāvu, gave him employment in the royal castle. Observing how wisely the youth acted, how modest he was and yet punctilious in the performance of his work, the king very soon gave him a position of trust.   25

"Now it came to pass that the king went hunting and became separated from his retinue, young Dīghāvu alone remaining with him. And the king worn out from the hunt laid his head in the lap of young Dīghāvu and slept.   26

"And Dīghāvu thought: 'People will forgive great wrongs which they have suffered, but they will never be at ease about the wrongs which they themselves have done. They will persecute their victims to the bitter end. This king Brahmadatta has done us great injury; he robbed us of our kingdom and slew my father and my mother. He is now in my power.' Thinking thus he unsheathed his sword. 27

"Then Dīghāvu thought of the last words of his father: 'Be not far-sighted, be not near-sighted. For not by hatred is hatred appeased. Hatred is appeased by not-hatred alone.' Thinking thus, he put his sword back into the sheath. 28

"The king became restless in his sleep and he awoke, and when the youth asked, 'Why art thou frightened, O king?' he replied: 'My sleep is always restless because I often dream that young Dīghāvu is coming upon me with his sword. While I lay here with my head in thy lap I dreamed the dreadful dream again; and I awoke full of terror and alarm.' 29

"Then the youth, laying his left hand upon the defenceless king's head and with his right hand drawing his sword, said: 'I am Dīghāvu, the son of king Dīghīti, whom thou hast robbed of his kingdom and slain together with his queen, my mother. I know that men overcome the hatred entertained for wrongs which they have suffered much more easily than for the wrongs which they have done, and so I cannot expect that thou wilt take pity on me; but now a chance for revenge has come to me.' 30

"The king seeing that he was at the mercy of young Dīghāvu raised his hands and said: 'Grant me my life, my dear Dīghāvu, grant me my life. I shall be forever grateful to thee.' 31

"And Dīghāvu said without bitterness or ill-will: 'How can I grant thee thy life, O king, since my life is endangered by thee. I do not mean to take thy life. It is thou, O king, who must grant me my life.' 32

"And the king said: 'Well, my dear Dīghāvu, then grant me my life, and I will grant thee thine.' 33

"Thus, king Brahmadatta of Kāsi and young Dīghāvu granted each other's life and took each other's hand and swore an oath not to do any harm to each other. 34

"And king Brahmadatta of Kāsi said to young Dīghāvu:

'Why did thy father say to thee in the hour of his death: "Be not far-sighted, be not near-sighted, for hatred is not appeased by hatred. Hatred is appeased by not-hatred alone,"—what did thy father mean by that?' 35

"The youth replied: 'When my father, O king, in the hour of his death said: "Be not far-sighted," he meant, Let not thy hatred go far. And when my father said, "Be not nearsighted," he meant, Be not hasty to fall out with thy friends. And when he said, "For not by hatred is hatred appeased; hatred is appeased by not-hatred," he meant this: Thou hast killed my father and mother, O king, and if I should deprive thee of thy life, then thy partisans in turn would take away my life; my partisans again would deprive thine of their lives. Thus by hatred, hatred would not be appeased. But now, O king, thou hast granted me my life, and I have granted thee thine; thus by not-hatred hatred has been appeased.' 36

"Then king Brahmadatta of Kāsi thought: 'How wise is young Dīghāvu that he understands in its full extent the meaning of what his father spoke concisely.' And the king gave him back his father's kingdom and gave him his daughter in marriage." 37

Having finished the story, the Blessed One said: "Brethren, ye are my lawful sons in the faith, begotten by the words of my mouth. Children ought not to trample under foot the counsel given them by their father; do ye henceforth follow my admonitions." 38

Then the bhikkhus met in conference; they discussed their differences in mutual good will, and the concord of the Sangha was re-established. 39

XXXVIII.

THE BHIKKHUS REBUKED.

And it happened that the Blessed One walked up and down in the open air unshod.　　　1

When the elders saw that the Blessed One walked unshod, they put away their shoes and did likewise. But the novices did not heed the example of their elders and kept their feet covered.　　　2

Some of the brethren noticed the irreverent behavior of the novices and told the Blessed One; and the Blessed One rebuked the novices and said: "If the brethren, even now, while I am yet living, show so little respect and courtesy to one another, what will they do when I have passed away?"　　　3

And the Blessed One was filled with anxiety for the welfare of the truth; and he continued:　　　4

"Even the laymen, O bhikkhus, who move in the world, pursuing some handicraft that they may procure them a living, will be respectful, affectionate, and hospitable to their teachers. Do ye, therefore, O bhikkhus, so let your light shine forth, that ye, having left the world and devoted your entire life to religion and to religious discipline, may observe the rules of decency, be respectful, affectionate, and hospitable to your teachers and superiors, or those who rank as your teachers and superiors. Your demeanor, O bhikkhus, does not conduce to the conversion of the unconverted and to the increase of the number of the faithful. It serves, O bhikkhus, to repel the unconverted and to estrange them. I exhort you to be more considerate in the future, more thoughtful and more respectful"　　　5

XXXIX

DEVADATTA.

When Devadatta, the son of Suprabuddha and a brother of Yasodharā, became a disciple, he cherished the
hope of attaining the same distinctions and honors as Gotama Siddhattha. Being disappointed in his ambitions, he
conceived in his heart a jealous hatred, and, attempting to
excel the Perfect One in virtue, he found fault with his
regulations and reproved them as too lenient.   1

Devadatta went to Rājagaha and gained the ear of Ajātasattu, the son of King Bimbisāra. And Ajātasattu built
a new vihāra for Devadatta, and founded a sect whose
disciples were pledged to severe rules and self-mortification.   2

Soon afterwards the Blessed One himself came to Rājagaha and stayed at the Veluvana vihāra.   3

Devadatta called on the Blessed One, requesting him to
sanction his rules of greater stringency, by which a greater
holiness might be procured. "The body," he said, "consists of its thirty-two parts and has no divine attributes. It
is conceived in sin and born in corruption. Its attributes
are liability to pain and dissolution, for it is impermanent.
It is the receptacle of karma which is the curse of our
former existences; it is the dwelling-place of sin and diseases and its organs constantly discharge disgusting secre-
tions. Its end is death and its goal the charnel house. Such
being the condition of the body it behooves us to treat it
as a carcass full of abomination and to clothe it in such
rags only as have been gathered in cemeteries or upon
dung-hills."   4

The Blessed One said: "Truly, the body is full of impurity and its end is the charnel house, for it is impermanent and destined to be dissolved into its elements. But
being the receptacle of karma, it lies in our power to make

it a vessel of truth and not of evil. It is not good to indulge in the pleasures of the body, but neither is it good to neglect our bodily needs and to heap filth upon impurities. The lamp that is not cleansed and not filled with oil will be extinguished, and a body that is unkempt, unwashed, and weakened by penance will not be a fit receptacle for the light of truth. Attend to your body and its needs as you would treat a wound which you care for without loving it. Severe rules will not lead the disciples on the middle path which I have taught. Certainly, no one can be prevented from keeping more stringent rules, if he sees fit to do so, but they should not be imposed upon any one, for they are unnecessary." 5

Thus the Tathāgata refused Devadatta's proposal; and Devadatta left the Buddha and went into the vihāra speaking evil of the Lord's path of salvation as too lenient and altogether insufficient. 6

When the Blessed One heard of Devadatta's intrigues, he said: "Among men there is no one who is not blamed. People blame him who sits silent and him who speaks, they also blame the man who preaches the middle path." 7

Devadatta instigated Ajātasattu to plot against his father Bimbisāra, the king, so that the prince would no longer be subject to him; Bimbisāra was imprisoned by his son in a tower where he died leaving the kingdom of Magadha to his son Ajātasattu. 8

The new king listened to the evil advice of Devadatta, and he gave orders to take the life of the Tathāgata. However, the murderers sent out to kill the Lord could not perform their wicked deed, and became converted as soon as they saw him and listened to his preaching. The rock hurled down from a precipice upon the great Master split in twain, and the two pieces passed by on either side without doing any harm. Nalagiri, the wild elephant let loose to destroy the Lord, became gentle in his presence; and Ajātasattu, suffering greatly from the pangs of his conscience, went to the Blessed One and sought peace in his distress.   9

The Blessed One received Ajātasattu kindly and taught him the way of salvation; but Devadatta still tried to become the founder of a religious school of his own.   10

Devadatta did not succeed in his plans and having been abandoned by many of his disciples, he fell sick, and then repented. He entreated those who had remained with him to carry his litter to the Buddha, saying: "Take me, children, take me to him; though I have done evil to him, I am his brother-in-law. For the sake of our relationship the Buddha will save me." And they obeyed, although reluctantly.   11

And Devadatta in his impatience to see the Blessed One rose from his litter while his carriers were washing their hands. But his feet burned under him; he sank to the ground; and, having chanted a hymn on the Buddha, died.   12

XL.

NAME AND FORM.

On one occasion the Blessed One entered the assembly hall and the brethren hushed their conversation.   1

When they had greeted him with clasped hands, they sat down and became composed. Then the Blessed One said: "Your minds are inflamed with intense interest; what was the topic of your discussion?"   2

And Sāriputta rose and spake: "World-honored master, we were discussing the nature of man's own existence. We were trying to grasp the mixture of our own being which is called Name and Form. Every human being consists of conformations, and there are three groups which are not corporeal. They are sensation, perception, and the dispositions, all three constitute consciousness and mind, being comprised under the term Name. And there are four elements, the earthy element, the watery element, the fiery element, and the gaseous element, and these four elements constitute man's bodily form, being held together so that this machine moves like a puppet. How does this name and form endure and how can it live?" 3

Said the Blessed One: "Life is instantaneous and living is dying. Just as a chariot-wheel in rolling rolls only at one point of the tire, and in resting rests only at one point; in exactly the same way, the life of a living being lasts only for the period of one thought. As soon as that thought has ceased the being is said to have ceased.   4

"As it has been said:—'The being of a past moment of thought has lived, but does not live, nor will it live. The being of a future moment of thought will live, but has not lived, nor does it live. The being of the present moment of thought does live, but has not lived, nor will it live.'"   5

"As to Name and Form we must understand how they interact. Name has no power of its own, ·nor can it go on of its own impulse, either to eat, or to drink, or to utter sounds, or to make a movement. Form also is without power and cannot go on of its own impulse. It has no desire to eat, or to drink, or to utter sounds, or to make a movement. But Form goes on when supported by Name, and Name when supported by Form. When Name has a desire to eat, or to drink, or to utter sounds, or to make a movement, then Form eats, drinks, utters sounds, makes a movement.   6

"It is as if two men, the one blind from birth and the other a cripple, were desirous of going traveling, and the man blind from birth were to say to the cripple as follows: 'See here! I am able to use my legs, but I have no eyes with which to see the rough and the smooth places in the road.'   7

"And the cripple were to say to the man blind from birth as follows: 'See here! I am able to use my eyes, but I have no legs with which to go forward and back.' 8

"And the man blind from birth, pleased and delighted, were to mount the cripple on his shoulders. And the cripple sitting on the shoulders of the man blind from birth were to direct him, saying, 'Leave the left and go to the right; leave the right and go to the left.' 9

"Here the man blind from birth is without power of his own, and weak, and cannot go of his own impulse or might. The cripple also is without power of his own, and weak, and cannot go of his own impulse or might. Yet when they mutually support one another it is not impossible for them to go. 10

"In exactly the same way Name is without power of its own, and cannot spring up of its own might, nor perform this or that action. Form also is without power of its own, and cannot spring up of its own might, nor perform this or that action. Yet when they mutually support one another it is not impossible for them to spring up and go on. 11

"There is no material that exists for the production of Name and Form; and when Name and Form cease, they do not go anywhither in space. After Name and Form have ceased, they do not exist anywhere in the shape of heaped-up music material. Thus when a lute is played upon, there is no previous store of sound; and when the music ceases it does not go anywhither in space. When it has ceased, it exists nowhere in a stored-up state. Having previously been non-existent, it came into existence on account of the structure and stem of the lute and the exertions of the performer; and as it came into existence so it passes away. In exactly the same way, all the elements of being, both corporeal and non-corporeal come into existence after having previously been non-existent; and having come into existence pass away. 12

"There is not a self residing in Name and Form, but the cooperation of the conformations produces what people call a man.   13

"Just as the word 'chariot' is but a mode of expression for axle, wheels, the chariot-body and other constituents in their proper combination, so a living being is the appearance of the groups with the four elements as they are joined in a unit. There is no self in the carriage and there is no self in man.   14

"O bhikkhus, this doctrine is sure and an eternal truth, that there is no self outside of its parts. This self of ours which constitutes Name and Form is a combination of the groups with the four elements, but there is no ego entity, no self in itself.   15

"Paradoxical though it may sound: There is a path to walk on, there is walking being done, but there is no traveler. There are deeds being done, but there is no doer. There is a blowing of the air, but there is no wind that does the blowing. The thought of self is an error and all existences are as hollow as the plantain tree and as empty as twirling water bubbles.   16

"Therefore, O bhikkhus, as there is no self, there is no transmigration of a self; but there are deeds and the continued effect of deeds. There is a rebirth of karma; there is reincarnation. This rebirth, this reincarnation, this reappearance of the conformations is continuous and depends on the law of cause and effect. Just as a seal is impressed upon the wax reproducing the configurations of its device, so the thoughts of men, their characters, their aspirations are impressed upon others in continuous transference and continue their karma, and good deeds will continue in blessings while bad deeds will continue in curses.   17

"There is no entity here that migrates, no self is transferred from one place to another; but there is a voice uttered here and the echo of it comes back. The teacher pronounces a stanza and the disciple who attentively listens to his teacher's instruction, repeats the stanza. Thus the stanza is reborn in the mind of the disciple. 18

"The body is a compound of perishable organs. It is subject to decay; and we should take care of it as of a wound or a sore; we should attend to its needs without being attached to it, or loving it. 19

"The body is like a machine, and there is no self in it that makes it walk or act, but the thoughts of it, as the windy elements, cause the machine to work. 20

"The body moves about like a cart. Therefore 'tis said: 21

> "As ships are by the wind impelled,
> As arrows from their bowstrings speed,
> So likewise when the body moves
> The windy element must lead. 22

> "Machines are geared to work by ropes;
> So too this body is, in fact,
> Directed by a mental pull
> Whene'er it stand or sit or act. 23

> "No independent self is here
> That could intrinsic forces prove
> To make man act without a cause,
> To make him stand or walk or move. 24

"He only who utterly abandons all thought of the ego escapes the snares of the Evil One; he is out of the reach of Māra. 25

"Thus says the pleasure-promising tempter: 26

> "So long as to the things
> Called 'mine' and 'I' and 'me'
> Thine anxious heart still clings,
> My snares thou canst not flee." 27

"The faithful disciple replies:

> "Naught's mine and naught of me,
> The self I do not mind!
> Thus Māra, I tell thee,
> My path thou canst not find."

"Dismiss the error of the self and do not cling to possessions which are transient but perform deeds that are good, for deeds are enduring and in deeds your karma continues.

"Since then, O bhikkhus, there is no self, there can not be any after life of a self. Therefore abandon all thought of self. But since there are deeds and since deeds continue, be careful with your deeds.

"All beings have karma as their portion: they are heirs of their karma; they are sprung from their karma; their karma is their kinsman; their karma is their refuge; karma allots beings to meanness or to greatness.

> "Assailed by death in life's last throes
> On quitting all thy joys and woes
> What is thine own, thy recompense?
> What stays with thee when passing hence?
> What like a shadow follows thee
> And will Beyond thine heirloom be?

> "T'is deeds, thy deeds, both good and bad;
> Naught else can after death be had.
> Thy deeds are thine, thy recompense;
> They are thine own when going hence;
> They like a shadow follow thee
> And will Beyond thine heirloom be.

> "Let all then here perform good deeds,
> For future weal a treasure store;
> There to reap crops from noble seeds,
> A bliss increasing evermore."

XLI.

THE GOAL.

And the Blessed One thus addressed the bhikkhus: 1
"It is through not understanding the four noble truths,
O bhikkhus, that we had to wander so long in the weary
path of samsāra, both you and I.   2

"Through contact thought is born from sensation, and
is reborn by a reproduction of its form. Starting from
the simplest forms, the mind rises and falls according to
deeds, but the aspirations of a Bodhisatta pursue the
straight path of wisdom and righteousness, until they reach
perfect enlightenment in the Buddha.   3

"All creatures are what they are through the karma of
their deeds done in former and in present existences.   4

"The rational nature of man is a spark of the true light;
it is the first step on the upward road. But new births
are required to insure an ascent to the summit of existence,
the enlightenment of mind and heart, where the immeasurable light of moral comprehension is gained which is the
source of all righteousness.   5

"Having attained this higher birth, I have found the
truth and have taught you the noble path that leads to
the city of peace.   6

"I have shown you the way to the lake of Ambrosia,
which washes away all evil desire.   7

"I have given you the refreshing drink called the perception of truth, and he who drinks of it becomes free
from excitement, passion, and wrong-doing.   8

"The very gods envy the bliss of him who has escaped
from the floods of passion and has climbed the shores of
Nirvāna. His heart is cleansed from all defilement and
free from all illusion.   9

"He is like unto the lotus which grows in the water,
yet not a drop of water adheres to its petals.   10

"The man who walks in the noble path lives in the world, and yet his heart is not defiled by worldly desires. 11

"He who does not see the four noble truths, he who does not understand the three characteristics and has not grounded himself in the uncreate, has still a long path to traverse by repeated births through the desert of ignorance with its mirages of illusion and through the morass of wrong. 12

"But now that you have gained comprehension, the cause of further migrations and aberrations is removed. The goal is reached. The craving of selfishness is destroyed, and the truth is attained. 13

"This is true deliverance; this is salvation; this is heaven and the bliss of a life immortal." 14

XLII.

MIRACLES FORBIDDEN.

Jotikkha, the son of Subhadda, was a householder living in Rājagaha. Having received a precious bowl of sandalwood decorated with jewels, he erected a long pole before his house and put the bowl on its top with this legend: "Should a samana take this bowl down without using a ladder or a stick with a hook, or without climbing the pole, but by magic power, he shall receive as reward whatever he desires." 1

And the people came to the Blessed One, full of wonder and their mouths overflowing with praise, saying: "Great is the Tathāgata. His disciples perform miracles. Kassapa, the disciple of the Buddha, saw the bowl on Jotikkha's pole, and, stretching out his hand, he took it down, carrying it away in triumph to the vihāra." 2

When the Blessed One heard what had happened, he went to Kassapa, and, breaking the bowl to pieces, forbade his disciples to perform miracles of any kind.   3

Soon after this it happened that in one of the rainy seasons many bhikkhus were staying in the Vajjī territory during a famine. And one of the bhikkhus proposed to his brethren that they should praise one another to the householders of the village, saying: "This bhikkhu is a saint; he has seen celestial visions; and that bhikkhu possesses supernatural gifts; he can work miracles." And the villagers said: "It is lucky, very lucky for us, that such saints are spending the rainy season with us." And they gave willingly and abundantly, and the bhikkhus prospered and did not suffer from the famine.   4

When the Blessed One heard it, he told Ānanda to call the bhikkhus together, and he asked them: "Tell me, O bhikkhus, when does a bhikkhu cease to be a bhikkhu?"   5

And Sāriputta replied: 6

"An ordained disciple must not commit any unchaste act. The disciple who commits an unchaste act is no longer a disciple of the Sakyamuni.   7

"Again, an ordained disciple must not take except what has been given him. The disciple who takes, be it so little as a penny's worth, is no longer a disciple of the Sakyamuni.   8

"And lastly, an ordained disciple must not knowingly and malignantly deprive any harmless creature of life, not even an earth-worm or an ant. The disciple who knowingly and malignantly deprives any harmless creature of its life is no longer a disciple of the Sakyamuni.   9

"These are the three great prohibitions."   10

And the Blessed One addressed the bhikkhus and said: 11

"There is another great prohibition which I declare to you: 12

"An ordained disciple must not boast of any super-human perfection. The disciple who with evil intent and from covetousness boasts of a superhuman perfection, be it celestial visions or miracles, is no longer a disciple of the Sakyamuni. 13

"I forbid you, O bhikkhus, to employ any spells or supplications, for they are useless, since the law of karma governs all things. He who attempts to perform miracles has not understood the doctrine of the Tathāgata." 14

XLIII.

THE VANITY OF WORLDLINESS.

There was a poet who had acquired the spotless eye of truth, and he believed in the Buddha, whose doctrine gave him peace of mind and comfort in the hour of affliction. 1

And it happened that an epidemic swept over the country in which he lived, so that many died, and the people were terrified. Some of them trembled with fright, and in anticipation of their fate were smitten with all the horrors of death before they died, while others began to be merry, shouting loudly, "Let us enjoy ourselves to-day, for we know not whether to-morrow we shall live"; yet was their laughter no genuine gladness, but a mere pretence and affectation. 2

Among all these worldly men and women trembling with anxiety, the Buddhist poet lived in the time of the pestilence, as usual, calm and undisturbed, helping wherever he could and ministering unto the sick, soothing their pains by medicine and religious consolation. 3

And a man came to him and said: "My heart is nervous and excited, for I see people die. I am not anxious about others, but I tremble because of myself. Help me; cure me of my fear."   4

The poet replied: "There is help for him who has compassion on others, but there is no help for thee so long as thou clingest to thine own self alone. Hard times try the souls of men and teach them righteousness and charity. Canst thou witness these sad sights around thee and still be filled with selfishness? Canst thou see thy brothers, sisters, and friends suffer, yet not forget the petty cravings and lust of thine own heart?"   5

Noticing the desolation in the mind of the pleasure-seeking man, the Buddhist poet composed this song and taught it to the brethren in the vihāra: 6

"Unless refuge you take in the Buddha and find in Nirvāna rest
Your life is but vanity—empty and desolate vanity.
To see the world is idle, and to enjoy life is empty.
The world, including man, is but like a phantom, and the
                                   hope of heaven is as a mirage.   7

"The worldling seeks pleasures fattening himself like a
                                   caged fowl.
But the Buddhist saint flies up to the sun like the wild crane.
The fowl in the coop has food but will soon be boiled
                                   in the pot.
No provisions are given to the wild crane, but the heavens
                                   and the earth are his."   8

The poet said: "The times are hard and teach the people a lesson; yet do they not heed it." And he composed another poem on the vanity of worldliness: 9

"It is good to reform, and it is good to exhort people to
                                   reform.
The things of the world will all be swept away.
Let others be busy and buried with care.
My mind all unvexed shall be pure.   10

"After pleasures they hanker and find no satisfaction;
Riches they covet and can never have enough.
They are like unto puppets held up by a string.
When the string breaks they come down with a shock.   11

"In the domain of death there are neither great nor small;
Neither gold nor silver is used, nor precious jewels.
No distinction is made between the high and the low.
And daily the dead are buried beneath the fragrant sod.   12

"Look at the sun setting behind the western hills.
You lie down to rest, but soon the cock will announce
                    morn.
Reform to-day and do not wait until it be too late.
Do not say it is early, for the time quickly passes by.   13

"It is good to reform and it is good to exhort people to
                    reform.
It is good to lead a righteous life and take refuge in the
                    Buddha's name.
Your talents may reach to the skies, your wealth may be
                    untold—
But all is in vain unless you attain the peace of Nirvāna."   14

XLIV.

SECRECY AND PUBLICITY.

The Buddha said: "Three things, O disciples, are char-
acterized by secrecy: love affairs, priestly wisdom, and
all aberrations from the path of truth.   1

"Women who are in love, O disciples, seek secrecy and
shun publicity; priests who claim to be in possession of
special revelations, O disciples, seek secrecy and shun

publicity; all those who stray from the path of truth, O disciples, seek secrecy and shun publicity. 2

"Three things, O disciples, shine before the world and cannot be hidden. What are the three? 3

"The moon, O disciples, illumines the world and cannot be hidden; the sun, O disciples, illumines the world and cannot be hidden; and the truth proclaimed by the Tathāgata illumines the world and cannot be hidden. These three things, O disciples, illumine the world and cannot be hidden. There is no secrecy about them." 4

XLV.

THE ANNIHILATION OF SUFFERING.

And the Buddha said: "What, my friends, is evil? 1

"Killing is evil; stealing is evil; yielding to sexual passion is evil; lying is evil; slandering is evil; abuse is evil; gossip is evil; envy is evil; hatred is evil; to cling to false doctrine is evil; all these things, my friends, are evil. 2

"And what, my friends, is the root of evil? 3

"Desire is the root of evil; hatred is the root of evil; illusion is the root of evil; these things are the root of evil. 4

"What, however, is good? 5

"Abstaining from killing is good; abstaining from theft is good; abstaining from sensuality is good; abstaining from falsehood is good; abstaining from slander is good; suppression of unkindness is good; abandoning gossip is good; letting go all envy is good; dismissing hatred is good; obedience to the truth is good; all these things are good. 6

"And what, my friends, is the root of the good? 7

"Freedom from desire is the root of the good; freedom from hatred and freedom from illusion; these things, my friends, are the root of the good. 8

"What, however, O brethren, is suffering? What is the origin of suffering? What is the annihilation of suffering?   9

"Birth is suffering; old age is suffering; disease is suffering; death is suffering; sorrow and misery are suffering; affliction and despair are suffering; to be united with loathsome things is suffering; the loss of that which we love and the failure in attaining that which is longed for are suffering; all these things, O brethren, are suffering.   10

"And what, O brethren, is the origin of suffering?   11

"It is lust, passion, and the thirst for existence that yearns for pleasure everywhere, leading to a continual rebirth! It is sensuality, desire, selfishness; all these things, O brethren, are the origin of suffering.   12

"And what is the annihilation of suffering?   13

"The radical and total annihilation of this thirst and the abandonment, the liberation, the deliverance from passion, that, O brethren, is the annihilation of suffering.   14

"And what, O brethren, is the path that leads to the annihilation of suffering?   15

"It is the holy eightfold path that leads to the annihilation of suffering, which consists of, right views, right decision, right speech, right action, right living, right struggling, right thoughts, and right meditation.   16

"In so far, O friends, as a noble youth thus recognizes suffering and the origin of suffering, as he recognizes the annihilation of suffering, and walks on the path that leads to the annihilation of suffering, radically forsaking passion, subduing wrath, annihilating the vain conceit of the "I-am," leaving ignorance, and attaining to enlightenment, he will make an end of all suffering even in this life."   17

XLVI.

AVOIDING THE TEN EVILS.

The Buddha said: "All acts of living creatures become bad by ten things, and by avoiding the ten things they become good. There are three evils of the body, four evils of the tongue, and three evils of the mind. 1

"The evils of the body are, murder, theft, and adultery; of the tongue, lying, slander, abuse, and idle talk; of the mind, covetousness, hatred, and error. 2

"I exhort you to avoid the ten evils: 3

"I. Kill not, but have regard for life. 4

"II. Steal not, neither do ye rob; but help everybody to be master of the fruits of his labor. 5

"III. Abstain from impurity, and lead a life of chastity. 6

"IV. Lie not, but be truthful. Speak the truth with discretion, fearlessly and in a loving heart. 7

"V. Invent not evil reports, neither do ye repeat them. Carp not, but look for the good sides of your fellow-beings, so that ye may with sincerity defend them against their enemies. 8

"VI. Swear not, but speak decently and with dignity. 9

"VII. Waste not the time with gossip, but speak to the purpose or keep silence. 10

"VIII. Covet not, nor envy, but rejoice at the fortunes of other people. 11

"IX. Cleanse your heart of malice and cherish no hatred, not even against your enemies; but embrace all living beings with kindness. 12

"X. Free your mind of ignorance and be anxious to learn the truth, especially in the one thing that is needful, lest you fall a prey either to scepticism or to errors. Scepticism will make you indifferent and errors will lead you astray, so that you shall not find the noble path that leads to life eternal." 13

XLVII.

THE PREACHER'S MISSION.

And the Blessed One said to his disciples: 1
"When I have passed away and can no longer address
you and edify your minds with religious discourse, select
from among you men of good family and education to
preach the truth in my stead. And let those men be in-
vested with the robes of the Tathāgata, let them enter
into the abode of the Tathāgata, and occupy the pulpit
of the Tathāgata. 2

"The robe of the Tathāgata is sublime forbearance and
patience. The abode of the Tathāgata is charity and love
of all beings. The pulpit of the Tathāgata is the comprehension of the good law in its abstract meaning as well
as in its particular application. 3

"The preacher must propound the truth with unshrink-
ing mind. He must have the power of persuasion rooted
in virtue and in strict fidelity to his vows. 4

"The preacher must keep in his proper sphere and be
steady in his course. He must not flatter his vanity by
seeking the company of the great, nor must he keep
company with persons who are frivolous and immoral.
When in temptation, he should constantly think of the
Buddha and he will conquer. 5

"All who come to hear the doctrine, the preacher must
receive with benevolence, and his sermon must be without
invidiousness. 6

"The preacher must not be prone to carp at others,
or to blame other preachers; nor speak scandal, nor
propagate bitter words. He must not mention by name
other disciples to vituperate them and reproach their
demeanor. 7

"Clad in a clean robe, dyed with good color, with
appropriate undergarments, he must ascend the pulpit

with a mind free from blame and at peace with the wole world. 8

"He must not take delight in quarrelous disputations or engage in controversies so as to show the superiority of his talents, but be calm and composed. 9

"No hostile feelings shall reside in his heart, and he must never abandon the disposition of charity toward all beings. His sole aim must be that all beings become Buddhas. 10

"Let the preacher apply himself with zeal to his work, and the Tathāgata will show to him the body of the holy law in its transcendent glory. He shall be honored as one whom the Tathāgata has blessed. The Tathāgata blesses the preacher and also those who reverently listen to him and joyfully accept the doctrine. 11

"All those who receive the truth will find perfect enlightenment. And, verily, such is the power of the doctrine that even by the reading of a single stanza, or by reciting, copying, and keeping in mind a single sentence of the good law, persons may be converted to the truth and enter the path of righteousness which leads to deliverance from evil. 12

"Creatures that are swayed by impure passions, when they listen to the voice, will be purified. The ignorant who are infatuated with the follies of the world will, when pondering on the profundity of the doctrine, acquire wisdom. Those who act under the impulse of hatred will, when taking refuge in the Buddha, be filled with good-will and love. 13

"A preacher must be full of energy and cheerful hope, never tiring and never despairing of final success. 14

"A preacher must be like a man in quest of water who digs a well in an arid tract of land. So long as he sees that the sand is dry and white, he knows that the water is still far off. But let him not be troubled or give up the task as hopeless. The work of removing the dry sand must be done so that he can dig down deeper into the ground. And often the deeper he has to dig, the cooler and purer and more refreshing will the water be. 15

"When after some time of digging he sees that the sand becomes moist, he accepts it as a token that the water is near. 16

"So long as the people do not listen to the words of truth, the preacher knows that he has to dig deeper into their hearts; but when they begin to heed his words he apprehends that they will soon attain enlightenment. 17

"Into your hands, O ye men of good family and education who take the vow of preaching the words of the Tathāgata, the Blessed One transfers, intrusts, and commends the good law of truth. 18

"Receive the good law of truth, keep it, read and re-read it, fathom it, promulgate it, and preach it to all beings in all the quarters of the universe. 19

"The Tathāgata is not avaricious, nor narrow-minded, and he is willing to impart the perfect Buddha-knowledge unto all who are ready and willing to receive it. Be ye like unto him. Imitate him and follow his example in bounteously giving, showing, and bestowing the truth. 20

"Gather round you hearers who love to listen to the benign and comforting words of the law; rouse the unbelievers to accept the truth and fill them with delight and joy. Quicken them, edify them, and lift them higher and higher until they see the truth face to face in all its splendor and infinite glory." 21

When the Blessed One had thus spoken, the disciples said: 22

"O thou who rejoicest in kindness having its source in compassion, thou great cloud of good qualities and of benevolent mind, thou quenchest the fire that vexeth living beings, thou pourest out nectar, the rain of the law! 23

"We shall do, O Lord, what the Tathāgata commands. We shall fulfil his behest; the Lord shall find us obedient to his words." 24

And this vow of the disciples resounded through the universe, and like an echo it came back from all the Bodhisattas who are to be and will come to preach the good law of Truth to future generations. 25

And the Blessed One said: "The Tathāgata is like unto a powerful king who rules his kingdom with righteousness, but being attacked by envious enemies goes out to wage war against his foes. When the king sees his soldiers fight he is delighted with their gallantry and will bestow upon them donations of all kinds. Ye are the soldiers of the Tathāgata, while Māra, the Evil One, is the enemy who must be conquered. And the Tathāgata will give to his soldiers the city of Nirvāna, the great capital of the good law. And when the enemy is overcome, the Dharma-rāja, the great king of truth, will bestow upon all his disciples the most precious crown which jewel brings perfect enlightenment, supreme wisdom, and undisturbed peace."

O. KOPETZKY

THE TEACHER.

XLVIII.

THE DHAMMAPADA.

THIS is the Dhammapada, the path of religion pursued
by those who are followers of the Buddha: 1

Creatures from mind their character derive; mind-mar-
shalled are they, mind-made.   Mind is the source either
of bliss or of corruption.   2

By oneself evil is done; by oneself one suffers; by oneself evil is left undone; by oneself one is purified. Purity
and impurity belong to oneself, no one can purify another. 3

You yourself must make an effort.   The Tathāgatas are
only preachers.   The thoughtful who enter the way are
freed from the bondage of Māra.   4

He who does not rouse himself when it is time to rise;
who, though young and strong, is full of sloth; whose
will and thoughts are weak; that lazy and idle man will
never find the way to enlightenment.   5

If a man hold himself dear, let him watch himself carefully; the truth guards him who guards himself. 6

If a man makes himself as he teaches others to be, then, being himself subdued, he may subdue others; one's own self is indeed difficult to subdue. 7

If some men conquer in battle a thousand times a thousand men, and if another conquer himself, he is the greatest of conquerors. 8

It is the habit of fools, be they laymen or members of the clergy, to think, "this is done by me. May others be subject to me. In this or that transaction a prominent part should be played by me." Fools do not care for the duty to be performed or the aim to be reached, but think of their self alone. Everything is but a pedestal of their vanity. 9

Bad deeds, and deeds hurtful to ourselves, are easy to do; what is beneficial and good, that is very difficult. 10

If anything is to be done, let a man do it, let him attack it vigorously! 11

Before long, alas! this body will lie on the earth, despised, without understanding, like a useless log; yet our thoughts will endure. They will be thought again, and will produce action. Good thoughts will produce good actions, and bad thoughts will produce bad actions. 12

Earnestness is the path of immortality, thoughtlessness the path of death. Those who are in earnest do not die; those who are thoughtless are as if dead already. 13

Those who imagine they find truth in untruth, and see untruth in truth, will never arrive at truth, but follow vain desires. They who know truth in truth, and untruth in untruth, arrive at truth, and follow true desires. 14

As rain breaks through an ill-thatched house, passion will break through an unreflecting mind. As rain does not break through a well-thatched house, passion will not break through a well-reflecting mind. 15

Well-makers lead the water wherever they like; fletchets bend the arrow; carpenters bend a log of wood; wise people fashion themselves; wise people falter not amidst blame and praise. Having listened to the law, they become serene, like a deep, smooth, and still lake.   16

If a man speaks or acts with an evil thought, pain follows him as the wheel follows the foot of the ox that draws the carriage.   17

An evil deed is better left undone, for a man will repent of it afterwards; a good deed is better done, for having done it one will not repent.   18

If a man commits a wrong let him not do it again; let him not delight in wrongdoing; pain is the outcome of evil. If a man does what is good, let him do it again; let him delight in it; happiness is the outcome of good. 19

Let no man think lightly of evil, saying in his heart, "It will not come nigh unto me." As by the falling of water-drops a water-pot is filled, so the fool becomes full of evil, though he gather it little by little.   20

Let no man think lightly of good, saying in his heart, "It will not come nigh unto me." As by the falling of water-drops a water-pot is filled, so the wise man becomes full of good, though he gather it little by little.   21

He who lives for pleasure only, his senses uncontrolled, immoderate in his food, idle, and weak, him Māra, the tempter, will certainly overthrow, as the wind throws down a weak tree. He who lives without looking for pleasures, his senses well-controlled, moderate in his food, faithful and strong, him Māra will certainly not overthrow, any more than the wind throws down a rocky mountain. 22

The fool who knows his foolishness, is wise at least so far. But a fool who thinks himself wise, he is a fool indeed.   23

To the evil-doer wrong appears sweet as honey; he looks upon it as pleasant so long as it bears no fruit; but when its fruit ripens, then he looks upon it as wrong. And so the good man looks upon the goodness of the Dharma as a burden and an evil so long as it bears no fruit; but when its fruit ripens, then he sees its goodness. 24

A hater may do great harm to a hater, or an enemy to an enemy; but a wrongly-directed mind will do greater mischief unto itself. A mother, a father, or any other relative will do much good; but a well-directed mind will do greater service unto itself. 25

He whose wickedness is very great brings himself down to that state where his enemy wishes him to be. He himself is his greatest enemy. Thus a creeper destroys the life of a tree on which it finds support. 26

Do not direct thy thought to what gives pleasure, that thou mayest not cry out when burning, "This is pain." The wicked man burns by his own deeds, as if burnt by fire. 27

Pleasures destroy the foolish; the foolish man by his thirst for pleasures destroys himself as if he were his own enemy. The fields are damaged by hurricanes and weeds; mankind is damaged by passion, by hatred, by vanity, and by lust. 28

Let no man ever take into consideration whether a thing is pleasant or unpleasant. The love of pleasure begets grief and the dread of pain causes fear; he who is free from the love of pleasure and the dread of pain knows neither grief nor fear. 29

He who gives himself to vanity, and does not give himself to meditation, forgetting the real aim of life and grasping at pleasure, will in time envy him who has exerted himself in meditation. 30

The fault of others is easily noticed, but that of oneself is difficult to perceive. A man winnows his neighbor's faults like chaff, but his own fault he hides, as a cheat hides the false die from the gambler. 31

If a man looks after the faults of others, and is always inclined to take offence, his own passions will grow, and he is far from the destruction of passions. 32

Not about the perversities of others, not about their sins of commission or omission, but about his own misdeeds and negligences alone should a sage be worried. 33

Good people shine from afar, like the snowy mountains; had people are concealed, like arrows shot by night. 34

If a man by causing pain to others, wishes to obtain pleasure for himself, he, entangled in the bonds of selfishness, will never be free from hatred. 35

Let a man overcome anger by love, let him overcome evil by good; let him overcome the greedy by liberality, the liar by truth! 36

For hatred does not cease by hatred at any time; hatred ceases by not-hatred, this is an old rule. 37

Speak the truth, do not yield to anger; give, if thou art asked; by these three steps thou wilt become divine. 38

Let a wise man blow off the impurities of his self, as a smith blows off the impurities of silver, one by one, little by little, and from time to time. 39

Lead others, not by violence, but by righteousness and equity. 40

He who possesses virtue and intelligence, who is just, speaks the truth, and does what is his own business, him the world will hold dear. 41

As the bee collects nectar and departs without injuring the flower, or its color or scent, so let a sage dwell in the community. 42

If a traveller does not meet with one who is his better, or his equal, let him firmly keep to his solitary journey; there is no companionship with fools. 43

Long is the night to him who is awake; long is a mile to him who is tired; long is life to the foolish who do not know the true religion. 44

Better than living a hundred years, not seeing the highest truth, is one day in the life of a man who sees the highest truth. 45

Some form their Dharma arbitrarily and fabricate it artificially; they advance complex speculations and imagine that good results are attainable only by the acceptance of their theories; yet the truth is but one; there are not different truths in the world. Having reflected on the various theories, we have gone into the yoke with him who has shaken off all sin. But shall we be able to proceed together with him? 46

The best of ways is the eightfold path. This is the path. There is no other that leads to the purifying of intelligence. Go on this path! Everything else is the deceit of Māra, the tempter. If you go on this path, you will make an end of pain! Says the Tathāgata, The path was preached by me, when I had understood the removal of the thorn in the flesh. 47

Not only by discipline and vows, not only by much learning, do I earn the happiness of release which no worldling can know. Bhikkhu, be not confident as long as thou hast not attained the extinction of thirst. The extinction of evil desire is the highest religion. 48

The gift of religion exceeds all gifts; the sweetness of religion exceeds all sweetness; the delight in religion exceeds all delights; the extinction of thirst overcomes all pain. 49

Few are there among men who cross the river and reach the goal. The great multitudes are running up and down the shore; but there is no suffering for him who has finished his journey. 50

As the lily will grow full of sweet perfume and delight upon a heap of rubbish, thus the disciple of the truly enlightened Buddha shines forth by his wisdom among those who are like rubbish, among the people that walk in darkness. 51

Let us live happily then, not hating those who hate us! Among men who hate us let us dwell free from hatred! 52

Let us live happily then, free from all ailments among the ailing! Among men who are ailing let us dwell free from ailments! 53

Let us live happily, then, free from greed among the greedy! Among men who are greedy let us dwell free from greed! 54

The sun is bright by day, the moon shines by night, the warrior is bright in his armor, thinkers are bright in their meditation; but among all the brightest with splendor day and night is the Buddha, the Awakened, the Holy, Blessed. 55

XLIX.

THE TWO BRAHMANS.

At one time when the Blessed One was journeying through Kosala he came to the Brahman village which is called Manasākata. There he stayed in a mango grove. 1

And two young Brahmans came to him who were of different schools. One was named Vāsettha and the other Bhāradvāja. And Vāsettha said to the Blessed One: 2

"We have a dispute as to the true path. I say the straight path which leads unto a union with Brahmā is that which has been announced by the Brahman Pokkharasāti, while my friend says the straight path which leads unto a union with Brahmā is that which has been announced by the Brahman Tārukkha. 3

"Now, regarding thy high reputation, O samana, and knowing that thou art called the Enlightened One, the teacher of men and gods, the Blessed Buddha, we have come to ask thee, are all these paths paths of salvation? There are many roads all around our village, and all lead to Manasākata. Is it just so with the paths of the sages? Are all paths paths to salvation, and do they all lead to a union with Brahmā? 4

And the Blessed One proposed these questions to the two Brahmans: "Do you think that all paths are right?" 5

Both answered and said: "Yes, Gotama, we think so." 6

"But tell me," continued the Buddha, "has any one of the Brahmans, versed in the Vedas, seen Brahmā face to face?" 7

"No, sir!" was the reply. 8

"But, then," said the Blessed One, "has any teacher of the Brahmans, versed in the Vedas, seen Brahmā face to face?" 9

The two Brahmans said: "No, sir." 10

"But, then," said the Blessed One, "has any one of the authors of the Vedas seen Brahmā face to face?" 11

Again the two Brahmans answered in the negative and exclaimed: "How can any one see Brahmā or understand him, for the mortal cannot understand the immortal." And the Blessed One proposed an illustration, saying: 12

"It is as if a man should make a staircase in the place where four roads cross, to mount up into a mansion. And people should ask him, 'Where, good friend, is this mansion, to mount up into which you are making this staircase? Knowest thou whether it is in the east, or in the south, or in the west, or in the north? Whether it is high, or low, or of medium size?' And when so asked he should answer, 'I know it not.' And people should say to him, 'But, then, good friend, thou art making a staircase to mount up into something—taking it for a mansion—which all the while thou knowest not, neither hast thou seen it.' And when so asked he should answer, 'That is exactly what I do; yea I know that I cannot know it.' What would you think of him? Would you not say that the talk of that man was foolish talk?" 13

"In sooth, Gotama," said the two Brahmans, "it would be foolish talk!" 14

The Blessed One continued: "Then the Brahmans should say, 'We show you the way unto a union of what we know not and what we have not seen.' This being the substance of Brahman lore, does it not follow that their task is vain?" 15

"It does follow," replied Bhāradvāja. 16

Said the Blessed One: "Thus it is impossible that Brahmans versed in the three Vedas should be able to show the way to a state of union with that which they neither know nor have seen. Just as when a string of blind men are clinging one to the other. Neither can the foremost see, nor can those in the middle see, nor can the hindmost see. Even so, methinks, the talk of the Brahmans versed in the three Vedas is but blind talk; it is ridiculous, consists of mere words, and is a vain and empty thing." 17

"Now suppose," added the Blessed One, "that a man should come hither to the bank of the river, and, having some business on the other side, should want to cross. Do you suppose that if he were to invoke the other bank of the river to come over to him on this side, the bank would come on account of his praying?" 18

"Certainly not, Gotama." 19

"Yet this is the way of the Brahmans. They omit the practice of those qualities which really make a man a Brahman, and say, 'Indra, we call upon thee; Soma, we call upon thee; Varuna, we call upon thee; Brahmā, we call upon thee.' Verily, it is not possible that these Brahmahns, on account of their invocations, prayers, and praises, should after death be united with Brahmā." 20

"Now tell me," continued the Buddha, "what do the Brahmans say of Brahmā? Is his mind full of lust?" 21

And when the Brahmans denied this, the Buddha asked: "Is Brahmā's mind full of malice, sloth, or pride?" 22

"No, sir!" was the reply. "He is the opposite of all this." 23

And the Buddha went on: "But are the Brahmans free from these vices?" 24

"No, sir!" said Vāsettha. 25

The Holy One said: "The Brahmans cling to the five things leading to worldliness and yield to the temptations of the senses; they are entangled in the five hindrances, lust, malice, sloth, pride, and doubt. How can they be united to that which is most unlike their nature? Therefore the threefold wisdom of the Brahmans is a waterless desert, a pathless jungle, and a hopeless desolation." 26

When the Buddha had thus spoken, one of the Brahmans said: "We are told, Gotama, that the Sakyamuni knows the path to a union with Brahmā." 27

And the Blessed One said: "What do you think, O Brahmans, of a man born and brought up in Manasākata? Would he be in doubt about the most direct way from this spot to Manasākata?" 28

"Certainly not, Gotama." 29

"Thus," replied the Buddha, "the Tathāgata knows the straight path that leads to a union with Brahmā. He knows it as one who has entered the world of Brahmā and has been born in it. There can be no doubt in the Tathāgata." 30

And the two young Brahmans said: "If thou knowest the way show it to us." 31

And the Buddha said: 32

"The Tathāgata sees the universe face to face and understands its nature. He proclaims the truth both in its letter and in its spirit, and his doctrine is glorious in its origin, glorious in its progress, glorious in its consummation. The Tathāgata reveals the higher life in its purity and perfection. He can show you the way to that which is contrary to the five great hindrances. 33

"The Tathāgata lets his mind pervade the four quarters of the world with thoughts of love. And thus the whole wide world, above, below, around, and everywhere will continue to be filled with love, far-reaching, grown great, and beyond measure. 34

"Just as a mighty trumpeter makes himself heard—and that without difficulty—in all the four quarters of the earth; even so is the coming of the Tathāgata: there is not one living creature that the Tathāgata passes by or leaves aside, but regards them all with mind set free, and deep-felt love. 35

"And this is the sign that a man follows the right path: Uprightness is his delight, and he sees danger in the least of those things which he should avoid. He trains himself in the commands of morality, he encompasseth himself with holiness in word and deed; he sustains his life by means that are quite pure; good is his conduct, guarded is the door of his senses; mindful and self-possessed, he is altogether happy. 36

"He who walks in the eightfold noble path with unswerving determination is sure to reach Nirvāna. The Tathāgata anxiously watches over his children and with loving care helps them to see the light. 37

"When a hen has eight or ten or twelve eggs, over which she has properly brooded, the wish arises in her heart, 'O would that my little chickens would break open the egg-shell with their claws, or with their beaks, and come forth into the light in safety!' yet all the while those little chickens are sure to break the egg-shell and will come forth into the light in safety. Even so, a brother who with firm determination walks in the noble path is sure to come forth into the light, sure to reach up to the higher wisdom, sure to attain to the highest bliss of enlightenment." 38

L.

GUARD THE SIX QUARTERS.

While the Blessed One was staying at the bamboo grove near Rājagaha, he once met on his way Sigāla, a householder, who, clasping his hands, turned to the four quarters of the world, to the zenith above, and to the nadir below. And the Blessed One, knowing that this was done according to the traditional religious superstition to avert evil, asked Sigāla: "Why performest thou these strange ceremonies?"   1

And Sigāla in reply said: "Dost thou think it strange that I protect my home against the influences of demons? I know thou wouldst fain tell me, O Gotama Sakyamuni, whom people call the Tathāgata and the Blessed Buddha, that incantations are of no avail and possess no saving power. But listen to me and know, that in performing this rite I honor, reverence, and keep sacred the words of my father."   2

Then the Tathāgata said: 3

Thou dost well, O Sigāla, to honor, reverence, and keep sacred the words of thy father; and it is thy duty to protect thy home, thy wife, thy children, and thy children's children against the hurtful influences of evil spirits. I find no fault with the performance of thy father's rite. But I find that thou dost not understand the ceremony. Let the Tathāgata, who now speaks to thee as a spiritual father and loves thee no less than did thy parents, explain to thee the meaning of the six directions.   4

"To guard thy home by mysterious ceremonies is not sufficient; thou must guard it by good deeds. Turn to thy parents in the East, to thy teachers in the South, to thy wife and children in the West, to thy friends in the North, and regulate the zenith of thy religious relations above thee, and the nadir of thy servants below thee.   5

"Such is the religion thy father wants thee to have, and the performance of the ceremony shall remind thee of thy duties."   6

And Sigāla looked up to the Blessed One with reverence as to his father and said: "Truly, Gotama, thou art the Buddha, the Blessed One, the holy teacher. I never knew what I was doing, but now I know. Thou hast revealed to me the truth that was hidden as one who bringeth a lamp into the darkness. I take my refuge in the Enlightened Teacher, in the truth that enlightens, and in the community of brethren who have been taught the truth."   7

LI.

SIMHA'S QUESTION CONCERNING ANNIHILATION.

At that time many distinguished citizens were sitting together assembled in the town-hall and spoke in many ways in praise of the Buddha, of the Dharma, and of the Sangha. Simha, the general-in-chief, a disciple of the Niggantha sect, was sitting among them. And Simha thought: "Truly, the Blessed One must be the Buddha, the Holy One. I will go and visit him."   1

Then Simha, the general, went to the place where the Niggantha chief, Nātaputta, was; and having approached him, he said: "I wish, Lord, to visit the samana Gotama."   2

Nātaputta said: "Why should you, Simha, who believe in the result of actions according to their moral merit, go to visit the samana Gotama, who denies the result of actions? The samana Gotama, O Simha, denies the result of actions; he teaches the doctrine of non-action; and in this doctrine he trains his disciples."   3

Then the desire to go and visit the Blessed One, which had arisen in Simha, the general, abated.   4

Hearing again the praise of the Buddha, of the Dharma, and of the Sangha, Simha asked the Niggantha chief a second time; and again Nātaputta persuaded him not to go.   5

When a third time the general heard some men of distinction extol the merits of the Buddha, the Dharma, and the Sangha, the general thought: "Truly the samana Gotama must be the Holy Buddha. What are the Nigganthas to me, whether they give their consent or not? I shall go without asking their permission to visit him, the Blessed One, the Holy Buddha."   6

And Simha, the general, said to the Blessed One: "I have heard, Lord, that the samana Gotama denies the result of actions; he teaches the doctrine of non-action, saying that the actions of sentient beings do not receive their reward, for he teaches annihilation and the contemptibleness of all things; and in this doctrine he trains his disciples. Teachest thou the doing away of the soul and the burning away of man's being? Pray tell me, Lord, do those who speak thus say the truth, or do they bear false witness against the Blessed One, passing off a spurious Dharma as thy Dharma?"   7

The Blessed One said: 8

"There is a way, Simha, in which one who says so, is speaking truly of me; on the other hand, Simha, there is a way in which one who says the opposite is speaking truly of me, too. Listen, and I will tell thee: 9

"I teach, Simha, the not-doing of such actions as are unrighteous, either by deed, or by word, or by thought; I teach the not-bringing about of all those conditions of heart which are evil and not good. However, I teach, Simha, the doing of such actions as are righteous, by deed, by word, and by thought; I teach the bringing about of all those conditions of heart which are good and not evil. 10

"I teach, Simha, that all the conditions of heart which are evil and not good, unrighteous actions by deed, by word, and by thought, must be burnt away. He who has freed himself, Simha, from all those conditions of heart which are evil and not good, he who has destroyed them as a palm-tree which is rooted out, so that they cannot grow up again, such a man has accomplished the eradication of self. 11

"I proclaim, Simha, the annihilation of egotism, of lust, of ill-will, of delusion. However, I do not proclaim the annihilation of forbearance, of love, of charity, and of truth. 12

"I deem, Simha, unrighteous actions contemptible, whether they be performed by deed, or by word, or by thought; but I deem virtue and righteousness praiseworthy." 13

And Simha said: "One doubt still lurks in my mind concerning the doctrine of the Blessed One. Will the Blessed One consent to clear the cloud away so that I may understand the Dharma as the Blessed One teaches it?" 14

The Tathāgata having given his consent, Simha continued: "I am a soldier, O Blessed One, and am appointed by the king to enforce his laws and to wage his wars. Does the Tathāgata who teaches kindness without end and compassion with all sufferers, permit the punishment of the criminal? and further, does the Tathāgata declare that it is wrong to go to war for the protection of our homes, our wives, our children, and our property? Does the Tathāgata teach the doctrine of a complete self-surrender, so that I should suffer the evil-doer to do what he pleases and yield submissively to him who threatens to take by violence what is my own? Does the Tathāgata maintain that all strife, including such warfare as is waged for a righteous cause, should be forbidden?" 15

The Buddha replied: "He who deserves punishment must be punished, and he who is worthy of favor must be favored. Yet at the same time he teaches to do no injury to any living being but to be full of love and kindness. These injunctions are not contradictory, for whosoever must be punished for the crimes which he has committed, suffers his injury not through the ill-will of the judge but on account of his evil-doing. His own acts have brought upon him the injury that the executer of the law inflicts. When a magistrate punishes, let him not harbor hatred in his breast, yet a murderer, when put do death, should consider that this is the fruit of his own act. As soon as he will understand that the punishment will purify his soul, he will no longer lament his fate but rejoice at it." 16

And the Blessed One continued: "The Tathāgata teaches that all warfare in which man tries to slay his brother is lamentable, but he does not teach that those who go to war in a righteous cause after having exhausted all means to preserve the peace are blameworthy. He must be blamed who is the cause of war. 17

"The Tathāgata teaches a complete surrender of self, but he does not teach a surrender of anything to those powers that are evil, be they men or gods or the elements of nature. Struggle must be, for all life is a struggle of some kind. But he that struggles should look to it lest he struggle in the interest of self against truth and righteousness. 18

"He who struggles in the interest of self, so that he himself may be great or powerful or rich or famous, will have no reward, but he who struggles for righteousness and truth, will have great reward, for even his defeat will be a victory. 19

"Self is not a fit vessel to receive any great success; self is small and brittle and its contents will soon be spilt for the benefit, and perhaps also for the curse, of others. 20

"Truth, however, is large enough to receive the yearnings and aspirations of all selves and when the selves break like soap-bubbles, their contents will be preserved and in the truth they will lead a life everlasting.   21

"He who goeth to battle, O Simha, even though it be in a righteous cause, must be prepared to be slain by his enemies, for that is the destiny of warriors; and should his fate overtake him he has no reason for complaint.   22

"But he who is victorious should remember the instability of earthly things. His success may be great, but be it ever so great the wheel of fortune may turn again and bring him down into the dust.   23

"However, if he moderates himself and, extinguishing all hatred in his heart lifts his down-trodden adversary up and says to him, 'Come now and make peace and let us be brothers,' he will gain a victory that is not a transient success, for its fruits will remain forever.   24

"Great is a successful general, O Simha, but he who has conquered self is the greater victor.   25

"The doctrine of the conquest of self, O Simha, is not taught to destroy the souls of men, but to preserve them. He who has conquered self is more fit to live, to be successful, and to gain victories than he who is the slave of self.   26

"He whose mind is free from the illusion of self, will stand and not fall in the battle of life.   27

"He whose intentions are righteousness and justice, will meet with no failure, but be successful in his enterprises and his success will endure.   28

"He who harbors in his heart love of truth will live and not die, for he has drunk the water of immortality.   29

"Struggle then, O general, courageously; and fight thy battles vigorously, but be a soldier of truth and the Tathāgata will bless thee."   30

When the Blessed One had spoken thus, Simha, the general, said: "Glorious Lord, glorious Lord! Thou hast revealed the truth. Great is the doctrine of the Blessed One. Thou, indeed, art the Buddha, the Tathāgata, the Holy One. Thou art the teacher of mankind. Thou showest us the road of salvation, for this indeed is true deliverance. He who follows thee will not miss the light to enlighten his path. He will find blessedness and peace. I take my refuge, Lord, in the Blessed One, and in his doctrine, and in his brotherhood. May the Blessed One receive me from this day forth while my life lasts as a disciple who has taken refuge in him." 31

And the Blessed One said: "Consider first, Simha, what thou doest. It is becoming that persons of rank like thyself should do nothing without due consideration." 32

Simha's faith in the Blessed One increased. He replied: "Had other teachers, Lord, succeeded in making me their disciple, they would carry around their banners through the whole city of Vesālī, shouting: 'Simha, the general has become our disciple! For the second time, Lord, I take my refuge in the Blessed One, and in the Dharma, and in the Sangha; may the Blessed One receive me from this day forth while my life lasts as a disciple who has taken his refuge in him." 33

Said the Blessed One: "For a long time, Simha, offerings have been given to the Nigganthas in thy house. Thou shouldst therefore deem it right also in the future to give them food when they come to thee on their alms-pilgrimage." 34

And Simha's heart was filled with joy. He said: "I have been told, Lord: 'The samana Gotama says: To me alone and to nobody else should gifts be given. My pupils alone and the pupils of no one else should receive offerings.' But the Blessed One exhorts me to give also to the Nigganthas. Well, Lord, we shall see what is season-

able. For the third time, Lord, I take my refuge in the
Blessed One, and in his Dharma, and in his fraternity." 35

LII.

ALL EXISTENCE IS SPIRITUAL.

And there was an officer among the retinue of Simha
who had heard of the discourses of the Blessed One, and
there was some doubt left in his heart. 1

This man came to the Blessed One and said: "It is said,
O Lord, that the samana Gotama denies the existence
of the soul. Do they who say so speak the truth, or do
they bear false witness against the Blessed One?" 2

And the Blessed One said: "There is a way in which
those who say so are speaking truly of me; on the other
hand, there is a way in which those who say so do not
speak truly of me. 3

"The Tathāgata teaches that there is no self. He who
says that the soul is his self and that the self is the thinker
of our thoughts and the actor of our deeds, teaches a
wrong doctrine which leads to confusion and darkness. 4

"On the other hand, the Tathāgata teaches that there is
mind. He who understands by soul mind, and says that
mind exists, teaches the truth which leads to clearness and
enlightenment." 5

The officer said: "Does, then, the Tathāgata maintain
that two things exist? that which we perceive with our
senses and that which is mental?" 6

Said the Blessed One: "Verily, I say unto thee, thy mind
is spiritual, but neither is the sense-perceived void of spiri-
tuality. The bodhi is eternal and it dominates all existence
as the good law guiding all beings in their search for truth.
It changes brute nature into mind, and there is no being
that cannot be transformed into a vessel of truth." 7

LIII.

IDENTITY AND NON-IDENTITY.

Kūtadanta, the head of the Brahmans in the village of Dānamatī having approached the Blessed One respectfully, greeted him and said: "I am told, O samana, that thou art the Buddha, the Holy One, the Allknowing, the Lord of the world. But if thou wert the Buddha, wouldst thou not come like a king in all thy glory and power?"   1

Said the Blessed One: "Thine eyes are holden. If the eye of thy mind were undimmed thou couldst see the glory and the power of truth."   2

Said Kūtadanta: "Show me the truth and I shall see it. But thy doctrine is without consistency. If it were consistent, it would stand; but as it is not, it will pass away."   3

The Blessed One replied: "The truth will never pass away."   4

Kūtadanta said: "I am told that thou teachest the law, yet thou tearest down religion. Thy disciples despise rites and abandon immolation, but reverence for the gods can be shown only by sacrifices. The very nature of religion consists in worship and sacrifice."   5

Said the Buddha: "Greater than the immolation of bullocks is the sacrifice of self. He who offers to the gods his evil desires will see the uselessness of slaughtering animals at the altar. Blood has no cleansing power, but the eradication of lust will make the heart pure. Better than worshiping gods is obedience to the laws of righteousness."   6

Kūtadanta, being of a religious disposition and anxious about his fate after death, had sacrificed countless victims. Now he saw the folly of atonement by blood. Not yet satisfied, however, with the teachings of the Tathāgata, Kūtadanta continued: "Thou believest, O Master, that beings are reborn; that they migrate in the evolution of life; and that subject to the law of karma we must reap what we sow. Yet thou teachest the non-existence of the soul! Thy disciples praise utter self-extinction as the highest bliss of Nirvāna. If I am merely a combination of the sankhāras, my existence will cease when I die. If I am merely a compound of sensations and ideas and desires, wither can I go at the dissolution of the body?" 7

Said the Blessed One: "O Brahman, thou art religious and earnest. Thou art seriously concerned about thy soul. Yet is thy work in vain because thou art lacking in the one thing that is needful. 8

"There is rebirth of character, but no transmigration of a self. Thy thought-forms reappear, but there is no ego-entity transferred. The stanza uttered by a teacher is reborn in the scholar who repeats the words. 9

"Only through ignorance and delusion do men indulge in the dream that their souls are separate and self-existent entities. 10

"Thy heart, O Brahman, is cleaving still to self; thou art anxious about heaven but thou seekest the pleasures of self in heaven, and thus thou canst not see the bliss of truth and the immortality of truth. 11

"Verily I say unto thee: The Blessed One has not come to teach death, but to teach life, and thou discernest not the nature of living and dying. 12

"This body will be dissolved and no amount of sacrifice will save it. Therefore, seek thou the life that is of the mind. Where self is, truth cannot be; yet when truth comes, self will disappear. Therefore, let thy mind rest in the truth; propagate the truth, put thy whole will in it, and let it spread. In the truth thou shalt live forever. 13

"Self is death and truth is life. The cleaving to self is a perpetual dying, while moving in the truth is partaking of Nirvāna which is life everlasting." 14

Kūtadanta said: "Where, O venerable Master, is Nir-vāna?"   15

"Nirvāna is wherever the precepts are obeyed," replied the Blessed One.   16

"Do I understand thee aright," rejoined the Brahman, "that Nirvāna is not a place, and being nowhere it is with-out reality?"   17

"Thou dost not understand me aright," said the Blessed One, "Now listen and answer these questions: Where does the wind dwell?"   18

"Nowhere," was the reply.   19

Buddha retorted: "Then, sir, there is no such thing as wind."   20

Kūtadanta made no reply; and the Blessed One asked again: "Answer me, O Brahman, where does wisdom dwell? Is wisdom a locality?"   21

"Wisdom has no allotted dwelling-place," replied Kūta-danta.   22

Said the Blessed One: "Meanest thou that there is no wisdom, no enlightenment, no righteousness, and no sal-vation, because Nirvāna is not a locality? As a great and mighty wind which passeth over the world in the heat of the day, so the Tathāgata comes to blow over the minds of mankind with the breath of his love, so cool, so sweet, so calm, so delicate; and those tormented by fever assuage their suffering and rejoice at the refreshing breeze."   23

Said Kūtadanta: "I feel, O Lord, that thou proclaimest a great doctrine, but I cannot grasp it. Forbear with me that I ask again: Tell me, O Lord, if there be no ātman, how can there be immortality? The activity of the mind passeth, and our thoughts are gone when we have done thinking."   24

Buddha replied: "Our thinking is gone, but our thoughts continue. Reasoning ceases, but knowledge remains."   25

Said Kūtadanta: "How is that? Is not reasoning and knowledge the same?" 26

The Blessed One explained the distinction by an illustration: "It is as when a man wants, during the night, to send a letter, and, after having his clerk called, has a lamp lit, and gets the letter written. Then, when that has been done, he extinguishes the lamp. But though the writing has been finished and the light has been put out the letter is still there. Thus does reasoning cease and knowledge remain; and in the same way mental activity ceases, but experience, wisdom, and all the fruits of our acts endure." 27

Kūtadanta continued: "Tell me, O Lord, pray tell me, where, if the sankhāras are dissolved, is the identity of my self. If my thoughts are propagated, and if my soul migrates, my thoughts cease to be *my* thoughts and my soul ceases to be *my* soul. Give me an illustration, but pray, O Lord, tell me, where is the identity of my self?" 28

Said the Blessed One: "Suppose a man were to light a lamp; would it burn the night through?" 29

"Yes, it might do so," was the reply. 30

"Now, is it the same flame that burns in the first watch of the night as in the second?" 31

Kūtadanta hesitated. He thought "Yes, it is the same flame," but fearing the complications of a hidden meaning, and trying to be exact, he said: "No, it is not." 32

"Then," continued the Blessed One, "there are flames, one in the first watch and the other in the second watch." 33

"No, sir," said Kūtadanta. "In one sense it is not the same flame, but in another sense it is the same flame. It burns the same kind of oil, it emits the same kind of light, and it serves the same purpose." 34

„Very well," said the Buddha, "and would you call those flames the same that have burned yesterday and are burning now in the same lamp, filled with the same kind of oil, illuminating the same room?" 35

"They may have been extinguished during the day," suggested Kūtadanta. 36

Said the Blessed One: "Suppose the flame of the first watch had been extinguished during the second watch, would you call it the same if it burns again in the third watch?" 37

Replied Kūtadanta: "In one sense it is a different flame, in another it is not." 38

The Tathāgata asked again: "Has the time that elapsed during the extinction of the flame anything to do with its identity or non-identity?" 39

"No, sir," said the Brahman, "it has not. There is a difference and an identity, whether many years elapsed or only one second, and also whether the lamp has been extinguished in the meantime or not." 40

"Well, then, we agree that the flame of to-day is in a certain sense the same as the flame of yesterday, and in another sense it is different at every moment. Moreover, the flames of the same kind, illuminating with equal power the same kind of rooms, are in a certain sense the same." 41

"Yes, sir," replied Kūtadanta. 42

The Blessed One continued: "Now, suppose there is a man who feels like thyself, thinks like thyself, and acts like thyself, is he not the same man as thou?" 43

"No, sir," interrupted Kūtadanta. 44

Said the Buddha: "Dost thou deny that the same logic holds good for thyself that holds good for the things of the world?" 45

Kūtadanta bethought himself and rejoined slowly: "No, I do not. The same logic holds good universally; but there is a peculiarity about my self which renders it altogether different from everything else and also from other selves. There may be another man who feels exactly like me, thinks like me, and acts like me; suppose even he had the same name and the same kind of possessions, he would not be myself."   46

"True, Kūtadanta," answered Buddha, "he would not be thyself. Now, tell me, is the person who goes to school one, and that same person when he has finished his schooling another? Is it one who commits a crime, another who is punished by having his hands and feet cut off?"   47

"They are the same," was the reply.   48

"Then sameness is constituted by continuity only?" asked the Tathāgata.   49

"Not only by continuity," said Kūtadanta, "but also and mainly by identity of character."   50

"Very well," concluded the Buddha, "then thou agreest that persons can be the same, in the same sense as two flames of the same kind are called the same; and thou must recognize that in this sense another man of the same character and product of the same karma is the same as thou."   51

"Well, I do," said the Brahman.   52

The Buddha continued: "And in this same sense alone art thou the same to-day as yesterday. Thy nature is not constituted by the matter of which thy body consists, but by thy sankhāras, the forms of the body, of sensations, of thoughts. Thy person is the combination of the sankhāras. Wherever they are, thou art. Whithersoever they go, thou goest. Thus thou wilt recognize in a certain sense an identity of thy self, and in another sense a difference. But he who does not recognize the identity should deny all identity, and should say that the questioner is no longer the same person as he who a minute after receives the answer. Now consider the continuation of thy personality, which is preserved in thy karma. Dost thou call it death and annihilation, or life and continued life?"   53

"I call it life and continued life," rejoined Kūtadanta, "for it is the continuation of my existence, but I do not care for that kind of continuation. All I care for is the continuation of self in the other sense, which makes of every man, whether identical with me or not, an altogether different person." 54

"Very well," said Buddha. "This is what thou desirest and this is the cleaving to self. This is thy error. All compound things are transitory: they grow and they decay. All compound things are subject to pain: they will be separated from what they love and be joined to what they abhor. All compound things lack a self, an ātman, an ego." 55

"How is that?" asked Kūtadanta. 56

"Where is thy self?" asked the Buddha. And when Kūtadanta made no reply, he continued: "Thy self to which thou cleavest is a constant change. Years ago thou wast a small babe; then, thou wast a boy; then a youth, and now, thou art a man. Is there any identity of the babe and the man? There is an identity in a certain sense only. Indeed there is more identity between the flames of the first and the third watch, even though the lamp might have been extinguished during the second watch. Now which is thy true self, that of yesterday, that of to-day, or that of to-morrow, for the preservation of which thou clamorest?" 57

Kūtadanta was bewildered. "Lord of the world," he said, "I see my error, but I am still confused." 58

The Tathāgata continued: "It is by a process of evolution that sankhāras come to be. There is no sankhāra which has sprung into being without a gradual becoming. Thy sankhāras are the product of thy deeds in former existences. The combination of thy sankhāras is thy self. Wheresoever they are impressed thither thy self migrates. In thy sankhāras thou wilt continue to live and thou wilt reap in future existences the harvest sown now and in the past." 59

"Verily, O Lord," rejoined Kūtadanta, "this is not a fair retribution. I cannot recognize the justice that others after me will reap what I am sowing now." 60

The Blessed One waited a moment and then replied: "Is all teaching in vain? Dost thou not understand that those others are thou thyself? Thou thyself wilt reap what thou sowest, not others. 61

"Think of a man who is ill-bred and destitute, suffering from the wretchedness of his condition. As a boy he was slothful and indolent, and when he grew up he had not learned a craft to earn a living. Wouldst thou say his misery is not the product of his own action, because the adult is no longer the same person as was the boy? 62

"Verily, I say unto thee: Not in the heavens, not in the midst of the sea, not if thou hidest thyself away in the clefts of the mountains, wilt thou find a place where thou canst escape the fruit of thine evil actions. 63

"At the same time thou art sure to receive the blessings of thy good actions. 64

"The man who has long been traveling and who returns home in safety, the welcome of kinsfolk, friends, and acquaintances awaits. So, the fruits of his good works bid him welcome who has walked in the path of righteousness, when he passes over from the present life into the hereafter." 65

Kūtadanta said: "I have faith in the glory and excellency of thy doctrines. My eye cannot as yet endure the light; but I now understand that there is no self, and the truth dawns upon me. Sacrifices cannot save, and invocations are idle talk. But how shall I find the path to life everlasting? I know all the Vedas by heart and have not found the truth." 66

Said the Buddha: "Learning is a good thing; but it availeth

not. True wisdom can be acquired by practice only. Practise the truth that thy brother is the same as thou. Walk in the noble path of righteousness and thou wilt understand that while there is death in self, there is immortality in truth."   67

Said Kūtadanta: "Let me take my refuge in the Blessed One, in the Dharma, and in the brotherhood. Accept me as thy disciple and let me partake of the bliss of immortality."   68

LIV.

THE BUDDHA OMNIPRESENT.

And the Blessed One thus addressed the brethren: 1
"Those only who do not believe, call me Gotama, but you call me the Buddha, the Blessed One, the Teacher. And this is right, for I have in this life entered Nirvāna, while the life of Gotama has been extinguished.   2

"Self has disappeared and the truth has taken its abode in me. This body of mine is Gotama's body and it will be dissolved in due time, and after its dissolution no one, neither God nor man, will see Gotama again. But the truth remains. The Buddha will not die; the Buddha will continue to live in the holy body of the law.   3

"The extinction of the Blessed One will be by that passing away in which nothing remains that could tend to the formation of another self. Nor will it be possible to point out the Blessed One as being here or there. But it will be like a flame in a great body of blazing fire. That flame has ceased; it has vanished and it cannot be said that it is here or there. In the body of the Dharma, however, the Blessed One can be pointed out; for the Dharma has been preached by the Blessed One.   4

"Ye are my children, I am your father; through me have ye been released from your sufferings.   5

"I myself having reached the other shore, help others to cross the stream; I myself having attained salvation, am a saviour of others; being comforted, I comfort others and lead them to the place of refuge.   6

"I shall fill with joy all the beings whose limbs languish; I shall give happiness to those who are dying from distress; I shall extend to them succor and deliverance.   7

"I was born into the world as the king of truth for the salvation of the world.   8

"The subject on which I meditate is truth. The practice to which I devote myself is truth. The topic of my conversation is truth. My thoughts are always in the truth. For lo! my self has become the truth.   9

"Whosoever comprehendeth the truth will see the Blessed One, for the truth has been preached by the Blessed One."   10

LV.

ONE ESSENCE, ONE LAW, ONE AIM.

And the Tathāgata addressed the venerable Kassapa, to dispel the uncertainty and doubt of his mind, and he said: 1

"All things are made of one essence, yet things are different according to the forms which they assume under different impressions. As they form themselves so they act, and as they act so they are.   2

"It is, Kassapa, as if a potter made different vessels out of the same clay. Some of these pots are to contain sugar, others rice, others curds and milk; others still are vessels of impurity. There is no diversity in the clay used; the diversity of the pots is only due to the moulding hands of the potter who shapes them for the various uses that circumstances may require. 3

"And as all things originate from one essence, so they are developing according to one law and they are destined to one aim which is Nirvāna. 4

"Nirvāna comes to thee, Kassapa, when thou understandest thoroughly, and when thou livest according to thy understanding, that all things are of one essence and that there is but one law. Hence, there is but one Nirvāna as there is but one truth, not two or three. 5

"And the Tathāgata is the same unto all beings, differing in his attitude only in so far as all beings are different. 6

"The Tathāgata recreates the whole world like a cloud shedding its waters without distinction. He has the same sentiments for the high as for the low, for the wise as for the ignorant, for the noble-minded as for the immoral. 7

"The great cloud full of rain comes up in this wide universe covering all countries and oceans to pour down its rain everywhere, over all grasses, shrubs, herbs, trees of various species, families of plants of different names growing on the earth, on the hills, on the mountains, or in the valleys. 8

"Then, Kassapa, the grasses, shrubs, herbs, and wild trees suck the water emitted from that great cloud which is all of one essence and has been abundantly poured down; and they will, according to their nature, acquire a proportionate development, shooting up and producing blossoms and their fruits in season. 9

„Rooted in one and the same soil, all those families of plants and germs are quickened by water of the same essence. 10

"The Tathāgata, however, O Kassapa, knows the law whose essence is salvation, and whose end is the peace of Nirvāna. He is the same to all, and yet knowing the requirements of every single being, he does not reveal himself to all alike. He does not impart to them at once the fulness of omniscience, but pays attention to the disposition of various beings." 11

LVI.

THE LESSON GIVEN TO RĀHULA.

Before Rāhula, the son of Gotama Siddhattha and Yasodharā, attained to the enlightenment of true wisdom, his conduct was not always marked by a love of truth, and the Blessed One sent him to a distant vihāra to govern his mind and to guard his tongue. 1

After some time the Blessed One repaired to the place, and Rāhula was filled with joy. 2

And the Blessed One ordered the boy to bring him a basin of water and to wash his feet, and Rāhula obeyed. 3

When Rāhula had washed the Tathāgata's feet, the Blessed One asked: "Is the water now fit for drinking?" 4

"No, my Lord," replied the boy, "the water is defiled." 5

Then the Blessed One said: "Now consider thine own case. Although thou art my son, and the grandchild of a king, although thou art a samana who has voluntarily given up everything, thou art unable to guard thy tongue from untruth, and thus defilest thou thy mind." 6

And when the water had been poured away, the Blessed One asked again: "Is this vessel now fit for holding water to drink?" 7

"No, my Lord," replied Rāhula, "the vessel, too, has become unclean." 8

And the Blessed One said: "Now consider thine own case. Although thou wearest the yellow robe, art thou fit for any high purpose when thou hast become unclean like this vessel?" 9

Then the Blessed One, lifting up the empty basin and whirling it round, asked: "Art thou not afraid lest it should fall and break?" 10

"No, my Lord," replied Rāhula, "the vessel is but cheap, and its loss will not amount to much." 11

"Now consider thine own case," said the Blessed One. "Thou art whirled about in endless eddies of transmigration, and as thy body is made of the same substance as other material things that will crumble to dust, there is no loss if it be broken. He who is given to speaking untruths is an object of contempt to the wise." 12

Rāhula was filled with shame, and the Blessed One addressed him once more: "Listen, and I will tell thee a parable: 13

"There was a king who had a very powerful elephant, able to cope with five hundred ordinary elephants. When going to war, the elephant was armed with sharp swords on his tusks, with scythes on his shoulders, spears on his feet, and an iron ball at his tail. The elephant-master rejoiced to see the noble creature so well equipped, and, knowing that a slight wound by an arrow in the trunk would be fatal, he had taught the elephant to keep his trunk well coiled up. But during the battle the elephant stretched forth his trunk to seize a sword. His master was frightened and consulted with the king, and they decided that the elephant was no longer fit to be used in battle. 14

"O Rāhula! if men would only guard their tongues all would be well! Be like the fighting elephant who guards his trunk against the arrow that strikes in the center. 15

"By love of truth the sincere escape iniquity. Like the elephant well subdued and quiet, who permits the king to mount on his trunk, thus the man that reveres righteousness will endure faithfully throughout his life." 16

Rāhula hearing these words was filled with deep sorrow; he never again gave any occasion for complaint, and forthwith he sanctified his life by earnest exertions.   17

LVII.

THE SERMON ON ABUSE.

And the Blessed One observed the ways of society and noticed how much misery came from malignity and foolish offences done only to gratify vanity and self-seeking pride.   1

And the Buddha said: "If a man foolishly does me wrong, I will return to him the protection of my ungrudging love; the more evil comes from him, the more good shall go from me; the fragrance of goodness always comes to me, and the harmful air of evil goes to him."   2

A foolish man learning that the Buddha observed the principle of great love which commends the return of good for evil, came and abused him. The Buddha was silent, pitying his folly.   3

When the man had finished his abuse, the Buddha asked him, saying: "Son, if a man declined to accept a present made to him, to whom would it belong?" And he answered: "In that case it would belong to the man who offered it."   4

"My son," said the Buddha, "thou hast railed at me, but I decline to accept thy abuse, and request thee to keep it thyself. Will it not be a source of misery to thee? As the echo belongs to the sound, and the shadow to the substance, so misery will overtake the evil-doer without fail."   5

The abuser made no reply, and Buddha continued: 6

"A wicked man who reproaches a virtuous one is like one who looks up and spits at heaven; the spittle soils not the heaven, but comes back and defiles his own person. 7

"The slanderer is like one who flings dust at another when the wind is contrary; the dust does but return on him who threw it. The virtuous man cannot be hurt and the misery that the other would inflict comes back on himself." 8

The abuser went away ashamed, but he came again and took refuge in the Buddha, the Dharma, and the Sangha. 9

LVIII.

THE BUDDHA REPLIES TO THE DEVA.

On a certain day when the Blessed One dwelt at Jeta-vana, the garden of Anāthapindika, a celestial deva came to him in the shape of a Brahman whose countenance was bright and whose garments were white like snow. The deva asked questions which the Blessed One answered. 1

The deva said: "What is the sharpest sword? What is is the deadliest poison? What is the fiercest fire? What is the darkest night?" 2

The Blessed One replied: "A word spoken in wrath is the sharpest sword; covetousness is the deadliest poison; passion is the fiercest fire; ignorance is the darkest night." 3

The deva said: "Who gains the greatest benefit? Who loses most? Which armor is invulnerable? What is the best weapon?" 4

The Blessed One replied: "He is the greatest gainer who gives to others, and he loses most who greedily receives without gratitude. Patience is an invulnerable armor; wisdom is the best weapon." 5

The deva said: "Who is the most dangerous thief? What is the most precious treasure? Who is most successful in taking away by violence not only on earth, but also in heaven? What is the securest treasure-trove?"   6

The Blessed One replied: "Evil thought is the most dangerous thief; virtue is the most precious treasure. The mind takes possession of everything not only on earth, but also in heaven, and immortality is its securest treasure-trove."   7

The deva said: "What is attractive? What is disgusting? What is the most horrible pain? What is the greatest enjoyment?"   8

The Blessed One replied: "Good is attractive; evil is disgusting. A bad conscience is the most tormenting pain; deliverance is the height of bliss."   9

The deva asked: "What causes ruin in the world? What breaks off friendships? What is the most violent fever? Who is the best physician?"   10

The Blessed One replied: "Ignorance causes the ruin of the world. Envy and selfishness break off friendships. Hatred is the most violent fever, and the Buddha is the best physician."   11

The deva then asked and said: "Now I have only one doubt to be solved; pray, clear it away: What is it fire can neither burn, nor moisture corrode, nor wind crush down, but is able to reform the whole world?"   12

The Blessed Once replied: "Blessing! Neither fire, nor moisture, nor wind can destroy the blessing of a good deed, and blessings reform the whole world."   13

The deva, having heard the words of the Blessed One, was full of exceeding joy. Clasping his hands, he bowed down before him in reverence, and disappeared suddenly from the presence of the Buddha.   14

LIX.

WORDS OF INSTRUCTION.

The bhikkhus came to the Blessed One, and having saluted him with clasped hands they said: 1

"O Master, thou all-seeing one, we all wish to learn; our ears are ready to hear, thou art our teacher, thou art incomparable. Cut off our doubt, inform us of the blessed Dharma, O thou of great understanding; speak in the midst of us, O thou who art all-seeing, as is the thousand-eyed Lord of the gods. 2

"We will ask the muni of great understanding, who has crossed the stream, gone to the other shore, is blessed and of a firm mind: How does a bhikkhu wander rightly in the world, after having gone out from his house and driven away desire?" 3

The Buddha said: 4

"Let the bhikkhu subdue his passion for human and celestial pleasures, then, having conquered existence, he will command the Dharma. Such a one will wander rightly in the world. 5

"He whose lusts have been destroyed, who is free from pride, who has overcome all the ways of passion, is subdued, perfectly happy, and of a firm mind. Such a one will wander rightly in the world. 6

"Faithful is he who is possessed of knowledge, seeing the way that leads to Nirvāna; he who is not a partisan; he who is pure and virtuous, and has removed the veil from his eyes. Such a one will wander rightly in the world." 7

Said the bhikkhus: "Certainly, O Bhagavat, it is so: whichever bhikkhu lives in this way, subdued and having overcome all bonds, such a one will wander rightly in the world." 8

The Blessed One said: 9

"Whatever is to be done by him who aspires to attain the tranquillity of Nirvāna let him be able and upright, conscientious and gentle, and not proud. 10

"Let a man's pleasure be the Dharma, let him delight in the Dharma, let him stand fast in the Dharma, let him know how to inquire into the Dharma, let him not raise any dispute that pollutes the Dharma, and let him spend his time in pondering on the well-spoken truths of the Dharma. 11

"A treasure that is laid up in a deep pit profits nothing and may easily be lost. The real treasure that is laid up through charity and piety, temperance, self-control, or deeds of merit, is hid secure and cannot pass away. It is never gained by despoiling or wronging others, and no thief can steal it. A man, when he dies, must leave the fleeting wealth of the world, but this treasure of virtuous acts he takes with him. Let the wise do good deeds; they are a treasure that can never be lost." 12

And the bhikkhus praised the wisdom of the Tathāgata: 13

"Thou hast passed beyond pain; thou art holy, O Enlightened One, we consider thee one that has destroyed his passions. Thou art glorious, thoughtful, and of great understanding. O thou who puttest an end to pain, thou hast carried us across our doubt. 14

"Because thou sawst our longing and carriedst us across our doubt, adoration be to thee, O muni, who hast attained the highest good in the ways of wisdom. 15

"The doubt we had before, thou hast cleared away, O thou clearly-seeing one; surely thou art a great thinker, perfectly enlightened, there is no obstacle for thee. 16

"And all thy troubles are scattered and cut off; thou art calm, subdued, firm, truthful. 17

"Adoration be to thee, O noble sage, adoration be to thee, O thou best of beings; in the world of men and gods there is none equal to thee. 18

"Thou art the Buddha, thou art the Master, thou art the muni that conquers Māra; after having cut off desire thou hast crossed over and carriest this generation to the other shore."   19

LX.

AMITĀBHA.

One of the disciples came to the Blessed One with a trembling heart and his mind full of doubt. And he asked the Blessed One: "O Buddha, our Lord and Master, why do we give up the pleasures of the world, if thou forbiddest us to work miracles and to attain the supernatural? Is not Amitābha, the infinite light of revelation, the source of innumerable miracles?"   1

And the Blessed One, seeing the anxiety of a truth-seeking mind, said: "O sāvaka, thou art a novice among the novices, and thou art swimming on the surface of samsāra. How long will it take thee to grasp the truth? Thou hast not understood the words of the Tathāgata. The law of karma is irrefragable, and supplications have no effect, for they are empty words."   2

Said the disciple: "So sayest thou there are no miraculous and wonderful things?"   3

And the Blessed One replied: 4

"Is it not a wonderful thing, mysterious and miraculous to the worldling, that a man who commits wrong can become a saint, that he who attains to true enlightenment will find the path of truth and abandon the evil ways of selfisness?   5

"The bhikkhu who renounces the transient pleasures of the world for the eternal bliss of holiness, performs the only miracle that can truly be called a miracle.   6

"A holy man changes the curses of karma into blessings. The desire to perform miracles arises either from covetousness or from vanity. 7

"That mendicant does right who does not think: 'People should salute me'; who, though despised by the world, yet cherishes no ill-will towards it. 8

"That mendicant does right to whom omens, meteors, dreams, and signs are things abolished; he is free from all their evils. 9

"Amitābha, the unbounded light, is the source of wisdom, of virtue, of Buddhahood. The deeds of sorcerers and miracle-mongers are frauds, but what is more wondrous, more mysterious, more miraculous than Amitābha?" 10

"But, Master," continued the sāvaka, "is the promise of the happy region vain talk and a myth?" 11

"What is this promise?" asked the Buddha; and the disciple replied: 12

"There is in the west a paradise called the Pure Land, exquisitely adorned with gold and silver and precious gems. There are pure waters with golden sands, surrounded by pleasant walks and covered with large lotus flowers. Joyous music is heard, and flowers rain down three times a day. There are singing birds whose harmonious notes proclaim the praises of religion, and in the minds of those who listen to their sweet sounds, remembrance arises of the Buddha, the law, and the brotherhood. No evil birth is possible there, and even the name of hell is unknown. He who fervently and with a pious mind repeats the words 'Amitābha Buddha' will be transported to the happy region of this pure land, and when death draws nigh, the Buddha, with a company of saintly followers, will stand before him, and there will be perfect tranquillity." 13

"In truth," said the Buddha, "there is such a happy paradise. But the country is spiritual and it is accessible only to those that are spiritual. Thou sayest it lies in the west.

This means, look for it where he who enlightens the world resides. The sun sinks down and leaves us in utter darkness, the shades of night steal over us, and Māra, the evil one, buries our bodies in the grave. Sunset is nevertheless no extinction, and where we imagine we see extinction, there is boundless light and inexhaustible life." 14

"I understand," said the sāvaka, "that the story of the Western Paradise is not literally true." 15

"Thy description of paradise," the Buddha continued, "is beautiful; yet it is insufficient and does little justice to the glory of the pure land. The worldly can speak of it in a worldly way only; they use worldly similes and worldly words. But the pure land in which the pure live is more beautiful than thou canst say or imagine. 16

"However, the repetition of the name Amitābha Buddha is meritorious only if thou speak it with such a devout attitude of mind as will cleanse thy heart and attune thy will to do works of righteousness. He only can reach the happy land whose soul is filled with the infinite light of truth. He only can live and breathe in the spiritual atmosphere of the Western Paradise who has attained enlightenment. 17

"Verily I say unto thee, the Tathāgata lives in the pure land of eternal bliss even now while he is still in the body; and the Tathāgata preaches the law of religion unto thee and unto the whole world, so that thou and thy brethren may attain the same peace and the same happiness." 18

Said the disciple: "Teach me, O Lord, the meditations to which I must devote myself in order to let my mind enter into the paradise of the pure land." 19

Buddha said: "There are five meditations. 20

"The first meditation is the meditation of love in which thou must so adjust thy heart that thou longest for the weal and welfare of all beings, including the happiness of thine enemies. 21

"The second meditation is the meditation of pity, in which thou thinkest of all beings in distress, vividly representing in thine imagination their sorrows and anxieties so as to arouse a deep compassion for them in thy soul. 22

"The third meditation is the meditation of joy in which thou thinkest of the prosperity of others and rejoicest with their rejoicings. 23

"The fourth meditation is the meditation on impurity, in which thou considerest the evil consequences of corruption, the effects of wrongs and evils. How trivial is often the pleasure of the moment and how fatal are its consequences! 24

"The fifth meditation is the meditation on serenity, in which thou risest above love and hate, tyranny and thraldom, wealth and want, and regardest thine own fate with impartial calmness and perfect tranquillity. 25

"A true follower of the Tathāgata founds not his trust upon austerities or rituals but giving up the idea of self relies with his whole heart upon Amitābha, which is the unbounded light of truth." 26

The Blessed One after having explained his doctrine of Amitābha, the immeasurable light which makes him who receives it a Buddha, looked into the heart of his disciple and saw still some doubts and anxieties. And the Blessed One said: "Ask me, my son, the questions which weigh upon thy soul." 27

And the disciple said: "Can a humble monk, by sanctifying himself, acquire the talents of supernatural wisdom called Abhiññās and the supernatural powers called Iddhi? Show me the Iddhi-pāda, the path to the highest wisdom? Open to me the Jhānas which are the means of acquiring samādhi, the fixity of mind which enraptures the soul." 28

And the Blessed One said: "Which are the Abhiññās?" 29

The disciple replied: "There are six Abhiññās: (1) The celestial eye; (2) the celestial ear; (3) the body at will or the power of transformation; (4) the knowledge of the destiny of former dwellings, so as to know former states of existence; (5) the faculty of reading the thoughts of others; and (6) the knowledge of comprehending the finality of the stream of life." 30

And the Blessed One replied: "These are wondrous things; but verily, every man can attain them. Consider the abilities of thine own mind; thou wert born about two hundred leagues from here and canst thou not in thy thought, in an instant travel to thy native place and remember the details of thy father's home? Seest thou not with thy mind's eye the roots of the tree which is shaken by the wind without being overthrown? Does not the collector of herbs see in his mental vision, whenever he pleases, any plant with its roots, its stem, its fruits, leaves, and even the uses to which it can be applied? Cannot the man who understands languages recall to his mind any word whenever he pleases, knowing its exact meaning and import? How much more does the Tathāgata understand the nature of things; he looks into the hearts of men and reads their thoughts. He knows the evolution of beings and foresees their ends." 31

Said the disciple: "Then the Tathāgata teaches that man can attain through the Jhānas the bliss of Abhiññā." 32

And the Blessed One asked in reply: "Which are the Jhānas through which man reaches Abhiññā?" 33

The disciple replied: "There are four Jhānas. The first Jhāna is seclusion in which one must free his mind from sensuality; the second Jhāna is a tranquillity of mind full of joy and gladness; the third Jhāna is a taking delight in things spiritual; the fourth Jhāna is a state of perfect purity and peace in which the mind is above all gladness and grief." 34

"Good, my son," enjoined the Blessed One. "Be sober and abandon wrong practices which serve only to stultify the mind." 35

Said the disciple: "Forbear with me, O Blessed One, for I have faith without understanding and I am seeking the truth. O Blessed One, O Tathāgata, my Lord and Master, teach me the Iddhipāda." 36

The Blessed One said: "There are four means by which Iddhi is acquired; (1) Prevent bad qualities from arising. (2) Put away bad qualities which have arisen. (3) Produce goodness that does not yet exist. (4) Increase goodness which already exists.—Search with sincerity, and persevere in the search. In the end thou wilt find the truth." 37

LXI.

THE TEACHER UNKNOWN.

And the Blessed One said to Ānanda: 1

"There are various kinds of assemblies, O Ānanda; assemblies of nobles, of Brahmans, of householders, of bhikkhus, and of other beings. When I used to enter an assembly, I always became, before I seated myself, in color like unto the color of my audience, and in voice like unto their voice. I spoke to them in their language and then with religious discourse, I instructed, quickened, and gladdened them. 2

"My doctrine is like the ocean, having the same eight wonderful qualities. 3

"Both the ocean and my doctrine become gradually deeper. Both preserve their identity under all changes. Both cast out dead bodies upon the dry land. As the great rivers, when falling into the main, lose their names and are thenceforth reckoned as the great ocean, so all the castes, having renounced their lineage and entered the Sangha, become brethren and are reckoned the sons of Sakyamuni. The ocean is the goal of all streams and of the rain from the clouds, yet is it never overflowing and never emptied: so the Dharma is embraced by many milllions of people, yet it neither increases nor decreases. As the great ocean has only one taste, the taste of salt, so my doctrine has only one flavor, the flavor of emancipation. Both the ocean and the Dharma are full of gems and pearls and jewels, and both afford a dwelling-place for mighty beings.   4

"These are the eight wonderful qualities in which my doctrine resembles the ocean.   5

"My doctrine is pure and it makes no discrimination between noble and ignoble, rich and poor.   6

"My doctrine is like unto water which cleanses all without distinction.   7

"My doctrine is like unto fire which consumes all things that exist between heaven and earth, great and small.   8

"My doctrine is like unto the heavens, for there is room in it, ample room for the reception of all, for men and women, boys and girls, the powerful and the lowly.   9

"But when I spoke, they knew me not and would say, 'Who may this be who thus speaks, a man or a god?' Then having instructed, quickened, and gladdened them with religious discourse, I would vanish away. But they knew me not, even when I vanished away."   10

PARABLES AND STORIES.

LXII.

PARABLES.

AND the Blessed One thought: "I have taught the truth which is excellent in the beginning, excellent in the middle, and excellent in the end; it is glorious in its spirit and glorious in its letter. But simple as it is, the people cannot understand it. I must speak to them in their own language. I must adapt my thoughts to their thoughts. They are like unto children, and love to hear tales. Therefore, I will tell them stories to explain the glory of the Dharma. If they cannot grasp the truth in the abstract arguments by which I have reached it, they may nevertheless come to understand it, if it is illustrated in parables.   1

LXIII.

THE WIDOW'S TWO MITES AND THE PARABLE OF THE THREE MERCHANTS.

There was once a lone widow who was very destitute, and having gone to the mountain she beheld hermits holding a religious assembly. Then the woman was filled with joy, and uttering praises, said, "It is well, holy priests! but while others give precious things such as the ocean caves produce, I have nothing to offer." Having spoken thus and having searched herself in vain for something to give, she recollected that some time before she had found in a dungheap two coppers, so taking these she offered them forthwith as a gift to the priesthood in charity.   1

The superior of the priests, a saint who could read the hearts of men, disregarding the rich gifts of others and beholding the deep faith dwelling in the heart of this poor widow, and wishing the priesthood to esteem rightly her religious merit, burst forth with full voice in a canto. He raised his right hand and said, "Reverend priests attend!" and then he proceeded: 2

"The coppers of this poor widow
To all purpose are more worth
Than all the treasures of the oceans
And the wealth of the broad earth.   3
"As an act of pure devotion
She has done a pious deed;
She has attained salvation,
Being free from selfish greed."   4

The woman was mightily strengthened in her mind by this thought, and said, "It is even as the Teacher says: what I have done is as much as if a rich man were to give up all his wealth."   5

And the Teacher said: "Doing good deeds is like hoarding up treasures," and he expounded this truth in a parable: 6

"Three merchants set out on their travels, each with his capital; one of them gained much, the second returned with his capital, and the third one came home after having lost his capital. What is true in common life applies also to religion.   7

"The capital is the state a man has reached, the gain is heaven; the loss of his capital means that a man will be born in a lower state, as a denizen of hell or as an animal. These are the courses that are open to the sinner.   8

"He who brings back his capital, is like unto one who is born again as a man. Those who through the exercise of various virtues become pious householders will be born again as men, for all beings will reap the fruit of their actions. But he who increases his capital is like unto one who practises eminent virtues. The virtuous, excellent man attains in heaven to the glorious state of the gods."   9

LXIV.

THE MAN BORN BLIND.

There was a man born blind, and he said: "I do not believe in the world of light and appearance. There are no colors, bright or sombre. There is no sun, no moon, no stars. No one has witnessed these things."   1

His friends remonstrated with him, but he clung to his opinion: "What you say that you see," he objected, "are illusions. If colors existed I should be able to touch them. They have no substance and are not real. Everything real has weight, but I feel no weight where you see colors."   2

In those days there was a physician who was called to see the blind man. He mixed four simples, and when he applied them to the cataract of the blind man the gray film melted, and his eyes acquired the faculty of sight.   3

The Tathāgata is the physician, the cataract is the illusion of the thought "I am," and the four simples are the four noble truths.   4

LXV.

THE LOST SON.

There was a householder's son who went away into a distant country, and while the father accumulated immeasurable riches, the son became miserably poor. And the son while searching for food and clothing happened to come to the country in which his father lived. And the father saw him in his wretchedness, for he was ragged and brutalized by poverty, and ordered some of his servants to call him.   1

When the son saw the place to which he was conducted, he thought, "I must have evoked the suspicion of a powerful man, and he will throw me into prison." Full of apprehension he made his escape before he had seen his father.   2

Then the father sent messengers out after his son, who was caught and brought back in spite of his cries and lamentations. Thereupon the father ordered his servants to deal tenderly with his son, and he appointed a laborer of his son's rank and education to employ the lad as a helpmate on the estate. And the son was pleased with his new situation.   3

From the window of his palace the father watched the boy, and when he saw that he was honest and industrious, he promoted him higher and higher.   4

After some time, he summoned his son and called together all his servants, and made the secret known to them. Then the poor man was exceedingly glad and he was full of joy at meeting his father.   5

Little by little must the minds of men be trained for higher truths.   6

LXVI.

THE GIDDY FISH.

There was a bhikkhu who had great difficulty in keeping his senses and passions under control; so, resolving to leave the Order, he came to the Blessed One to ask him for a release from the vows. And the Blessed One said to the bhikkhu: 1

"Take heed, my son, lest thou fall a prey to the passions of thy misguided heart. For I see that in former existences, thou hast suffered much from the evil consequences of lust, and unless thou learnest to conquer thy sensual desire, thou wilt in this life be ruined through thy folly. 2

"Listen to a story of another existence of thine, as a fish. 3

"The fish could be seen swimming lustily in the river, playing with his mate. She, moving in front, suddenly perceived the meshes of a net, and slipping around escaped the danger; but he, blinded by love, shot eagerly after her and fell straight into the mouth of the net. The fisherman pulled the net up, and the fish, who complained bitterly of his sad fate, saying, 'this indeed is the bitter fruit of my folly,' would surely have died if the Bodhisatta had not chanced to come by, and, understanding the language of the fish, took pity on him. He bought the poor creature and said to him: 'My good fish, had I not caught sight of thee this day, thou wouldst have lost thy life. I shall save thee, but henceforth avoid the evil of lust.' With these words he threw the fish into the water. 4

"Make the best of the time of grace that is offered to thee in thy present existence, and fear the dart of passion which, if thou guard not thy senses, will lead thee to destruction." 5

LXVII.

THE CRUEL CRANE OUTWITTED.

A tailor who used to make robes for the brotherhood was wont to cheat his customers, and thus prided himself on being smarter than other men. But once, on entering upon an important business transaction with a stranger, he found his master in fraudulent practices, and suffered a heavy loss. 1

And the Blessed One said: "This is not an isolated incident in the greedy tailor's fate; in other incarnations he suffered similar losses, and by trying to dupe others ultimately ruined himself. 2

"This same greedy character lived many generations ago as a crane near a pond, and when the dry season set in he said to the fishes with a bland voice: 'Are you not anxious for your future welfare? There is at present very little water and still less food in this pond. What will you do should the whole pond become dry, in this drought?' 3

'Yes, indeed' said the fishes, 'what should we do?' 4

"Replied the crane: 'I know a fine, large lake, which never becomes dry. Would you not like me to carry you there in my beak?' When the fishes began to distrust the honesty of the crane, he proposed to have one of them sent over to the lake to see it; and a big carp at last decided to take the risk for the sake of the others, and the crane carried him to a beautiful lake and brought him back in safety. Then all doubt vanished, and the fishes gained confidence in the crane, and now the crane took them one by one out of the pond and devoured them on a big varana-tree. 5

"There was also a lobster in the pond, and when it listed the crane to eat him too, he said: 'I have taken all the fishes away and put them in a fine, large lake. Come along. I shall take thee, too!' 6

'But how wilt thou hold me to carry me along?' asked the lobster.   7

'I shall take hold of thee with my beak,' said the crane.   8

'Thou wilt let me fall if thou carry me like that. I will not go with thee!' replied the lobster.   9

'Thou needst not fear,' rejoined the crane; 'I shall hold thee quite tight all the way.'   10

"Then said the lobster to himself: 'If this crane once gets hold of a fish, he will certainly never let him go in a lake! Now if he should really put me into the lake it would be splendid; but if he does not, then I will cut his throat and kill him!' So he said to the crane: 'Look here, friend, thou wilt not be able to hold me tight enough; but we lobsters have a famous grip. If thou wilt let me catch hold of thee round the neck with my claws, I shall be glad to go with thee.'   11

"The crane did not see that the lobster was trying to outwit him, and agreed. So the lobster caught hold of his neck with his claws as securely as with a pair of black-smith's pincers, and called out: 'Ready, ready, go!'   12

"The crane took him and showed him the lake, and then turned off toward the varana-tree. 'My dear uncle!' cried the lobster, 'The lake lies that way, but thou art taking me this other way.'   13

"Answered the crane: 'Thinkest thou so? Am I thy dear uncle? Thou meanest me to understand, I suppose, that I am thy slave, who has to lift thee up and carry thee about with him, where thou pleasest! Now cast thine eye upon that heap of fish-bones at the root of yonder varana-tree. Just as I have eaten those fish, every one of them, just so will I devour thee also!'   14

'Ah! those fishes got eaten through their own stupidity,' answered the lobster, 'but I am not going to let thee kill me. On the contrary, it is thou that I am going to des-troy. For thou, in thy folly, hast not seen that I have outwitted thee. If we die, we both die together; for I will cut off this head of thine and cast it to the ground!' So saying, he gave the crane's neck a pinch with his claws as with a vise.   15

"Then gasping, and with tears trickling from his eyes, and trembling with the fear of death, the crane besought the lobster, saying: 'O, my Lord! Indeed I did not intend to eat thee. Grant me my life!'   16

'Very well! fly down and put me into the lake,' replied the lobster.   17

"And the crane turned round and stepped down into the lake, to place the lobster on the mud at its edge. Then the lobster cut the crane's neck through as clean as one would cut a lotus-stalk with a hunting-knife, and then entered the water!"   18

When the Teacher had finished this discoruse, he added: "Not now only was this man outwitted in this way, but in other existences, too, by his own intrigues."   19

LXVIII.

FOUR KINDS OF MERIT.

There was a rich man who used to invite all the Brahmans of the neighborhood to his house, and, giving them rich gifts, offered great sacrifices to the gods.   1

And the Blessed One said: "If a man each month repeat a thousand sacrifices and give offerings without ceasing, he is not equal to him who but for one moment fixes his mind upon righteousness."   2

The world-honored Buddha continued: "There are four kinds of offering: first, when the gifts are large and the merit small; secondly, when the gifts are small and the merit small; thirdly, when the gifts are small and the merit large; and fourthly, when the gifts are large and the merit is also large.   3

"The first is the case of the deluded man who takes away life for the purpose of sacrificing to the gods, accompanied by carousing and feasting. Here the gifts are great, but the merit is small indeed.   4

"The gifts are small and the merit is also small, when from covetousness and an evil heart a man keeps to himself a part of that which he intends to offer.   5

"The merit is great, however, while the gift is small, when a man makes his offering from love and with a desire to grow in wisdom and in kindness.   6

"Lastly, the gift is large and the merit is large, when a wealthy man, in an unselfish spirit and with the wisdom of a Buddha, gives donations and founds institutions for the best of mankind to enlighten the minds of his fellow-men and to administer unto their needs."   7

LXIX.

THE LIGHT OF THE WORLD.

There was a certain Brahman in Kosambī, a wrangler and well versed in the Vedas. As he found no one whom he regarded his equal in debate he used to carry a lighted torch in his hand, and when asked for the reason of his strange conduct, he replied: "The world is so dark that I carry this torch to light it up, as far as I can."   1

A samana sitting in the market-place heard these words and said: "My friend, if thine eyes are blind to the sight of the omnipresent light of the day, do not call the world dark. Thy torch adds nothing to the glory of the sun and thy intention to illumine the minds of others is as futile as it is arrogant."   2

Whereupon the Brahman asked: "Where is the sun of which thou speakest?" And the samana replied: "The wisdom of the Tathāgata is the sun of the mind. His radiancy is glorious by day and night, and he whose faith is strong will not lack light on the path to Nirvāna where he will inherit bliss everlasting."   3

LXX.

LUXURIOUS LIVING.

While the Buddha was preaching his doctrine for the conversion of the world in the neighborhood of Sāvatthi, a man of great wealth who suffered from many ailmemts came to him with clasped hands and said: "World-honored Buddha, pardon me for my want of respect in not saluting thee as I ought, but I suffer greatly from obesity, excessive drowsiness, and other complaints, so that I cannot move without pain."   1

The Tathāgata, seeing the luxuries with which the man was sourrounded asked him: "Hast thou a desire to know the cause of thy ailments?" And when the wealthy man expressed his willingness to learn, the Blessed One said: "There are five things which produce the condition of which thou complainest: opulent dinners, love of sleep, hankering after pleasure, thoughtlessness, and lack of occupation. Exercise self-control at thy meals, and take upon thyself some duties that will exercise thy abilities and make thee useful to thy fellow-men. In following this advice thou wilt prolong thy life."   2

The rich man remembered the words of the Buddha and after some time having recovered his lightness of body and youthful buoyancy returned to the Worldhonored One and, coming afoot without horses and attendants, said to him:

"Master, thou hast cured my bodily ailments; I come now to seek enlightenment of my mind." 3

And the Blessed One said: "The worldling nourishes his body, but the wise man nourishes his mind. He who indulges in the satisfaction of his appetites works his own destruction; but he who walks in the path will have both the salvation from evil and a prolongation of life." 4

LXXI.

THE COMMUNICATION OF BLISS.

Annabhāra, the slave of Sumana, having just cut the grass on the meadow, saw a samana with his bowl begging for food. Throwing down his bundle of grass he ran into the house and returned with the rice that had been provided for his own food. 1

The samana ate the rice and gladdened him with words of religious comfort. 2

The daughter of Sumana having observed the scene from a window called out: "Good! Annabhāra, good! Very good!" 3

Sumana hearing these words inquired what she meant, and on being informed about Annabhāra's devotion and the words of comfort he had received from the samana, went to his slave and offered him money to divide the bliss of his offering. 4

"My lord," said Annabhāra, "let me first ask the venerable man." And approaching the samana, he said: "My master has asked me to share with him the bliss of the offering I made thee of my allowance of rice. Is it right that I should divide it with him?" 5

The samana replied in a parable. He said: "In a village of one hundred houses a single light was burning. Then a neighbor came with his lamp and lit it; and in this same way the light was communicated from house to house and the brightness in the village was increased. Thus the light of religion may be diffused without stinting him who communicates it. Let the bliss of thy offering also be diffused. Divide it." 6

Annabhāra returned to his master's house and said to him: "I present thee, my lord, with a share of the bliss of my offering. Deign to accept it." 7

Sumana accepted it and offered his slave a sum of money, but Annabhāra replied: "Not so, my lord; if I accept thy money it would appear as if I sold thee my share. Bliss cannot be sold; I beg thou wilt accept it as a gift." 8

The master replied: "Brother Annabhāra, from this day forth thou shalt be free. Live with me as my friend and accept this present as a token of my respect." 9

LXXII.

THE LISTLESS FOOL.

There was a rich Brahman, well advanced in years, who, unmindful of the impermanence of earthly things and anticipating a long life, had built himself a large house. 1

The Buddha wondered why a man so near to death had built a mansion with so many apartments, and he sent Ānanda to the rich Brahman to preach to him the four noble truths and the eightfold path of salvation. 2

The Brahman showed Ānanda his house and explained to him the purpose of its numerous chambers, but to the instruction of the Buddha's teachings he gave no heed. 3

Ānanda said: "It is the habit of fools to say, 'I have children and wealth.' He who says so is not even master of himself; how can he claim possession of children, riches, and servants? Many are the anxieties of the worldly, but they know nothing of the changes of the future." 4

Scarcely had Ānanda left, when the old man was stricken with apoplexy and fell dead. The Buddha said, for the instruction of those who were ready to learn: "A fool, though he live in the company of the wise, understands nothing of the true doctrine, as a spoon tastes not the flavor of the soup. He thinks of himself only, and unmindful of the advice of good counsellors is unable to deliver himself." 5

LXXIII.

RESCUE IN THE DESERT.

There was a disciple of the Blessed One, full of energy and zeal for the truth, who, living under a vow to complete a meditation in solitude, flagged in a moment of weakness. He said to himself: "The Teacher said there are several kinds of men; I must belong to the lowest class and fear that in this birth there will be neither path nor fruit for me. What is the use of a forest life if I cannot by my constant endeavor attain the insight of meditation to which I have devoted myself?" And he left the solitude and returned to the Jetavana. 1

When the brethren saw him they said to him: "Thou hast done wrong, O brother, after taking a vow, to give up the attempt of carrying it out;" and they took him to the Master. 2

When the Blessed One saw them he said: "I see, O mendicants, that you have brought this brother here against his will. What has he done?" 3

"Lord, this brother, having taken the vows of so sanctifying a faith, has abandoned the endeavor to accomplish the aim of a member of the order, and has come back to us." 4

Then the Teacher said to him: "Is it true that thou hast given up trying?" 5

"It is true, O Blessed One!" was the reply. 6

The Master said: "This present life of thine is a time of grace. If thou fail now to reach the happy state thou wilt have to suffer remorse in future existences. How is it, brother, that thou hast proved so irresolute? Why, in former states of existence thou wert full of determination. By thy energy alone the men and bullocks of five hundred wagons obtained water in the sandy desert, and were saved. How is it that thou now givest up?" 7

By these few words that brother was re-established in his resolution. But the others besought the Blessed One, saying: "Lord! Tell us how this was." 8

"Listen, then, O mendicants!" said the Blessed One; and having thus excited their attention, he made manifest a thing concealed by change of birth. 9

Once upon a time, when Brahmadatta was reigning in Kāsi, the Bodhisatta was born in a merchant's family; and when he grew up, he went about trafficking with five hundred carts. 10

One day he arrived at a sandy desert many leagues across. The sand in that desert was so fine that when taken in the closed fist it could not be kept in the hand. After the sun had risen it became as hot as a mass of burning embers, so that no man could walk on it. Those, therefore, who had to travel over it took wood, and water, and oil, and rice in their carts, and traveled during the night. And at daybreak they formed an encampment and spread an awning over it, and, taking their meals early, they passed the day lying in the shade. At sunset they supped, and when the ground had become cool they yoked their oxen and went on. The traveling was like a voyage over the sea: a desert-pilot had to be chosen, and he brought the caravan safe to the other side by his knowledge of the stars. 11

Thus the merchant of our story traversed the desert. And when he had passed over fifty-nine leagues he thought, "Now, in one more night we shall get out of the sand," and after supper he directed the wagons to be yoked, and so set out. The pilot had cushions arranged on the foremost cart and lay down, looking at the stars and directing the men where to drive. But worn out by want of rest during the long march, he fell asleep, and did not perceive that the oxen had turned round and taken the same road by which they had come. 12

The oxen went on the whole night through. Towards dawn the pilot woke up, and, observing the stars, called out: "Stop the wagons, stop the wagons!" The day broke just as they stopped and were drawing up the carts in a line. Then the men cried out: "Why this is the very encampment we left yesterday! We have but little wood left and our water is all gone! We are lost!" And unyoking the oxen and spreading the canopy over their heads, they lay down in despondency, each one under his wagon. But the Bodhisatta said to himself, "If I lose heart, all these will perish," and walked about while the morning was yet cool. On seeing a tuft of kusa-grass, he thought: "This could have grown only by soaking up some water which must be beneath it." 13

And he made them bring a spade and dig in that spot. And they dug sixty cubits deep. And when they had got thus far, the spade of the diggers struck on a rock; and as soon as it struck, they all gave up in despair. But the Bodhisatta thought, "There must be water under that rock," and descending into the well he got upon the stone, and stooping down applied his ear to it and tested the sound of it. He heard the sound of water gurgling beneath, and when he got out he called his page. "My lad, if thou givest up now, we shall all be lost. Do not lose heart. Take this iron hammer, and go down into the pit, and give the rock a good blow." 14

The lad obeyed, and though they all stood by in despair, he went down full of determination and struck at the stone. The rock split in two and fell below, so that it no longer blocked the stream, and water rose till its depth from the bottom to the brim of the well was equal to the height of a palm-tree. And they all drank of the water, and bathed in it. Then they cooked rice and ate it, and fed their oxen with it. And when the sun set, they put a flag in the well, and went to the place appointed. There they sold their merchandise at a good profit and returned to their home, and when they died they passed away according to their deeds. And the Bodhisatta gave gifts and did other virtuous acts, and he also passed away according to his deeds. 15

After the Teacher had told the story he formed the connection by saying in conclusion, "The caravanleader was the Bodhisatta, the future Buddha; the page who at that time despaired not, but broke the stone, and gave water to the multitude, was this brother without perseverance; and the other men were attendants on the Buddha." 16

LXXIV.

THE SOWER.

Bhāradvāja, a wealthy Brahman farmer, was celebrating his harvest-thanksgiving when the Blessed One came with his alms-bowl, begging for food. 1

Some of the people paid him reverence, but the Brahman was angry and said: "O samana, it would be more fitting for thee to go to work than to beg. I plough and sow, and having ploughed and sown, I eat. If thou didst likewise, thou, too, wouldst have something to eat."　2

The Tathāgata answered him and said: "O Brahman, I, too, plough and sow, and having ploughed and sown, I eat."　3

"Dost thou profess to be a husbandman?" replied the Brahman. "Where, then, are thy bullocks? Where is the seed and the plough?"　4

The Blessed One said: "Faith is the seed I sow: good works are the rain that fertilizes it; wisdom and modesty are the plough; my mind is the guiding-rein; I lay hold of the handle of the law; earnestness is the goad I use, and exertion is my draught-ox. This ploughing is ploughed to destroy the weeds of illusion. The harvest it yields is the immortal fruit of Nirvāna, and thus all sorrow ends."　5

Then the Brahman poured rice-milk into a golden bowl and offered it to the Blessed One, saying: "Let the Teacher of mankind partake of the rice-milk, for the venerable Gotama ploughs a ploughing that bears the fruit of immortality."　6

LXXV.

THE OUTCAST.

When Bhagavat dwelt at Sāvatthi in the Jetavana, he went out with his alms-bowl to beg for food and approached the house of a Brahman priest while the fire of an offering was blazing upon the altar. And the priest said: "Stay there, O shaveling; stay there, O wretched samana; thou art an outcast."　1

The Blessed One replied: "Who is an outcast?　2

"An outcast is the man who is angry and bears hatred; the man who is wicked and hypocritical, he who embraces error and is full of deceit. 3

"Whosoever is a provoker and is avaricious, has evil desires, is envious, wicked, shameless, and without fear to commit wrong, let him be known as an outcast. 4

"Not by birth does one become an outcast, not by birth does one become a Brahman; by deeds one becomes an outcast, by deeds one becomes a Brahman." 5

LXXVI.

THE WOMAN AT THE WELL.

Ānanda, the favorite disciple of the Buddha, having been sent by the Lord on a mission, passed by a well near a village, and seeing Pakati, a girl of the Mātanga caste, he asked her for water to drink. 1

Pakati said: "O Brahman, I am too humble and mean to give thee water to drink, do not ask any service of me lest thy holiness be contaminated, for I am of low caste." 2

And Ānanda replied: "I ask not for caste but for water;" and the Mātanga girl's heart leaped joyfully and she gave Ānanda to drink. 3

Ānanda thanked her and went away; but she followed him at a distance. 4

Having heard that Ānanda was a disciple of Gotama Sakyamuni, the girl repaired to the Blessed One and cried: "O Lord help me, and let me live in the place where Ānanda thy disciple dwells, so that I may see him and minister unto him, for I love Ānanda." 5

And the Blessed One understood the emotions of her heart and he said: "Pakati, thy heart is full of love, but thou understandest not thine own sentiments. It is not Ānanda that thou lovest, but his kindness. Accept, then, the kindness thou hast seen him practise unto thee, and in the humility of thy station practise it unto others. 6

"Verily there is great merit in the generosity of a king when he is kind to a slave; but there is a greater merit in the slave when he ignores the wrongs which he suffers and cherishes kindness and good-will to all mankind. He will cease to hate his oppressors, and even when powerless to resist their usurpation will with compassion pity their arrogance and supercilious demeanor. 7

"Blessed art thou, Pakati, for though thou art a Mātanga thou wilt be a model for noblemen and noblewomen. Thou art of low caste, but Brahmans may learn a lesson from thee. Swerve not from the path of justice and righteousness and thou wilt outshine the royal glory of queens on the throne." 8

LXXVII.

THE PEACEMAKER.

It is reported that two kingdoms were on the verge of war for the possession of a certain embankment which was disputed by them. 1

And the Buddha seeing the kings and their armies ready to fight, requested them to tell him the cause of their quarrels. Having heard the complaints on both sides, he said: 2

"I understand that the embankment has value for some of your people; has it any intrinsic value aside from its service to your men?" 3

"It has no intrinsic value whatever," was the reply. The Tathāgata continued: "Now when you go to battle is it not sure that many of your men will be slain and that you yourselves, O kings, are liable to lose your lives?" 4

And they said: "Verily, it is sure that many will be slain and our own lives be jeopardized." 5

"The blood of men, however," said Buddha, "has it less intrinsic value than a mound of earth?" 6

"No," the kings said, "the lives of men and above all the lives of kings, are priceless." 7

Then the Tathāgata concluded: "Are you going to stake that which is priceless against that which has no intrinsic value whatever?" 8

The wrath of the two monarchs abated, and they came to a peaceable agreement. 9

LXXVIII.

THE HUNGRY DOG.

There was a great king who oppressed his people and was hated by his subjects; yet when the Tathāgata came into his kingdom, the king desired much to see him. So he went to the place where the Blessed One stayed and asked: "O Sakyamuni, canst thou teach a lesson to the king that will divert his mind and benefit him at the same time?" 1

And the Blessed One said: "I shall tell thee the parable of the hungry dog: 2

"There was a wicked tyrant; and the god Indra, assuming the shape of a hunter, came down upon earth with the demon Mātali, the latter appearing as a dog of enormous size. Hunter and dog entered the palace, and the dog howled so wofully that the royal buildings shook by the sound to their very foundations. The tyrant had the awe-inspiring hunter brought before his throne and inquired after the cause of the terrible bark. The hunter said, "The dog is hungry," whereupon the frightened king ordered food for him. All the food prepared at the royal banquet disappeared rapidly in the dog's jaws, and still he howled with portentous significance. More food was sent for, and all the royal store-houses were emptied, but in vain. Then the tyrant grew desperate and asked: 'Will nothing satisfy the cravings of that woful beast?' 'Nothing,' replied the hunter, 'nothing except perhaps the flesh of all his enemies.' 'And who are his enemies?' anxiously asked the tyrant. The hunter replied: 'The dog will howl as long as there are people hungry in the kingdom, and his enemies are those who practise injustice and oppress the poor.' The oppressor of the people, remembering his evil deeds, was seized with remorse, and for the first time in his life he began to listen to the teachings of righteousness."   3

Having ended his story, the Blessed One addressed the king, who had turned pale, and said to him: 4

"The Tathāgata can quicken the spiritual ears of the powerful, and when thou, great king, hearest the dog bark, think of the teachings of the Buddha, and thou mayst still learn to pacify the monster."   5

LXXIX.

THE DESPOT.

King Brahmadatta happened to see a beautiful woman, the wife of a Brahman merchant, and, conceiving a passion for her ordered a precious jewel secretly to be dropped into the merchant's carriage. The jewel was missed, searched for, and found. The merchant was arrested on the charge of stealing, and the king pretended to listen with great attention to the defence, and with seeming regret ordered the merchant to be executed, while his wife was consigned to the royal harem.   1

Brahmadatta attended the execution in person, for such sights were wont to give him pleasure, but when the doomed man looked with deep compassion at his infamous judge, a flash of the Buddha's wisdom lit up the king's passion-beclouded mind; and while the executioner raised the sword for the fatal stroke, Brahmadatta felt the effect in his own mind, and he imagined he saw himself on the block. "Hold, executioner!" shouted Brahmadatta, "it is the king whom thou slayest!" But it was too late! The executioner had done the bloody deed.   2

The king fell back in a swoon, and when he awoke a change had come over him. He had ceased to be the cruel despot and henceforth led a life of holiness and rectitude. The people said that the character of the Brahman had been impressed into his mind.   3

O ye who commit murders and robberies! The veil of self-delusion covers your eyes. If ye could see things as they are, not as they appear, ye would no longer inflict injuries and pain on your own selves. Ye see not that ye will have to atone for your evil deeds, for what ye sow that will ye reap.   4

LXXX.

VÂSAVADATTÂ.

There was a courtesan in Mathurā named Vāsavadattā. She happened to see Upagutta, one of Buddha's disciples, a tall and beautiful youth, and fell desperately in love with him. Vāsavadattā sent an invitation to the young man, but he replied: "The time has not yet arrived when Upagutta will visit Vāsavadattā."   1

The courtesan was astonished at the reply, and she sent again for him, saying: "Vāsavadattā desires love, not gold, from Upagutta." But Upagutta made the same enigmatic reply and did not come. 2

A few months later Vāsavadattā had a love-intrigue with the chief of the artisans, and at that time a wealthy merchant came to Mathurā, who fell in love with Vāsavadattā. Seeing his wealth, and fearing the jealousy of her other lover, she contrived the death of the chief of the artisans, and concealed his body under a dunghill. 3

When the chief of the artisans had disappeared, his relatives and friends searched for him and found his body. Vāsavadattā, however, was tried by a judge, and condemned to have her ears and nose, her hands and feet cut off, and flung into a graveyard. 4

Vāsavadattā had been a passionate girl, but kind to her servants, and one of her maids followed her, and out of love for her former mistress ministered unto her in her agonies, and chased away the crows. 5

Now the time had arrived when Upagutta decided to visit Vāsavadattā. 6

When he came, the poor woman ordered her maid to collect and hide under a cloth her severed limbs; and he greeted her kindly, but she said with petulance: "Once this body was fragrant like the lotus, and I offered thee my love. In those days I was covered with pearls and fine muslin. Now I am mangled by the executioner and covered with filth and blood." 7

"Sister," said the young man, "it is not for my pleasure that I approach thee. It is to restore to thee a nobler beauty than the charms which thou hast lost. 8

"I have seen with mine eyes the Tathāgata walking upon earth and teaching men his wonderful doctrine. But thou wouldst not have listened to the words of righteousness while surrounded with temptations, while under the spell of passion and yearning for worldly pleasures. Thou wouldst not have listened to the teachings of the Tathāgata, for thy heart was wayward, and thou didst set thy trust on the sham of thy transient charms.   9

"The charms of a lovely form are treacherous, and quickly lead into temptations, which have proved too strong for thee. But there is a beauty which will not fade, and if thou wilt but listen to the doctrine of our Lord, the Buddha, thou wilt find that peace which thou wouldst have found in the restless world of sinful pleasures."   10

Vāsavadattā became calm and a spiritual happiness soothed the tortures of her bodily pain; for where there is much suffering there is also great bliss.   11

Having taken refuge in the Buddha, the Dharma, and the Sangha, she died in pious submission to the punishment of her crime.   12

LXXXI.

THE MARRIAGE-FEAST IN JAMBŪNADA.

There was a man in Jambūnada who was to be married the next day, and he thought, "Would that the Buddha, the Blessed One, might be present at the wedding."   1

And the Blessed One passed by his house and met him, and when he read the silent wish in the heart of the bridegroom, he consented to enter.   2

When the Holy One appeared with the retinue of his many bhikkhus, the host whose means were limited received them as best he could, saying: "Eat, my Lord, and all thy congregation, according to your desire."   3

While the holy men ate, the meats and drinks remained undiminished, and the host thought to himself: "How wondrous is this! I should have had plenty for all my

O.KOPETZKV

relatives and friends. Would that I had invited them all." 4

When this thought was in the host's mind, all his relatives and friends entered the house; and although the hall in the house was small there was room in it for all of them. They sat down at the table and ate, and there was more than enough for all of them. 5

The Blessed One was pleased to see so many guests full of good cheer and he quickened them and gladdened them with words of truth, proclaiming the bliss of righteousness: 6

"The greatest happiness which a mortal man can imagine is the bond of marriage that ties together two loving hearts. But there is a greater happiness still: it is the embrace of truth. Death will separate husband and wife, but death will never affect him who has espoused the truth. 7

"Therefore be married unto the truth and live with the truth in holy wedlock. The husband who loves his wife and desires for a union that shall be everlasting must be faithful to her so as to be like truth itself, and she will rely upon him and revere him and minister unto him. And the wife who loves her husband and desires a union that shall be everlasting must be faithful to him so as to be like truth itself; and he will place his trust in her, he will provide for her. Verily, I say unto you, their children will become like unto their parents and will bear witness to their happiness. 8

"Let no man be single, let every one be wedded in holy love to the truth. And when Māra, the destroyer, comes to separate the visible forms of your being, you will continue to live in the truth, and you will partake of the life everlasting, for the truth is immortal." 9

There was no one among the guests but was strengthened in his spiritual life, and recognized the sweetness

of a life of righteousness; and they took refuge in
Buddha, the Dharma, and the Sangha.

LXXXII.

A PARTY IN SEARCH OF A THIEF.

Having sent out his disciples, the Blessed One himself
wandered from place to place until he reached Uruvelā. 1

On his way he sat down in a grove to rest, and it
happened that in that same grove there was a party of
thirty friends who were enjoying themselves with their
wives; and while they were sporting, some of their goods
were stolen. 2

Then the whole party went in search of the thief and,
meeting the Blessed One sitting under a tree, saluted him
and said: "Pray, Lord, didst thou see the thief pass by
with our goods?" 3

And the Blessed One said: "Which is better for you,
that you go in search for the thief or for yourselves?"
And the youths cried: "In search for ourselves!" 4

"Well, then," said the Blessed One, "sit down and I will
preach the truth to you." 5

And the whole party sat down and they listened eagerly
to the words of the Blessed One. Having grasped the
truth, they praised the doctrine and took refuge in the
Buddha. 6

LXXXIII.

IN THE REALM OF YAMARĀJA.

There was a Brahman, a religious man and fond in his
affections but without deep wisdom. He had a son of great
promise, who, when seven years old, was struck with a

fatal disease and died. The unfortunate father was unable to control himself; he threw himself upon the corpse and lay there as one dead.   1

The relatives came and buried the dead child and when the father came to himself, he was so immoderate in his grief that he behaved like an insane person. He no longer gave way to tears but wandered about asking for the residence of Yamaraja, the king of death, humbly to beg of him that his child might be allowed to return to life.   2

Having arrived at a great Brahman temple the sad father went through certain religious rites and fell asleep. While wandering on in his dream he came to a deep mountain pass where he met a number of samanas who had acquired supreme wisdom. "Kind sirs," he said, "can you not tell me where the residence of Yamaraja is?" And they asked him, "Good friend, why wouldst thou know?" Whereupon he told them his sad story and explained his intentions. Pitying his self-delusion, the samanas said: "No mortal man can reach the place where Yama reigns, but some four hundred miles westward lies a great city in which many good spirits live; every eighth day of the month Yama visits the place, and there mayst thou see him who is the King of Death and ask him for a boon."   3

The Brahman rejoicing at the news went to the city and found it as the samanas had told him. He was admitted to the dread presence of Yama, the King of Death, who, on hearing his request, said: "Thy son now lives in the eastern garden where he is disporting himself; go there and ask him to follow thee."   4

Said the happy father: "How does it happen that my son, without having performed one good work, is now living in paradise?" Yamaraja replied: "He has obtained celestial happiness not for performing good deeds, but because he died in faith and in love to the Lord and

Master, the most glorious Buddha. The Buddha says: 'The heart of love and faith spreads as it were a beneficent shade from the world of men to the world of gods.' This glorious utterance is like the stamp of a king's seal upon a royal edict."   5

The happy father hastened to the place and saw his beloved child playing with other children, all transfigured by the peace of the blissful existence of a heavenly life. He ran up to his boy and cried with tears running down his cheeks: "My son, my son, dost thou not remember me, thy father who watched over thee with loving care and tended thee in thy sickness? Return home with me to the land of the living." But the boy, while struggling to go back to his playmates, upbraided him for using such strange expressions as father and son. "In my present state," he said, "I know no such words, for I am free from delusion."   6

On this, the Brahman departed, and when he woke from his dream he bethought himself of the Blessed Master of mankind, the great Buddha, and resolved to go to him, lay bare his grief, and seek consolation.   7

Having arrived at the Jetavana, the Brahman told his story and how his boy had refused to recognize him and to go home with him.   8

And the World-honored One said: "Truly thou art deluded. When man dies the body is dissolved into its elements, but the spirit is not entombed. It leads a higher mode of life in which all the relative terms of father, son, wife, mother, are at an end, just as a guest who leaves his lodging has done with it, as though it were a thing of the past. Men concern themselves most about that which passes away; but the end of life quickly comes as a burning torrent sweeping away the transient in a moment. They are like a blind man set to look after a burning lamp. A wise man, understanding the transiency of worldly relations, destroys the cause of grief, and escapes from the seething whirlpool of sorrow. Religious wisdom lifts a man above the pleasures and pains of the world and gives him peace everlasting." 9

The Brahman asked the permission of the Blessed One to enter the community of his bhikkhus, so as to acquire that heavenly wisdom which alone can give comfort to an afflicted heart. 10

LXXXIV.

THE MUSTARD SEED.

There was a rich man who found his gold suddenly transformed into ashes; and he took to his bed and refused all food. A friend, hearing of his sickness, visited the rich man and learned the cause of his grief. And the friend said: "Thou didst not make good use of thy wealth. When thou didst hoard it up it was not better than ashes. Now heed my advice. Spread mats in the bazaar; pile up these ashes, and pretend to trade with them." 1

The rich man did as his friend had told him, and when his neighbors asked him, "Why sellest thou ashes?" he said: "I offer my goods for sale." 2

After some time a young girl, named Kisā Gotamī, an orphan and very poor, passed by, and seeing the rich man in the bazaar, said: "My lord, why pilest thou thus up gold and silver for sale." 3

And the rich man said: "Wilt thou please hand me that gold and silver?" And Kisā Gotamī took up a handful of ashes, and lo! they changed back into gold. 4

Considering that Kisā Gotamī had the mental eye of spiritual knowledge and saw the real worth of things, the rich man gave her in marriage to his son, and he said:

"With many, gold is no better than ashes, but with Kisā Gotamī ashes become pure gold."   5

And Kisā Gotamī had an only son, and he died. In her grief she carried the dead child to all her neighbors, asking them for medicine, and the people said: "She has lost her senses. The boy is dead."   6

At length Kisā Gotamī met a man who replied to her request: "I cannot give thee medicine for thy child, but I know a physician who can."   7

And the girl said: "Pray tell me, sir; who is it?" And the man replied: "Go to Sakyamuni, the Buddha."   8

Kisā Gotamī repaired to the Buddha and cried: "Lord and Master, give me the medicine that will cure my boy."   9

The Buddha answered: "I want a handful of mustard-seed." And when the girl in her joy promised to procure it, the Buddha added: "The mustard-seed must be taken from a house where no one has lost a child, husband, parent, or friend."   10

Poor Kisā Gotamī now went from house to house, and the people pitied her and said: "Here is mustard-seed; take it!" But when she asked, "Did a son or daughter, a father or mother, die in your family?" They answered her: "Alas! the living are few, but the dead are many. Do not remind us of our deepest grief." And there was no house but some beloved one had died in it.   11

Kisā Gotamī became weary and hopeless, and sat down at the wayside, watching the lights of the city, as they flickered up and were extinguished again. At last the darkness of the night reigned everywhere. And she considered the fate of men, that their lives flicker up and are extinguished. And she thought to herself: "How selfish am I in my grief! Death is common to all; yet in this valley of desolation there is a path that leads him to immortality who has surrendered all selfishness."   12

Putting away the selfishness of her affection for her child, Kisā Gotamī had the dead body buried in the forest. Returning to the Buddha, she took refuge in him and found comfort in the Dharma, which is a balm that will soothe all the pains of our troubled hearts.   13

The Buddha said: 14

"The life of mortals in this world is troubled and brief and combined with pain. For there is not any means by which those that have been born can avoid dying; after reaching old age there is death; of such a nature are living beings.   15

"As ripe fruits are early in danger of falling, so mortals when born are always in danger of death.   16

"As all earthen vessels made by the potter end in being broken, so is the life of mortals.   17

"Both young and adult, both those who are fools and those who are wise, all fall into the power of death; all are subject to death.   18

"Of those who, overcome by death, depart from life, a father cannot save his son, nor kinsmen their relations.   19

"Mark! while relatives are looking on and lamenting deeply, one by one mortals are carried off, like an ox that is led to the slaughter.   20

"So the world is afflicted with death and decay, therefore the wise do not grieve, knowing the terms of the world.   21

"In whatever manner people think a thing will come to pass, it is often different when it happens, and great is the disappointment; see, such are the terms of the world.   22

"Not from weeping nor from grieving will any one obtain peace of mind; on the contrary, his pain will be the greater and his body will suffer. He will make himself sick and pale, yet the dead are not saved by his lamentation.   23

"People pass away, and their fate after death will be according to their deeds.   24

"If a man live a hundred years, or even more, he will at last be separated from the company of his relatives, and leave the life of this world.   25

"He who seeks peace should draw out the arrow of lamentation, and complaint, and grief.   26

"He who has drawn out the arrow and has become composed will obtain peace of mind; he who has overcome all sorrow will become free from sorrow, and be blessed."   27

LXXXV.

FOLLOWING THE MASTER OVER THE STREAM.

South of Sāvatthi is a great river, on the banks of which lay a hamlet of five hundred houses. Thinking of the salvation of the people, the World-honored One resolved to go to the village and preach the doctrine. Having come to the riverside he sat down beneath a tree, and the villagers seeing the glory of his appearance approached him with reverence; but when he began to preach, they believed him not.   1

When the world-honored Buddha had left Sāvatthi Sāriputta felt a desire to see the Lord and to hear him preach. Coming to the river where the water was deep and the current strong, he said to himself: "This stream shall not prevent me. I shall go and see the Blessed One," and he stepped upon the water which was as firm under his feet as a slab of granite.   2

When he arrived at a place in the middle of the stream where the waves were high, Sāriputta's heart gave way, and he began to sink. But rousing his faith and renewing his mental effort, he preceeded as before and reached the other bank.   3

The people of the village were astonished to see Sāriputta, and they asked how he could cross the stream where there was neither a bridge nor a ferry.   4

And Sāriputta replied: "I lived in ignorance until I heard the voice of the Buddha. As I was anxious to hear the doctrine of salvation, I crossed the river and I walked over its troubled waters because I had faith. Faith, nothing else, enabled me to do so, and now I am here in the bliss of the Master's presency."   5

The World-honored One added: "Sāriputta, thou hast spoken well. Faith like thine alone can save the world from the yawning gulf of migration and enable men to walk dryshod to the other shore."   6

And the Blessed One urged to the villagers the necessity of ever advancing in the conquest of sorrow and of casting off all shackles so as to cross the river of worldliness and attain deliverance from death.   7

Hearing the words of the Tathāgata, the villagers were filled with joy and believing in the doctrines of the Blessed One embraced the five rules and took refuge in his name.   8

LXXXVI.

THE SICK BHIKKHU.

An old bhikkhu of a surly disposition was afflicted with a loathsome disease the sight and smell of which was so nauseating that no one would come near him or help him in his distress. And it happened that the World-honored One came to the vihāra in which the unfortunate man lay; hearing of the case he ordered warm water to be prepared and went to the sick-room to administer unto the sores of the patient with his own hand, saying to his disciples: 1

"The Tathāgata has come into the world to befriend the poor, to succor the unprotected, to nourish those in bodily affliction, both the followers of the Dharma and unbelievers, to give sight to the blind and enlighten the minds of the deluded, to stand up for the rights of orphans as well as the aged, and in so doing to set an example to others. This is the consummation of his work, and thus he attains the great goal of life as the rivers that lose themselves in the ocean." 2

The World-honored One administered unto the sick bhikkhu daily so long as he stayed in that place. And the governor of the city came to the Buddha to do him reverence, and having heard of the service which the Lord did in the vihāra asked the Blessed One about the previous existence of the sick monk, and the Buddha said: 3

"In days gone by there was a wicked king who used to extort from his subjects all he could get; and he ordered one of his officers to lay the lash on a man of eminence. The officer little thinking of the pain he inflicted upon others, obeyed; but when the victim of the king's wrath begged for mercy, he felt compassion and laid the whip lightly upon him. Now the king was reborn as Devadatta, who was abandoned by all his followers, because they were no longer willing to stand his severity and he died miserable and full of penitence. The officer is the sick bhikkhu, who having often given offence to his brethren in the vihāra was left without assistance in his distress. The eminent man, however, who was unjustly beaten and begged for mercy was the Bodhisatta; he has been reborn as the Tathāgata. It is now the lot of the Tathāgata to help the wretched officer as he had mercy on him." 4

And the World-honored One repeated these lines: "He who inflicts pain on the gentle, or falsely accuses the innocent, will inherit one of the ten great calamities. But he who has learned to suffer with patience will be purified and will be the chosen instrument for the alleviation of suffering." 5

The diseased bhikkhu on hearing these words turned to the Buddha, confessed his ill-natured temper and repented, and with a heart cleansed from error did reverence unto the Lord. 6

LXXXVII.

THE PATIENT ELEPHANT.

While the Blessed One was residing in the Jetavana, there was a householder living in Sāvatthi known to all his neighbors as patient and kind, but his relatives were wicked and contrived a plot to rob him. One day they came to the householder and often worrying him with all kinds of threats took away a goodly portion of his property. He did not go to court, nor did he complain, but tolerated with great forbearance the wrongs he suffered. 1

The neighbors wondered and began to talk about it, and rumors of the affair reached the ears of the brethren in Jetavana. While the brethren discussed the occurrence in the assembly hall, the Blessed One entered and asked "What was the topic of your conversation?" And they told him. 2

Said the Blessed One: "The time will come when the wicked relatives will find their punishment. O brethren, this is not the first time that this occurrence took place; it has happened before", and he told them a world-old tale. 3

Once upon a time, when Brahmadatta was king of Benares, the Bodhisatta was born in the Himālaya region as an elephant. He grew up strong und big, and ranged the hills and mountains, the peaks and caves of the tortuous woods in the valleys. Once as he went he saw a pleasant tree, and took his food, standing under it.   4

Then some impertinent monkeys came down out of the tree, and jumping on the elephant's back, insulted and tormented him greatly; they took hold of his tusks, pulled his tail and disported themselves, thereby causing him much annoyance. The Bodhisatta, being full of patience, kindliness and mercy, took no notice at all of their misconduct which the monkeys repeated again and again.   5

One day the spirit that lived in the tree, standing upon the tree-trunk, addressed the elephant saying, "My lord elephant, why dost thou put up with the impudence of these bad monkeys?" And he asked the question in a couplet as follows: 6

"Why dost thou patiently endure each freak
These mischievous and selfish monkeys wreak?"   7

The Bodhisatta, on hearing this, replied, „If, Tree-sprite, I cannot endure these monkeys' ill treatment without abusing their birth, lineage and persons, how can I walk in the eightfold noble path? But these monkeys will do the same to others thinking them to be like me. If they do it to any rogue elephant, he will punish them indeed, and I shall be delivered both from their annoyance and the guilt of having done harm to others."   8

Saying this he repeated another stanza: 9

"If they will treat another one like me,
He will destroy them; and I shall be free."   10

A few days after, the Bodhisatta went elsewhither, and another elephant, a savage beast, came and stood in his place. The wicked monkeys thinking him to be like the old one, climbed upon his back and did as before. The rogue elephant seized the monkeys with his trunk, threw them upon the ground, gored them with his tusk and trampled them to mincemeat under his feet.   11

When the Master had ended this teaching, he declared the truths, and identified the births, saying: "At that time the mischievous monkeys were the wicked relatives of the good man, the rogue elephant was the one who will punish them, but the virtuous noble elephant was the Tathāgata himself in a former incarnation."   12

After this discourse one of the brethren rose and asked leave to propose a question and when permission was granted he said: "I have heard the doctrine that wrong should be met with wrong and the evil doer should be checked by being made to suffer, for if this were not done evil would increase and good would disappear. What shall we do?"   13

Said the Blessed One: "Nay, I will tell you: Ye who have left the world and have adopted this glorious faith of putting aside selfishness, ye shall not do evil for evil nor return hate for hate. Nor do ye think that ye can destroy wrong by retaliating evil for evil and thus increasing wrong. Leave the wicked to their fate and their evil deeds will sooner or later in one way or another bring on their own punishment." And the Tathāgata repeated these stanzas: 14

"Who harmeth him that doth no harm
And striketh him that striketh not,
Shall gravest punishment incur
The which his wickedness begot,—   15

"Some of the greatest ills in life
Either a loathsome dread disease,
Or dread old age, or loss of mind,
Or wretched pain without surcease,   16

"Or conflagration, loss of wealth;
Or of his nearest kin he shall
See some one die that's dear to him,
And then he'll be reborn in hell."   17

O.KOPETZKY.

THE LAST DAYS.

LXXXVIII.

THE CONDITIONS OF WELFARE.

WHEN the Blessed One was residing on the mount called Vulture's Peak, near Rājagaha, Ajātasattu the king of Magadha, who reigned in the place of Bimbisāra, planned an attack on the Vajjis, and he said to Vassa-kāra, his prime minister: "I will root out the Vajjis, mighty though they be. I will destroy the Vajjis; I will bring them to utter ruin! Come now, O Brahman, and go to the Blessed One; inquire in my name for his health, and tell him my purpose. Bear carefully in mind what the Blessed One may say, and repeat it to me, for the Buddhas speak nothing untrue." 1

When Vassakāra, the prime minister, had greeted the Blessed One and delivered his message, the venerable Ānanda stood behind the Blessed One and fanned him, and the Blessed One said to him: "Hast thou heard, Ānanda, that the Vajjis hold full and frequent public assemblies?" 2

"Lord, so I have heard," replied he. 3

"So long, Ānanda," said the Blessed One, "as the Vajjis hold these full and frequent public assemblies, they may be expected not to decline, but to prosper. So long as they meet together in concord, so long as they honor their elders, so long as they respect womanhood, so long as they remain religious, performing all proper rites, so long as they extend the rightful protection, defence and support to the holy ones, the Vajjis may be expected not to decline, but to prosper." 4

Then the Blessed One addressed Vassakāra and said: "When I stayed, O Brahman, at Vesālī, I taught the Vajjis these conditions of welfare, that so long as they should remain well instructed, so long as they will continue in the right path, so long as they live up to the precepts of righteousness, we could expect them not to decline, but to prosper." 5

As soon as the king's messenger had gone, the Blessed One had the brethren, that were in the neighborhood of Rājagaha, assembled in the service-hall, and addressed them, saying: 6

"I will teach you, O bhikkhus, the conditions of the welfare of a community. Listen well, and I will speak. 7

"So long, O bhikkhus, as the brethren hold full and frequent assemblies, meeting in concord, rising in concord, and attending in concord to the affairs of the Sangha; so long as they, O bhikkhus, do not abrogate that which experience has proved to be good, and introduce nothing except such things as have been carefully tested; so long as their elders practise justice; so long as the brethren esteem, revere, and support their elders, and hearken unto their words; so long as the brethren are not under the influence of craving, but delight in the blessings of religion, so that good and holy men shall come to them and dwell among them in quiet; so long as the brethren shall not be addicted to sloth and idleness; so long as the brethren shall exercise themselves in the sevenfold higher wisdom of mental activity, search after truth, energy, joy, modesty, self-control, earnest contemplation, and equanimity of mind, — so long the Sangha may be expected not to decline, but to prosper.   8

"Therefore, O bhikkhus, be full of faith, modest in heart, afraid of sin, anxious to learn, strong in energy, active in mind, and full of wisdom."   9

LXXXIX.

SĀRIPUTTA'S FAITH.

The Blessed One proceeded with a great company of the brethren to Nālandā; and there he stayed in a mango grove.   1

Now the venerable Sāriputta came to the place where the Blessed One was, and having saluted him, took his seat respectfully at his side, and said: "Lord! such faith have I in the Blessed One, that methinks there never has been, nor will there be, nor is there now any other, who is greater or wiser than the Blessed One, that is to say, as regards the higher wisdom."   2

Replied the Blessed One: "Grand and bold are the words of thy mouth, Sāriputta: verily, thou hast burst forth into a song of ecstasy! Surely then thou hast known all the Blessed Ones who in the long ages of the past have been holy Buddhas?"   3

"Not so, O Lord!" said Sāriputta.   4

And the Lord continued: "Then thou hast perceived all

the Blessed Ones who in the long ages of the future shall be holy Buddhas?" 5

"Not so, O Lord!" 6

"But at least then, O Sāriputta, thou knowest me as the holy Buddha now alive, and hast penetrated my mind." 7

"Not even that, O Lord!" 8

"Thou seest then, Sāriputta, that thou knowest not the hearts of the holy Buddhas of the past nor the hearts of those of the future. Why, therefore, are thy words so grand and bold? Why burstest thou forth into such a song of ecstasy?" 9

"O Lord! I have not the knowledge of the hearts of all the Buddhas that have been and are to come, and now are. I only know the lineage of the faith. Just as a king, Lord, might have a border city, strong in its foundations, strong in its ramparts and with one gate only; and the king might have a watchman there, clever, expert, and wise, to stop all strangers and admit only friends. And on going over the approaches all about the city, he might not be able so to observe all the joints and crevices in the ramparts of that city as to know where such a small creature as a cat could get out. That might well be. Yet all living beings of larger size that entered or left the city, would have to pass through that gate. Thus only is it, Lord, that I know the lineage of the faith. I know that the holy Buddhas of the past, putting away all lust, ill-will, sloth, pride, and doubt, knowing all those mental faults which make men weak, training their minds in the four kinds of mental activity, thoroughly exercising themselves in the sevenfold higher wisdom, received the full fruition of Enlightenment. And I know that the holy Buddhas of the times to come will do the same. And I know that the Blessed One, the holy Buddha of to-day, has done so now." 10

"Great is thy faith, O Sāriputta," replied the Blessed One, "but take heed that it be well grounded." 11

XC.

PĀTALIPUTTA.

When the Blessed One had stayed as long as convenient at Nālandā, he went to Pātaliputta, the frontier town of Magadha; and when the disciples at Pātaliputta heard of his arrival, they invited him to their village rest-house. And the Blessed One robed himself, took his bowl and went with the brethren to the rest-house. There he washed his feet, entered the hall, and seated himself against the center pillar, with his face towards the east. The brethren, also, having washed their feet, entered the hall, and took their seats round the Blessed One, against the western wall, facing the east. And the lay devotees of Pātaliputta, having also washed their feet, entered the hall, and took their seats opposite the Blessed One, against the eastern wall, facing towards the west. 1

Then the Blessed One addressed the lay-disciples of Pātaliputta, and he said: 2

"Fivefold, O householders, is the loss of the wrong-doer through his want of rectitude. In the first place, the wrong-doer, devoid of rectitude, falls into great poverty through sloth; in the next place, his evil repute gets noised abroad; thirdly, whatever society he enters, whether of Brahmans, nobles, heads of houses, or samanas, he enters shyly and confusedly; fourthly, he is full of anxiety when he dies; and lastly, on the dissolution of the body after death, his mind remains in an unhappy state. Wherever his karma continues, there will be suffering and woe. This, O householders, is the fivefold loss of the evil-doer! 3

"Fivefold, O householders, is the gain of the well-doer through his practice of rectitude. In the first place the well-doer, strong in rectitude, acquires property through his industry; in the next place, good reports of him are spread abroad; thirdly, whatever society he enters, whether of nobles, Brahmans, heads of houses, or members of the order, he enters with confidence and self-possession; fourthly, he dies without anxiety; and, lastly, on the dissolution of the body after death, his mind remains in a happy state. Wherever his karma continues, there will be heavenly bliss and peace. This, O householders, is the fivefold gain of the well-doer."   4

When the Blessed One had taught the disciples, and incited them, and roused them, and gladdened them far into the night with religious edification, he dismissed them, saying, "The night is far spent, O householders. It is time for you to do what ye deem most fit."   5

"Be it so, Lord!" answered the disciples of Pātaliputta, and rising from their seats, they bowed to the Blessed One, and keeping him on their right hand as they passed him, they departed thence.   6

While the Blessed One stayed at Pātaliputta, the king of Magadha sent a messenger to the governor of Pātaliputta to raise fortifications for the security of the town.   7

And the Blessed One seeing the laborers at work predicted the future greatness of the place, saying: "The men who build the fortress act as if they had consulted higher powers. For this city of Pātaliputta will be a dwelling-place of busy men and a center for the exchange of all kinds of goods. But three dangers hang over Pātaliputta, that of fire, that of water, that of dissension."   8

When the governor heard of the prophecy of Pātaliputta's future, he greatly rejoiced and named the city-gate through which the Buddha had gone towards the river Ganges, "The Gotama Gate."   9

Meanwhile the people living on the banks of the Ganges arrived in great numbers to pay reverence to the Lord of the world; and many persons asked him to do them the honor to cross over in their boats. But the Blessed One considering the number of the boats and their beauty did not want to show any partiality, and by accepting the invitation of one to offend all the others. He therefore crossed the river without any boat, signifying thereby that the rafts of asceticism and the gaudy gondolas of religious ceremonies were not staunch enough to weather the storms of Samsāra, while the Tathāgata can walk dry-shod over the ocean of worldliness.   10

And as the city gate was called after the name of the Tathāgata so the people called this passage of the river "Gotama Ford."   11

XCI.

THE MIRROR OF TRUTH.

The Blessed One proceeded to the village Nādikā with a great company of brethren and there he stayed at the Brick Hall. And the venerable Ānanda went to the Blessed One and mentioning to him the names of the brethren and sisters that had died, anxiously inquired about their fate after death, whether they had been reborn in animals or in hell, or as ghosts, or in any place of woe.   1

And the Blessed One replied to Ānanda and said: 2

"Those who have died after the complete destruction of the three bonds of lust, of covetousness and of the egotistical cleaving to existence, need not fear the state after death. They will not be reborn in a state of suffering; their minds will not continue as a karma of evil deeds or sin, but are assured of final salvation.   3

"When they die, nothing will remain of them but their good thoughts, their righteous acts, and the bliss that proceeds from truth and righteousness. As rivers must at last reach the distant main, so their minds will be reborn in higher states of existence and continue to be pressing on to their ultimate goal which is the ocean of truth, the eternal peace of Nirvāna.   4

"Men are anxious about death and their fate after death; but consider, it is not at all strange, Ānanda, that a human being should die. However, that thou shouldst inquire about them, and having heard the truth still be anxious about the dead, this is wearisome to the Blessed One. I will, therefore, teach thee the mirror of truth and let the faithful disciple repeat it: 5

"'Hell is destroyed for me, and rebirth as an animal, or a ghost, or in any place of woe. I am converted; I am no longer liable to be reborn in a state of suffering, and am assured of final salvation.'   6

"What, then, Ānanda, is this mirror of truth? It is the consciousness that the elect disciple is in this world possessed of faith in the Buddha, believing the Blessed One to be the Holy One, the Fully-englightened One, wise, upright, happy, world-knowing, supreme, the Bridler of men's wayward hearts, the Teacher of gods and men, the blessed Buddha.   7

"It is further the consciousness that the disciple is possessed of faith in the truth, believing the truth to have been proclaimed by the Blessed One, for the benefit of the world, passing not away, welcoming all, leading to salvation, to which through truth the wise will attain, each one by his own efforts.   8

"And, finally, it is the consciousness that the disciple is possessed of faith in the order, believing in the efficacy of a union among those men and women who are anxious to walk in the noble eightfold path; believing this church of the Buddha, of the righteous, the upright, the just, the law-abiding, to be worthy of honor, of hospitality, of gifts, and of reverence; to be the supreme sowing-ground of merit for the world; to be possessed of the virtues beloved by the good, virtues unbroken, intact, unspotted, unblemished, virtues which make men truly free, virtues which are praised by the wise, are untarnished by the desire of selfish aims, either now or in a future life, or by the belief in the efficacy of outward acts, and are conducive to high and holy thought.   9

"This is the mirror of truth which teaches the straightest way to enlightenment which is the common goal of all living creatures. He who possesses the mirror of truth is free from fear; he will find comfort in the tribulations of life, and his life will be a blessing to all his fellow-creatures."   10

XCII.

AMBAPĀLĪ.

Then the Blessed One proceeded with a great number of brethren to Vesālī, and he stayed at the grove of the courtesan Ambapālī. And he said to the brethren: "Let a brother, O bhikkhus, be mindful and thoughtful. Let a brother, whilst in the world, overcome the grief which arises from bodily craving, from the lust of sensations, and from the errors of wrong reasoning. Whatever you do, act always in full presence of mind. Be thoughtful in eating and drinking, in walking or standing, in sleeping or waking, while talking or being silent."   1

When the courtesan Ambapālī heard that the Blessed One was staying in her mango grove, she was exceedingly glad and went in a carriage as far as the ground was passable for carriages. There she alighted and thence proceeding to the place where the Blessed One was, she took her seat respectfully at his feet on one side. As a prudent woman goes forth to perform her religious duties, so she appeared in a simple dress without any ornaments, yet beautiful to look upon.   2

And the Blessed One thought to himself: "This woman moves in worldly circles and is a favorite of kings and princes; yet is her heart calm and composed. Young in years, rich, surrounded by pleasures, she is thoughtful and steadfast. This, indeed, is rare in the world. Women, as a rule, are scant in wisdom and deeply immersed in vanity; but she, although living in luxury, has acquired the wisdom of a master, taking delight in piety, and able to receive the truth in its completeness."   3

When she was seated, the Blessed One instructed, aroused, and gladdened her with religious discourse.   4

As she listened to the law, her face brightened with delight. Then she rose and said to the Blessed One: "Will the Blessed One do me the honor of taking his meal, together with the brethren, at my house to-morrow?" And the Blessed One gave, by silence, his consent.   5

Now, the Licchavi, a wealthy family of princely rank, hearing that the Blessed One had arrived at Vesāli and was staying at Ambapāli's grove, mounted their magnificent carriages, and proceeded with their retinue to the place where the Blessed One was. And the Licchavi were gorgeously dressed in bright colors and decorated with costly jewels.   6

And Ambapāli drove up against the young Licchavi, axle to axle, wheel to wheel, and yoke to yoke, and the Licchavi said to Ambapāli, the courtesan: "How is it, Ambapāli, that you drive up against us thus?"   7

"My lords," said she, "I have just invited the Blessed One and his brethren for their to-morrow's meal."   8

And the princes replied: "Ambapāli! give up this meal to us for a hundred thousand."   9

"My lords, were you to offer all Vesāli with its subject territory, I would not give up so great an honor!"   10

Then the Licchavi went on to Ambapāli's grove.   11

When the Blessed One saw the Licchavi approaching in the distance, he addressed the brethren, and said: "O

brethren, let those of the brethren who have never seen the gods gaze upon this company of the Licchavi, for they are dressed gorgeously, like immortals." 12

And when they had driven as far as the ground was passable for carriages, the Licchavi alighted and went on foot to the place where the Blessed One was, taking their seats respectfully by his side. And when they were thus seated, the Blessed One instructed, aroused, and gladdened them with religious discourse. 13

Then they addressed the Blessed One and said: "Will the Blessed One do us the honor of taking his meal, together with the brethren, at our palace to-morrow?" 14

"O Licchavi," said the Blessed One, "I have promised to dine to-morrow with Ambapālī, the courtesan." 15

Then the Licchavi, expressing their approval of the words of the Blessed One, arose from their seats and bowed down before the Blessed One, and, keeping him on their right hand as they passed him, they departed thence; but when they came home, they cast up their hands, saying: "A worldly woman has outdone us; we have been left behind by a frivolous girl!" 16

And at the end of the night Ambapālī, the courtesan, made ready in her mansion sweet rice and cakes, and on the next day announced through a messenger the time to the Blessed One, saying, "The hour, Lord, has come, and the meal is ready!" 17

And the Blessed One robed himself early in the morning, took his bowl, and went with the brethren to the place where Ambapālī's dwelling-house was; and when they had come there they seated themselves on the seats prepared for them. And Ambapālī, the courtesan, set the sweet rice and cakes before the order, with the Buddha at their head, and waited upon them till they refused to take more. 18

And when the Blessed One had finished his meal, the courtesan had a low stool brought, and sat down at his side, and addressed the Blessed One, and said: "Lord, I present this mansion to the order of bhikkhus, of which the Buddha is the chief." 19

And the Blessed One accepted the gift; and after instructing, arousing, and gladdening her with religious edification, he rose from his seat and departed thence. 20

XCIII.

THE BUDDHA'S FAREWELL ADDRESS.

When the Blessed One had remained as long as he wished at Ambapāli's grove, he went to Beluva, near Vesāli. There the Blessed One addressed the brethren, and said: "O mendicants, take up your abode for the rainy season round about Vesāli, each one according to the place where his friends and near companions may live. I shall enter upon the rainy season here at Beluva." 1

When the Blessed One had thus entered upon the rainy season there fell upon him a dire sickness, and sharp pains came upon him even unto death. But the Blessed One, mindful and self-possessed, bore his ailments without complaint. 2

Then this thought occurred to the Blessed One, "It would not be right for me to pass away from life without addressing the disciples, without taking leave of the order. Let me now, by a strong effort of the will, subdue this sickness, and keep my hold on life till the allotted time have come." 3

And the Blessed One, by a strong effort of the will subdued the sickness, and kept his hold on life till the time he fixed upon should come. And the sickness abated. 4

Thus the Blessed One began to recover; and when he had quite got rid of the sickness, he went out from the monastery, and sat down on a seat spread out in the open air. And the venerable Ānanda, accompanied by many other disciples, approached where the Blessed One was, saluted him, and taking a seat respectfully on one side, said: "I have beheld, Lord, how the Blessed One was in health, and I have beheld how the Blessed One had to suffer. And though at the sight of the sickness of the Blessed One my body became weak as a creeper, and the horizon became dim to me, and my faculties were no longer clear, yet notwithstanding I took some little comfort from the thought that the Blessed One would not pass away from existence until at least he had left instructions as touching the order."   5

And the Blessed One addressed Ānanda in behalf of the order, saying: 6

"What, then, Ānanda, does the order expect of me? I have preached the truth without making any distinction between exoteric and esoteric doctrine; for in respect of the truth, Ānanda, the Tathāgata has no such thing as the closed fist of a teacher, who keeps some things back.   7

"Surely, Ānanda, should there be any one who harbors the thought, 'It is I who will lead the brotherhood,' or, 'The order is dependent upon me,' he should lay down instructions in any matter concerning the order. Now the Tathāgata, Ānanda, thinks not that it is he who should lead the brotherhood, or that the order is dependent upon him. 8

"Why, then, should the Tathāgata leave instructions in any matter concerning the order?   9

"I am now grown old, O Ānanda, and full of years; my journey is drawing to its close, I have reached the sum of my days, I am turning eighty years of age.   10

"Just as a worn-out cart can not be made to move along without much difficulty, so the body of the Tathāgata can only be kept going with much additional care.   11

"It is only, Ānanda, when the Tathāgata, ceasing to

attend to any outward thing, becomes plunged in that devout meditation of heart which is concerned with no bodily object, it is only then that the body of the Tathāgata is at ease. 12

"Therefore, O Ānanda, be ye lamps unto yourselves. Rely on yourselves, and do not rely on external help. 13

"Hold fast to the truth as a lamp. Seek salvation alone in the truth. Look not for assistance to any one besides yourselves. 14

"And how, Ānanda, can a brother be a lamp unto himself, rely on himself only and not on any external help, holding fast to the truth as his lamp and seeking salvation in the truth alone, looking not for assistance to any one besides himself? 15

"Herein, O Ānanda, let a brother, as he dwells in the body, so regard the body that he, being strenuous, thoughtful, and mindful, may, whilst in the world, overcome the grief which arises from the body's cravings. 16

"While subject to sensations let him continue so to regard the sensations that he, being strenuous, thoughtful, and mindful, may, whilst in the world, overcome the grief which arises from the sensations. 17

"And so, also, when he thinks or reasons, or feels, let him so regard his thoughts that being strenuous, thoughtful, and mindful he may, whilst in the world, overcome the grief which arises from the craving due to ideas, or to reasoning, or to feeling. 18

"Those who, either now or after I am dead, shall be lamps unto themselves, relying upon themselves only and not relying upon any external help, but holding fast to the truth as their lamp, and seeking their salvation in the truth alone, and shall not look for assistance to any one besides themselves, it is they, Ānanda, among my bhikkhus, who shall reach the very topmost height! But they must be anxious to learn." 19

XCIV.

THE BUDDHA ANNOUNCES HIS DEATH.

Said the Tathāgata to Ānanda: "In former years, Ānanda, Māra, the Evil One, approached the holy Buddha three times to tempt him. 1

"And now, Ānanda, Māra, the Evil One, came again to-day to the place where I was, and, standing beside me, addressed me in the same words as he did when I was resting under the shepherd's Nigrodha tree on the bank of the Nerañjarā river: 'Be greeted, thou Holy One. Thou hast attained the highest bliss and it is time for thee to enter into the final Nirvāna.' 2

"And when Māra had thus spoken, Ānanda, I answered him and said: 'Make thyself happy, O wicked one; the final extinction of the Tathāgata shall take place before long.'" 3

And the venerable Ānanda addressed the Blessed One and said: "Vouchsafe, Lord, to remain with us, O Blessed One! for the good and the happiness of the great multitudes, out of pity for the world, for the good and the gain of makind!" 4

Said the Blessed One: "Enough now, Ānanda, beseech not the Tathāgata!" 5

And again, a second time, the venerable Ānanda besought the Blessed One in the same words. And he received from the Blessed One the same reply. 6

And again, the third time, the venerable Ānanda besought the Blessed One to live longer; and the Blessed One said: "Hast thou faith, Ānanda?" 7

Said Ānanda: "I have, my Lord!" 8

And the Blessed One, seeing the quivering eyelids of Ānanda, read the deep grief in the heart of his beloved disciple, and he asked again: "Hast thou, indeed, faith, Ānanda?" 9

And Ānanda said: "I have faith, my Lord." 10

Than the Blessed One continued: "If thou hast faith, Ānanda, in the wisdom of the Tathāgata, why, then, Ānanda, dost thou trouble the Tathāgata even until the third time? Have I not formerly declared to you that it is in the very nature of all compound things that they must be dissolved again. We must separate ourselves from all things near and dear to us, and must leave them. How then, Ānanda, can it be possible for me to remain, since everything that is born, or brought into being, and organized, contains within itself the inherent necessity of dissolution? How, then, can it be possible that this body of mine should not be dissolved? No such condition can exist! And this mortal existence, O Ānanda, has been relinquished, cast away, renounced, rejected, and abandoned by the Tathāgata." 11

And the Blessed One said to Ānanda: "Go now, Ānanda, and assemble in the Service Hall such of the brethren as reside in the neighborhood of Vesālī." 12

Then the Blessed One proceeded to the Service Hall, and sat down there on the mat spread out for him. And when he was seated, the Blessed One addressed the brethren, and said: 13

"O brethren, ye to whom the truth has been made known, having thoroughly made yourselves masters of it, practise it, meditate upon it, and spread it abroad, in order that pure religion may last long and be perpetuated, in order that it may continue for the good and happiness of the great multitudes, out of pity for the world, and to the good and gain of all living beings! 14

"Star-gazing and astrology, forecasting lucky or unfortunate events by signs, prognosticating good or evil, all these are things forbidden. 15

"He who lets his heart go loose without restraint shall not attain Nirvāna; therefore, must we hold the heart in check, and retire from worldly excitements and seek tranquillity of mind. 16

"Eat your food to satisfy your hunger, and drink to satisfy you thirst. Satisfy the necessities of life like the butterfly that sips the flower, without destroying its fragrance or its texture. 17

"It is through not understanding and grasping the four truths, O brethren, that we have gone astray so long, and wandered in this weary path of transmigrations, both you and I, until we have found the truth. 18

"Practise the earnest meditations I have taught you. Continue in the great struggle against sin. Walk steadily in the roads of saintship. Be strong in moral powers. Let the organs of your spiritual sense be quick. When the seven kinds of wisdom enlighten your mind, you will find the noble, eightfold path that leads to Nirvāna. 19

"Behold, O brethren, the final extinction of the Tathāgata will take place before long. I now exhort you, saying: 'All component things must grow old and be dissolved again. Seek ye for that which is permanent, and work out your salvation with diligence.'" 20

XCV.

CHUNDA, THE SMITH.

And the Blessed One went to Pāvā. 1

When Chunda, the worker in metals, heard that the Blessed One had come to Pāvā and was staying in his mango grove, he came to the Buddha and respectfully invited him and the brethren to take their meal at his house. And Chunda prepared rice-cakes and a dish of dried boar's meat. 2

When the Blessed One had eaten the food prepared by Chunda, the worker in metals, there fell upon him a dire sickness, and sharp pain came upon him even unto death.

But the Blessed One, mindful and self-possessed, bore it without complaint.　　3

And the Blessed One addressed the venerable Ānanda, and said: "Come, Ānanda, let us go on to Kusinārā."　　4

On his way the Blessed One grew tired, and he went aside from the road to rest at the foot of a tree, and said: "Fold the robe, I pray thee, Ānanda, and spread it out for me. I am weary, Ānanda, and must rest awhile!"　　5

"Be it so, Lord!" said the venerable Ānanda; and he spread out the robe folded fourfold.　　6

The Blessed One seated himself, and when he was seated he addressed the venerable Ānanda, and said: "Fetch me some water, I pray thee, Ānanda. I am thirsty, Ānanda, and would drink."　　7

When he had thus spoken, the venerable Ānanda said to the Blessed One: "But just now, Lord, five hundred carts have gone across the brook and have stirred the water; but a river, O Lord, is not far off. Its water is clear and pleasant, cool and transparent, and it is easy to get down to it. There the Blessed One may both drink water and cool his limbs."　　8

A second time the Blessed One addressed the venerable Ānanda, saying: "Fetch me some water, I pray thee Ānanda, I am thirsty, Ānanda, and would drink."　　9

And a second time the venerable Ānanda said: "Let us go to the river."　　10

Then the third time the Blessed One addressed the venerable Ānanda, and said: "Fetch me some water, I pray thee, Ānanda, I am thirsty, Ānanda, and would drink."　　11

"Be it so, Lord!" said the venerable Ānanda in assent to the Blessed One; and, taking a bowl, he went down to the streamlet. And lo! the streamlet, which, stirred up by wheels, had become muddy, when the venerable Ānanda came up to it, flowed clear and bright and free from all turbidity. And he thought: "How wonderful, how marvelous is the great might and power of the Tathā-gata!" 12

Ānanda brought the water in the bowl to the Lord, saying: "Let the Blessed One take the bowl. Let the Happy One drink the water. Let the Teacher of men and gods quench his thirst." 13

Then the Blessed One drank of the water. 14

Now, at that time a man of low caste, named Pukkusa, a young Malla, a disciple of Alāra Kālāma, was passing along the high road from Kusinārā to Pāvā. 15

And Pukkusa, the young Malla, saw the Blessed One seated at the foot of a tree. On seeing him, he went up to the place where the Blessed One was, and when he had come there, he saluted the Blessed One and took his seat respectfully on one side. Then the Blessed One instructed, edified, and gladdened Pukkusa, the young Malla, with religious discourse. 16

Aroused and gladdened by the words of the Blessed One, Pukkusa, the young Malla, addressed a certain man who happened to pass by, and said: "Fetch me, I pray thee, my good man, two robes of cloth of gold, burnished and ready for wear." 17

"Be it so, sir!" said that man in assent to Pukkusa, the young Malla; and he brought two robes of cloth of gold, burnished and ready for wear. 18

And the Malla Pukkusa presented the two robes of cloth of gold, burnished and ready for wear, to the Blessed One, saing: "Lord, these two robes of burnished cloth of gold are ready for wear. May the Blessed One show me favor and accept them at my hands!" 19

The Blessed One said: "Pukkusa, robe me in one, and Ānanda in the other." 20

And the Tathāgata's body appeared shining like a flame, and he was beautiful above all expression. 21

And the venerable Ānanda said to the Blessed One: "How wonderful a thing is it, Lord, and how marvellous, that the color of the skin of the Blessed One should be so clear, so exceedingly bright! When I placed this robe of burnished cloth of gold on the body of the Blessed One, lo! it seemed as if it had lost its splendor!" 22

The Blessed One said: "There are two occasions on which a Tathāgata's appearance becomes clear and exceeding bright. In the night, Ānanda, in which a Tathāgata attains to the supreme and perfect insight, and in the night in which he passes finally away in that utter passing away which leaves nothing whatever of his earthly existence to remain." 23

And the Blessed One addressed the venerable Ānanda, and said: "Now it may happen, Ānanda, that some one should stir up remorse in Chunda, the smith, by saying: 'It is evil to thee, Chunda, and loss to thee, that the Tathāgata died, having eaten his last meal from thy provision.' Any such remorse, Ānanda, in Chunda, the smith, should be checked by saying: 'It is good to thee, Chunda, and gain to thee, that the Tathāgata died, having eaten his last meal from thy provision. From the very mouth of the Blessed One, O Chunda, have I heard, from his own mouth have I received this saying, "These two offerings of food are of equal fruit and of much greater profit than any other: the offerings of food which a Tathāgata accepts when he has attained perfect enlightenment and when he passes away by the utter passing away in which nothing whatever of his earthly existence remains behind—these two offerings of food are of equal fruit and of equal profit, and of much greater fruit and much greater profit than any other. There has been laid up by Chunda, the smith, a karma redounding to length of life, redounding to good birth, redounding to good fortune, redounding to good fame, redounding to the inheritance of heaven and of great power." In this way,

Ānanda, should be checked any remorse in Chunda, the smith." 24

Then the Blessed One, perceiving that death was near, uttered these words: "He who gives away shall have real gain. He who subdues himself shall be free, he shall cease to be a slave of passions. The righteous man casts off evil; and by rooting out lust, bitterness, and illusion, do we reach Nirvāna." 25

XCVI.

METTEYYA.

The Blessed One proceeded with a great company of the brethren to the sāla grove of the Mallas, the Upavattana of Kusinārā on the further side of the river Hiraññavatī, and when he had arrived he addressed the venerable Ānanda, and said: "Make ready for me, I pray you, Ānanda, the couch with its head to the north, between the twin sāla trees. I am weary, Ānanda, and wish to lie down." 1

"Be it so, Lord!" said the venerable Ānanda, and he spread a couch with its head to the north, between the twin sāla trees. And the Blessed One laid himself down, and he was mindful and self-possessed. 2

Now, at that time the twin sāla trees were full of bloom with flowers out of season; and heavenly songs came wafted from the skies, out of reverence for the successor of the Buddhas of old. And Ānanda was filled with wonder that the Blessed One was thus honored. But the Blessed One said: "Not by such events, Ānanda, is the Tathāgata rightly honored, held sacred, or revered. But the brother or the sister, the devout man or the devout woman, who continually fulfils all the greater and the lesser duties, walking according to the precepts, it is they who rightly honor, hold sacred, and revere the Tathāgata with the worthiest homage. Therefore, O Ānanda, be ye 'constant in the fulfilment of the greater and of the lesser duties, and walk according to the precepts; thus, Ānanda, will ye honor the Master." 3

Then the venerable Ānanda went into the vihāra, and stood leaning against the doorpost, weeping at the thought: "Alas! I remain still but a learner, one who has yet to work out his own perfection. And the Master is about to pass away from me—he who is so kind!" 4

Now, the Blessed One called the brethren, and said: "Where, O brethren, is Ānanda?" 5

And one of the brethren went and called Ānanda. And Ānanda came and said to the Blessed One: "Deep darkness reigned for want of wisdom; the world of sentient creatures was groping for want of light; then the Tathāgata lit up the lamp of wisdom, and now it will be extinguished again, ere he has brought it out." 6

And the Blessed One said to the venerable Ānanda, as he sat there by his side: 7

"Enough, Ānanda! Let not thy self be troubled; do not weep! Have I not already, on former occasions, told you that it is in the very nature of all things most near and dear unto us that we must separate from them and leave them? 8

"The foolish man conceives the idea of 'self,' the wise man sees there is no ground on which to build the idea of 'self,' thus he has a right conception of the world and well concludes that all compounds amassed by sorrow will be dissolved again, but the truth will remain. 9

"Why should I preserve this body of flesh, when the body of the excellent law will endure? I am resolved; having accomplished my purpose and attended to the work set me, I look for rest! 10

"For a long time, Ānanda, thou hast been very near to

O. KOPETZKY.

me by thoughts and acts of such love as never varies and is beyond all measure. Thou hast done well, Ānanda! Be earnest in effort and thou too shalt soon be free from the great evils, from sensuality, from selfishness, from delusion, and from ignorance!" 11

And Ānanda, suppressing his tears, said to the Blessed One: "Who shall teach us when thou art gone?" 12

And the Blessed One replied: "I am not the first Buddha who came upon earth, nor shall I be the last. In due time another Buddha will arise in the world, a Holy One, a supremely enlightened One, endowed with wisdom in conduct, auspicious, knowing the universe, an incomparable leader of men, a master of angels and mortals. He will reveal to you the same eternal truths which I have taught you. He will preach his religion, glorious in its origin, glorious at the climax, and glorious at the goal, in the spirit and in the letter. He will proclaim a religious life, wholly perfect and pure; such as I now proclaim." 13

Ānanda said: "How shall we know him?" 14

The Blessed One said: "He will be known as Metteyya, which means 'he whose name is kindness.'" 15

XCVII.

THE BUDDHA'S FINAL ENTERING INTO NIRVĀNA.

Then the Mallas, with their young men and maidens and their wives, being grieved, and sad, and afflicted at heart, went to the Upavattana, the sāla grove of the Mallas, and wanted to see the Blessed One, in order to partake of the bliss that devolves upon those who are in the presence of the Holy One. 1

And the Blessed One addressed them and said: 2

"Seeking the way, ye must exert yourselves and strive

with diligence. It is not enough to have seen me! Walk as I have commanded you; free yourselves from the tangled net of sorrow. Walk in the path with steadfast aim.   3

"A sick man may be cured by the healing power of medicine and will be rid of all his ailments without beholding the physician.   4

"He who does not do what I command sees me in vain. This brings no profit. Whilst he who lives far off from where I am and yet walks righteously is ever near me.   5

"A man may dwell beside me, and yet, being disobedient, be far away from me. Yet he who obeys the Dharma will always enjoy the bliss of the Tathāgata's presence."   6

Then the mendicant Subhadda went to the sāla grove of the Mallas and said to the venerable Ānanda: "I have heard from fellow mendicants of mine, who were deep stricken in years and teachers of great experience: 'Sometimes and full seldom to Tathāgatas appear in the world, the holy Buddhas.' Now it is said that to-day in the last watch of the night, the final passing away of the samana Gotama will take place. My mind is full of uncertainty, yet have I faith in the samana Gotama and trust he will be able so to present the truth that I may become rid of my doubts. O that I might be allowed to see the samana Gotama!"   7

When he had thus spoken the venerable Ānanda said to the mendicant Subhadda: "Enough! friend Subhadda. Trouble not the Tathāgata. The Blessed One is weary."   8

Now the Blessed One overheard this conversation of the venerable Ānanda with the mendicant Subhadda. And the Blessed One called the venerable Ānanda, and said: "Ānanda! Do not keep out Subhadda. Subhadda may be allowed to see the Tathāgata. Whatever Subhadda will ask of me, he will ask from a desire for knowledge, and not to annoy me, and whatever I may say in answer to his questions, that he will quickly understand."   9

Then the venerable Ānanda said to Subhadda the mendicant: "Step in, friend Subhadda; for the Blessed One gives thee leave." 10

When the Blessed One had instructed Subhadda, and aroused and gladdened him with words of wisdom and comfort, Subhadda said to the Blessed One: 11

"Glorious Lord, glorious Lord! Most excellent are the words of thy mouth, most excellent! They set up that which has been overturned, they reveal that which has been hidden. They point out the right road to the wanderer who has gone astray. They bring a lamp into the darkness so that those who have eyes to see can see. Thus, Lord, the truth has been made known to me by the Blessed One and I take my refuge in the Blessed One, in the Truth, and in the Order. May the Blessed One accept me as a disciple and true believer, from this day forth as long as life endures." 12

And Subhadda, the mendicant, said to the venerable Ānanda: "Great is thy gain, friend Ānanda, great is thy good fortune, that for so many years thou hast been sprinkled with the sprinkling of discipleship in this brotherhood at the hands of the Master himself!" 13

Now the Blessed One addressed the venerable Ananda, and said: "It may be, Ānanda, that in some of you the thought may arise, 'The word of the Master is ended, we have no teacher more!' But it is not thus, Ānanda, that you should regard it. It is true that no more shall I receive a body, for all future sorrow has now forever passed away. But though this body will be dissolved, the Tathāgata remains. The truth and the rules of the order which I have set forth and laid down for you all, let them, after I am gone, be a teacher unto you. When I am gone, Ānanda, let the order, if it should so wish, abolish all the lesser and minor precepts." 14

Then the Blessed One addressed the brethren, and said:

"There may be some doubt or misgiving in the mind of a brother as to the Buddha, or the truth, or the path. Do not have to reproach yourselves afterwards with the thought, 'We did not inquire of the Blessed One when we were face to face with him.' Therefore inquire now, O brethren, inquire freely." 15

And the brethren remained silent. 16

Then the venerable Ānanda said to the Blessed One: "Verily, I believe that in this whole assembly of the brethren there is not one brother who has any doubt or misgiving as to the Buddha, or the truth, or the path!" 17

Said the Blessed One: "It is out of the fullness of faith that thou hast spoken, Ānanda! But, Ānanda, the Tathāgata knows for certain that in this whole assembly of the brethren there is not one brother who has any doubt or misgiving as to the Buddha, or the truth, or the path! For even the most backward, Ānanda, of all these brethren has become converted, and is assured of final salvation." 18

Then the Blessed One addressed the brethren and said: "If ye now know the Dharma, the cause of all suffering, and the path of salvation, O disciples, will ye then say: 'We respect the Master, and out of reverence for the Master do we thus speak?'" 19

The brethren replied: "That we shall not, O Lord." 20

And the Holy One continued: 21

"Of those beings who live in ignorance, shut up and confined, as it were, in an egg, I have first broken the eggshell of ignorance and alone in the universe obtained the most exalted, universal Buddhahood. Thus, O disciples, I am the eldest, the noblest of beings. 22

"But what ye speak, O disciples, is it not even that which ye have yourselves known, yourselves seen, yourselves realised?" 23

Ānanda and the brethren said: "It is, O Lord." 24

Once more the Blessed One began to speak: "Behold

now, brethren," said he, "I exhort you, saying, 'Decay is inherent in all component things, but the truth will remain forever!' Work out your salvation with diligence!" This was the last word of the Tathāgata. Then the Tathāgata fell into a deep meditation, and having passed through the four jhānas, entered Nirvāna.   25

When the Blessed One entered Nirvāna there arose, at his passing out of existence, a mighty earthquake, terrible and awe-inspiring: and the thunders of heaven burst forth, and of those of the brethren who were not yet free from passions some stretched out their arms and wept, and some fell headlong on the ground, in anguish at the thought: "Too soon has the Blessed One died! Too soon has the Happy One passed away from existence! Too soon has the Light of the world gone out!"   26

Then the venerable Anuruddha exhorted the brethren and said: "Enough, my brethren! Weep not, neither lament! Has not the Blessed One formerly declared this to us, that it is in the very nature of all things near and dear unto us, that we must separate from them and leave them, since everything that is born, brought into being, and organized, contains within itself the inherent necessity of dissolution? How then can it be possible that the body of the Tathāgata should not be dissolved? No such condition can exist! Those who are free from passion will bear the loss, calm and self-possessed, mindful of the truth he has taught us."   27

And the venerable Anuruddha and the venerable Ānanda spent the rest of the night in religious discourse.   28

Then the venerable Anuruddha said to the venerable Ānanda: "Go now, brother Ānanda, and inform the Mallas of Kusinārā saying, 'The Blessed One has passed away: do, then, whatsoever seemeth to you fit!'"   29

And when the Mallas had heard this saying they were grieved, and sad, and afflicted at heart.   30

Then the Mallas of Kusinārā gave orders to their atten
dants, saying, "Gather together perfumes and garlands, and
all the music in Kusinārā!" And the Mallas of Kusinārā
took the perfumes and garlands, and all the musical instruments, and five hundred garments, and went to the sāla
grove where the body of the Blessed One lay. There they
passed the day in paying honor and reverence to the remains of the Blessed One, with hymns, and music, and
with garlands and perfumes, and in making canopies of
their garments, and preparing decorative wreaths to hang
thereon. And they burned the remains of the Blessed One
as they would do to the body of a king of kings. 31

When the funeral pyre was lit, the sun and moon withdrew their shining, the peaceful streams on every side were
torrent-swollen, the earth quaked, and the sturdy forests
shook like aspen leaves, whilst flowers and leaves fell un-
timely to the ground, like scattered rain, so that all Kusinārā
became strewn knee-deep with mandāra flowers raining
down from heaven. 32

When the burning ceremonies were over, Devaputta
said to the multitudes that were assembled round the
pyre: 33

"Behold, O brethren, the earthly remains of the Blessed
One have been dissolved, but the truth which he has taught
us lives in our minds and cleanses us from all error. 34

"Let us, then, go out into the world, as compassionate
and merciful as our great master, and preach to all living
beings the four noble truths and the eightfold path of
righteousness, so that all mankind may attain to a final salvation, taking refuge in the Buddha, the Dharma, and the
Sangha." 35

And when the Blessed One had entered into Nirvāna,
and the Mallas had burned the body with such ceremonies
as would indicate that he was the great king of kings, am-
bassadors came from all the empires that at the time had

embraced his doctrine, to claim a share of the relics; and
the relics were divided into eight parts and eight dāgobas
were erected for their preservation. One dāgoba was erected
by the Mallas and seven others by the seven kings of those
countries, whose people had taken refuge in the Buddha. 36

CONCLUSION.

XCVIII.

THE THREE PERSONALITIES OF THE BUDDHA.

WHEN the Blessed One had passed away into Nirvāna, the disciples came together and consulted what to do in order to keep the Dharma pure and uncorrupted by heresies. 1

And Upāli rose, saying: 2

"Our great Master used to say to the brethren: 'O bhikkhus! after my final entrance into Nirvāna you must reverence and obey the law. Regard the law as your master. The law is like unto a light that shines in the darkness, pointing out the way; it is also like unto a precious jewel to gain which you must shun no trouble, and be ready to bring any sacrifice, even, should it be needed, your own lives. Obey the Dharma which I have revealed to you;

follow it carefully and regard it in no way different from myself.' 3

"Such were the words of the Blessed One. 4

"The law, accordingly, which the Buddha has left us as a precious inheritance has now become the visible body of the Tathāgata. Let us, therefore, revere it and keep it sacred. For what is the use of erecting dāgobas for relics, if we neglect the spirit of the Master's teachings?" 5

And Anuruddha arose and said: 6

"Let us bear in mind, O brethren, that Gotama Siddhattha has revealed the truth to us. He was the Holy One and the Perfect One and the Blessed One, because the eternal truth had taken abode in him. 7

"The Tathāgata taught us that the truth existed before he was born into this world, and will exist after he has entered into the bliss of Nirvāna. 8

"The Tathāgata said: 9

"'The truth is omnipresent and eternal, endowed with excellencies innumerable, above all human nature, and ineffable in its holiness.' 10

"Now, let us bear in mind that not this or that law which is revealed to us in the Dharma is the Buddha, but the entire truth, the truth which is eternal, omnipresent, immutable, and most excellent. 11

"Many regulations of the Sangha are temporary; they were prescribed because they suited the occasion and were needed for some transient emergency. The truth, however, is not temporary. 12

"The truth is not arbitrary nor a matter of opinion, but can be investigated, and he who earnestly searches for the truth will find it. 13

"The truth is hidden to the blind, but he who has the mental eye sees the truth. The truth is Buddha's essence, and the truth will remain the ultimate standard by which we can discern false and true doctrines. 14

"Let us, then, revere the truth; let us inquire into the truth and state it, and let us obey the truth. For the truth is Buddha our Master, our Teacher, our Lord." 15

And Kassapa rose and said: 16

"Truly thou hast spoken well, O brother Anuruddha. Neither is there any conflict of opinion on the meaning of our religion. For the Blessed One possesses three personalities, and every one of them is of equal importance to us. 17

"There is the Dharma Kāya. There is the Nirmāna Kāya. There is the Sambhoga Kāya. 18

"Buddha is the all-excellent truth, eternal, omnipresent, and immutable. This is the Sambhoga Kāya which is in a state of perfect bliss. 19

"Buddha is the all-loving teacher assuming the shape of the beings whom he teaches. This is the Nirmāna Kāya, his apparitional body. 20

"Buddha is the all-blessed dispensation of religion. He is the spirit of the Sangha and the meaning of the commands which he has left us in his sacred word, the Dharma. This is the Dharma Kāya, the body of the most excellent law. 21

"If Buddha had not appeared to us as Gotama Sakyamuni, how could we have the sacred traditions of his doctrine? And if the generations to come did not have the sacred traditions preserved in the Sangha, how could they know anything of the great Sakyamuni? And neither we nor others would know anything about the most excellent truth which is eternal, omnipresent, and immutable. 22

"Let us then keep sacred and revere the traditions; let us keep sacred the memory of Gotama Sakyamuni, so that people may find the truth; for he whose spiritual eye is open will discover it, and it is the same to every one who possesses the comprehension of a Buddha to recognize it and to expound it." 23

Then the brethren decided to convene a synod in Rājagaha in order to lay down the pure doctrines of the
Blessed One, to collect and collate the sacred writings, and
to establish a canon which should serve as a source of instruction for future generations.   24

XCIX.

THE PURPOSE OF BEING.

Eternal verities dominate the formation of worlds and
constitute the cosmic order of natural laws. But when,
through the conflicting motion of masses, the universe was
illumined with blazing fire, there was no eye to see the
light, no ear to listen to reason's teachings, no mind to
perceive the significance of being; and in the immeasurable
spaces of existence no place was found where the truth
could abide in all its glory.   1

In the due course of evolution sentiency appeared and
sense-perception arose. There was a new realm of being,
the realm of soul-life, full of yearning, with powerful passions and of unconquerable energy. And the world split
in twain: there were pleasures and pains, self and notself,
friends and foes, hatred and love. The truth vibrated
through the world of sentiency, but in all its infinite po-
tentialities no place could be found where the truth could
abide in all its glory.   2

And reason came forth in the struggle for life. Reason
began to guide the instinct of self, and reason took the
sceptre of the creation and overcame the strength of the
brutes and the power of the elements. Yet reason seemed
to add new fuel to the flame of hatred, increasing the turmoil of conflicting passions; and brothers slew their brothers

for the sake of satisfying the lust of a fleeting moment. And the truth repaired to the domains of reason, but in all its recesses no place was found where the truth could abide in all its glory. 3

Now reason, as the helpmate of self, implicated all living beings more and more in the meshes of lust, hatred, and envy, and from lust, hatred, and envy the evils of wrong-doing originated. Men broke down under the burdens of life, until the saviour appeared, the great Buddha, the Holy Teacher of men and gods. 4

And the Buddha taught men the right use of sentiency, and the right application of reason; and he taught men to see things as they are, without illusions, and they learned to act according to truth. He taught righteousness and thus changed rational creatures into humane beings, just, kind-hearted, and faithful. And now at last a place was found where the truth might abide in all its glory, and this place is the heart of mankind. 5

Buddha, O Blessed One, O Holy One, O Perfect One, thou hast revealed the truth, and the truth has appeared upon earth and the kingdom of truth has been founded. 6

There is not room for truth in space, infinite though it be. 7

There is not room for truth in sentiency, neither in its pleasures nor in its pains; sentiency is the first footstep of truth, but there is not room in it for the truth, though sentiency may beam with the blazing glow of beauty and life. 8

Neither is there any room for truth in rationality. Rationality is a two-edged sword and serves the purpose of love equally as well as the purpose of hatred. Rationality is the platform on which the truth standeth. No truth is attainable without reason. Nevertheless, in mere rationality there is no room for truth, though it be the instrument that masters the things of the world. 9

The throne of truth is righteousness; and love and justice and good-will are its ornaments. 10

Righteousness is the place in which truth dwells, and here in the hearts of mankind aspiring after the realization of righteousness, there is ample space for a rich and ever richer revelation of the truth. 11

This is the Gospel of the Blessed One. This is the revelation of the Englightened One. This is the bequest of the Holy One. 12

Those who accept the truth and have faith in the truth, take refuge in the Buddha, the Dharma, and the Sangha. 13

Receive us, O Buddha, as thy disciples from this day hence, so long as our life lasts. 14

Comfort, O holy Teacher, compassionate and all-loving, the afflicted and the sorrow-laden, illumine those who go astray, and let us all gain more and more in comprehension and in holiness. 15

The truth is the end and aim of all existence, and the worlds originate so that the truth may come and dwell therein. 16

Those who fail to aspire for the truth have missed the purpose of life. 17

Blessed is he who rests in the truth, for all things will pass away, but the truth abideth forever. 18

The world is built for the truth, but false combinations of thought misrepresent the true state of things and bring forth errors. 19

Errors can be fashioned as it pleases those who cherish them; therefore they are pleasant to look upon, but they are unstable and contain the seeds of dissolution. 20

Truth cannot be fashioned. Truth is one and the same; it is immutable. 21

Truth is above the power of death; it is omnipresent, eternal, and most glorious. 22

Illusions, errors, and lies are the daughters of Māra, and great power is given unto them to seduce the minds of men and lead them astray upon the path of evil.   23

The nature of delusions, errors, and lies is death; and wrong-doing is the way to perdition.   24

Delusions, errors, and lies are like huge, gaudy vessels, the rafters of which are rotten and wormeaten, and those who embark in them are fated to be shipwrecked.   25

There are many who say: "Come error, be thou my guide," and when they are caught in the meshes of selfishness, lust, and evil desires, misery is begot.   26

Yet does all life yearn for the truth and the truth only can cure our diseases and give peace to our unrest.   27

Truth is the essence of life, for truth endureth beyond the death of the body. Truth is eternal and will still remain even though heaven and earth shall pass away. 28

There are not different truths in the world, for truth is one and the same at all times and in every place.   29

Truth teaches us the noble eightfold path of righteousness, and it is a straight path easily found by the truth-loving. Happy are those who walk in it."   30

C.

THE PRAISE OF ALL THE BUDDHAS.

All the Buddhas are wonderful and glorious.
There is not their equal upon earth.
They reveal to us the path of life.
And we hail their appearance with pious reverence.   1

All the Buddhas teach the same truth.
They point out the path to those who go astray.

The Truth is our hope and comfort.
We gratefully accept its illimitable light. 2

All the Buddhas are one in essence,
Which is omnipresent in all modes of being,
Sanctifying the bonds that tie all souls together,
And we rest in its bliss as our final refuge. 3

TABLE OF REFERENCE.

THE GOSPEL OF BUDDHA CHAPTER AND VERSE	SOURCES	PARALLELISMS
I—III	*EA*	
Descent from heaven	*LV.*	Klopstock's *Messias*
omitted	*rGya*, III—v	Gesang I.
IV	*Fo, vv.* 1—147	
IV, 6	*B St, p.* 64	Mark VII, 32, 37 Matth. XI, 5
IV, 9	*Fo, vv.* 22—24	Matth. II, 1
IV, 12	*Fo, vv.* 39—40	Luke II, 36
IV, 17	*RB* 150; *RHB* 52	Pseudo Matth. 23
IV, 27	*Fo, v.* 147	Luke II, 52
Omitted	*RHB, pp.* 103—108 . . .	Matth. II, 16
V	*HM, p.* 156; *RB, p.* 83; *rGya*, XII	
	Fo vv. 152—156	Luke II, 46—47
V, 9	*Fo, v.* 164	Matth. III, 16
VI	*Fo, vv.* 191—322	
VI, 19—20	*B St, pp.* 79—80 . . . . . . *RB, p.* 23	Luke XI, 27—28
VII	*Fo, vv.* 335—417	
VII, 7	*B St, p.* 5—6	

THE GOSPEL OF BUDDHA CHAPTER AND VERSE	SOURCES	PARALLELISMS
VII, 18—19	*BSt, p.* 18	Matth. xxiv, 35 Luke xxi, 33 Luke xvi, 17
VII, 23—24	*BSt, p.* 84	Luke iv, 5—8 [See also Matth. iv, 1—7 and Mark i, 13]
VIII	*Fo, vv.* 778—918	
VIII, 15	*DP, v.* 178	
IX	*Fo, vv.* 919—1035	
	Cf. "Arāda and Udraka" in Rhys Davids's *Dialogue*	Compare the results of modern psychology
IX, 6	*MV.* 1, 6, §§ 36—38 [*SB*, xiii, *p.* 100]	
IX, 14	*QKM, pp.* 83—86	Evolution theory
IX, 15	*QKM, p.* 133	
IX, 16	*QKM, p.* 111	
X	*Fo, vv.* 1000—1023	
X, 4, 5	*SN, vv.* 425, 439 . . . . . *SN, v.* 445	Luke iv, 2—4 John iii, 46
X, 11	*Fo, v.* 1024 . . . . . . : . . *Fo, vv.* 1222—1224	Luke vii, 19 Matth. ii, 3
XI [See LXXXIX, 1—6]	*Fo. vv.* 1026—1110	Luke iv, 2 Matth. iv, 1—7 Mark i, 13
XII	*Fo, vv.* 1111—1199	
XII, 8	*QKM, p.* 79 *SDP*, vii [*SB*, xxi, *p.*172]	
XII, 11—15	*SDP*, iii [*SB*, xxi, *p.* 90] *MV,* 1, 6 §§ 19—28 Cf. *Old, G, pp.* 227—228, *Old, E, p.* 211 *RhDB, pp.* 106—107	
XII, 16	*BSt, pp.* 103—104 Cf. *DP, pp.* 153—154 *Dh, p.* 12	
XII, 20	*rGya,* 355	Matth. v, 3—11

THE GOSPEL OF BUDDHA CHAPTER AND VERSE	SOURCES	PARALLELISMS
XIII	*MV*, I, 4	
XIV	*MV*, I, 5	
XIV, 2	*MV*, I, 3, § 4	
XIV, 14	*MPN*, III, 44, 45 Cf. *W*, *p*. 87	
XV	{ *Fo*, *vv*. 1200—1217 { *MV*, I, 6, §§ 1—9	
XVI	{ *Fo*, *vv*. 1217—1279 { *MV*, I, 6, §§ 10—47	
XVI, 5	*SN*, *v*. 248	
XVI, 6	*RbDB p*. 131	
XVI, 7	*SN*, *v*. 241	Matth. xv, 10
XVII	*MV*, I, 6, § 10—47	
XVII, 10—12	*Samyuttaka Nikāya, vol*. III, fol. sâ, quoted by *Old*, G, 364; *Old, E, p*. 339	
XVII, 13—18	{ *MV*, I, 11 { *Fo*, *vv*. 1297—1300	{ Luke IX, 1—6 { Luke x, 1—24
XVII, 15	{ *QKM, p*. 264 . . . . { *QKM, p*. 266	Matth. v, 16 Matth. vII, 6
XVIII	{ *MV*, I, 7, 8, 9 . . . . } { *Fo*, *vv*. 1280—1296 . . . . }	John III, 2
XVIII, 8	*Fo*, *vv*. 1289—1290	
XVIII, 10	*Fo*, *v*. 1292	
XIX	{ *Fo*, *vv*. 1300—1334 { *MV*, I, 20—21	
XX	{ *Fo*, *vv*. 1335—1379 { *MV*, I, 22	
XX, 19—20	{ *SN*, *v*. 148 { *Metta Sutta*. [An often { quoted sentence. *RbD* { *B*, *p*. 109, Hardy, "Le- { gends and Theories of { the Buddhas," *p*. 212	
XX, 23	*Rb D B, p*. 62	
XX, 28	*Fo*, *v*. 1733	

THE GOSPEL OF BUDDHA CHAPTER AND VERSE	SOURCES	PARALLELISMS
XXI	*Fo, vv.* 1380—1381 . . . . *MV,* I, 22, §§ 15—18 . . .	Matth. XXI, 1—11 Mark XI, 1—10 Luke XIX, 28—38 John XII, 12—15
XXII	*Fo, vv.* 1382—1431 *MV* I, 23—24, *W, p.* 89	
XXII, 3—5	*MV,* I, 23, §§ 13—14 ..	Matth. XXI, 9 Mark XI, 9 John XII, 13
XXIII	*Fo, vv.* 1432—1495	
XXIII, 10—20	*EA,*	
XXIV	*Fo vv.* 1496—1521	
XXV, 4	*Fo, vv.* 1516—1517	Acts XX, 35
XXV	*Fo, vv.* 1522—1533 1611—1671	
XXVI, 1—7	*AN,* III, 134	Compare the results of modern psychology
XXVI, 8—13	*US, p.* 112 *W, p.* XIV	
XXVII	*Fo, vv.* 1534—1610 *HM, p.* 204	
XXVIII	*HM, p.* 203 et seqq. *BSt, pp.* 125—126	
XXIX	*MV,* I, 54 *HM,* 208—209	
XXX	*MV,* VIII, 23—36 [*SB,* XVII, *pp.* 193—194]	
XXXI	*Fo vv.* 1672—1673	
XXXII	*HM, pp.* 353—354	
XXXII, 4—6	*W, pp.* 443—444	
XXXIII	*S* 42 *S* . . . . *Fo, vv.* 1757—1766 . . . . *BP, p.* 153	Matth. v, 28
XXXIII, 9—11	*Fo vv.* 1762—1763 . . . . *Fo, vv.* 1763	Eph. VI, 13—17 Mark IX, 47 Matth. v, 29 Matth. XVIII, 9

THE GOSPEL OF BUDDHA CHAPTER AND VERSE	SOURCES	PARALLELISMS
XXXIV	*MV*, VIII, 15. [*SB*, XVII, *pp.* 219—225.]	
XXXIV, 24 [Last part of the verse.]	*Bgt, p.* 211	{ Luke VIII, 2 Matth. XIII, 24—27
XXXV	*MV*, II	
XXXVI	*MV*, X, 1, 2, § 1—2; § 20 *C*, vol. III, *p.* 139	
XXXVII	*MV*, X, 5—6, 2 § 3—20	
XXXVIII	*MV*, V, 4	
XXXVIII, 3	*BSt, p.* 311	
XXXVIII, 5	*MV*, V, 4, 2. [*SB*, XVII, *p.* 18.]	Matth. V, 46—47
XXXIX	{ *Fo, vv.* 1713—1734 *HM, pp.* 337—340	
XXXIX, 4	*BSt, p.* 200	
XXXIX, 7	*DP, v.* 227; *SB*, X, *p.* 58 (cf. *ChD, p.* 122)	Matth. XI, 16, 19
XL	{ *V*, XVIII, XX *W, pp.* 184—186	
XLI	*MV*, VI, 29. [*SB*, XVII, *pp.* 104—105.]	
XLI, 12—13	{ *Metta Sutta* *SN, v.* 148. [Cf. *RhDB, p.* 109.]	
XLII	*RB, pp.* 68—69. [Cf. *RhD B, p.* 71 and *Old, G,* 376—378.]	{ Mark III, 14 Luke IX, 2
	Bgt, 212	{ Matth. XIII, 3 et seq. Mark IV, 3—20
XLIV	*TPN, p.* 129	
XLV	*TPN, pp.* 22—23 and *p.* 25	
XLVI	*S42S*, 4	
XLVII	*SDP*, X, XIII, XXVII	
XLVII, 23	*SDP*, XXIV, 22. [*SB*, XXI, *p.* 416.]	
XLVIII	*DP* in *SB*, X	

THE GOSPEL OF BUDDHA CHAPTER AND VERSE	SOURCES	PARALLELISMS
XLVIII, 36—37	*DP, v.* 5	Matth. v, 44
XLVIII, 46	*SN, vv.* 784—785, 885—888, 834. [*SB*, x, 149, 159, 169.]	Matth. xi, 29—30
XLVIII, 47	*DP, v.* 275	II Cor. vii, 7
XLVIII, 55	*DP, v.* 387	
XLIX	*SB*, xi, *pp.* 157—203	
XLIX, 17	*SB*, xi, *pp.* 173—174 . . .	Matth. xv, 14
L	*SSP, pp.* 297—320. [Cf. *RbDB*, 143.]	
LI, 1—14 } LI, 31—35 }	*MV*, vi, 31. [*SB*, xvii, *pp.* 108—113.]	
LI, 15—30	*EA* [cf. *QKM, pp.* 254—257]	
LII	*EA* [cf. *CBS, p.* 15 and also *MY*, v]	
LIII	Compiled from *HM, pp.* 280 et seq., *Fo, v,* 1682, 1683, *W, p.* 239, and *QKM*, pass.	
LIII, 18—23*a*	*QKM, p.* 120	
LIII, 23*b*	*QKM, p.* 148	John iii, 8
LIII, 26—27	*QKM, p.* 67	
LIII, 29—32	*QKM, pp.* 73—74	
LIII, 47—59	*QKM, pp.* 63, 83—86	
LIII, 53	*US* and *W*, motto	
LIV, 1—2	*Fo, vv.* 1208, 1228	Matth. v, 3—11
LIV, 3	*Brahmajāla Sutta*, quoted by *RbD, p.* 99	{John xvi, 16 {Matth. xxiv, 23
LIV, 4	*QKM, p.* 114	
LIV, 5	*Fo, v.* 1231	
LIV, 6—8	*rGya, p.* 372	Matth. xi, 28
LIV, 9	*S42S*, 16	
LIV, 10	*QKM, p.* 110	{John xiv, 6 {John xviii, 37
LV	*SDP*, v	
LVI	*Mahā Rāhula Sutta*	

THE GOSPEL OF BUDDHA CHAPTER AND VERSE	SOURCES	PARALLELISMS
LVII	*S 42 S*	
LVIII	*Buddhist Catena*	
LIX	*SN, pp.* 58—62; *p.* 25; *p.* 147; *p.* 54 *MV,* I, 3, § 4 [cf. *Old, E, p.* 118] *Nidhikanda Sutta,* quoted by *Rh D B, p.* 127....	Matth. VI, 20
LX, 7—8	*Rh D B, p.* 156	
LX, 12	Beal, *Buddhism of China,* chap. XII	
LX, 18—23	*Rh D B, p.* 170	
LX, 27—28	*EH*	
LX, 29	*Q KM, p.* 127	
LX, 31	*Rh D B, pp.* 175—176	
LX, 33	*Rh D B, p.* 173	
LXI	*MP N,* III, 22. [*SB,* xx, *p.* 48—49.]	
LXI, 3—5	*Chullavagga* IX, 1—4. [*SB,* XX, 301—305]	Matth. V, 13
LXI, 6—9	*Sutra Dsanglun* [cf. R. Seydel "*Das Ev. v. Jesu in s. Verh. z. Buddha-Sage*" *pp.* 184—185]	Matth. V, 1—2
LXII	*EA*	
LXIII	See *O. C.* XVII, *pp.* 353—354	
LXIII, 7—9	*UG,* VII, 14 seq.	Matth. XXV, 14 et seq.
LXIV	*DDP,* V	
LXV	*SDP,* IV	Luke XV, 11 et seq.
LXVI	*B St, pp.* 211, 299. [See *PT,* II, 58.]	
LXVII	*B St, pp.* 315 et seq.	
LXVIII	*Ch D, pp.* 88—89	
LXVIII, 6	*Ch D*	Mark XII, 42—44
LXIX	*Ch D, p.* 46	The Story ot Diogenes and his Lantern

THE GOSPEL OF BUDDHA CHAPTER AND VERSE	SOURCES	PARALLELISMS
LXX	*ChD, p.* 134	
LXXI	*BgP, pp.* 107 et seq.	
LXXII	*ChD, p.* 77	Luke XII, 20
LXXIII	*BSt, p.* 147	
LXXIII, 15	*BSt.*	Exodus XVII, 6
LXXIV	*SN, pp.* 11—15	{ Matth. XIII, 3 et seq. Mark IV, 14
LXXV	*SN, pp.* 20 et seq.	
LXXVI	*Bf, p.* 205	John V, 5 et seq.
LXXVII	*HM, pp.* 317—319	
LXXVIII LXXIX	} *Jātaka Tales*	
LXXX	*Bf, pp.* 146 et seq.	
LXXXI	*Fu-Pen-Hing-tsi-King,* tr. by S. Beal	
LXXXI, 7—10	*EA*	John II, 1 et seq.
LXXXII	*MV,* I, 14	
LXXXIII	*ChD, p.* 130 et seq.	
LXXXIII, 5	*BP, p.* 16	
LXXXIII, 5, 6, 9	*ChD* and *SS*	Matth. XXII, 30
LXXXIV, 1—14	*BP, pp.* 98 et seqq.	Greek versions quoted by Jacob H. Thiesen, *LKG.*
LXXXIV, 15—28	*SB,* x, *p.* 106	
LXXXV	*ChD, pp.* 50—51	Matth. V, 25, 29
LXXXV, 6	*ChD,* cf *OC* No. 470 . . .	Rom. III, 28
LXXXVI	*ChD, pp.* 94—98	
LXXXVII	*C,* II *p.* 262	
LXXXVIII	*MPN,* I [*SB,* XI, *p.* 1 et seqq.]	
LXXXIX	{ *MPN,* I, 19, 22 *MV,* VI, 28	
XC	*MPN,* I, 16	
XCI	*MPN,* II, 9	
XCI, 6	*MPN*	I Cor. 15, 55
XCII	{ *MPN,* II, 12—24 *Fo, vv.* 1749—1753; 1768 —1782	

THE GOSPEL OF BUDDHA CHAPTER AND VERSE	SOURCES	PARALLELISMS
XCIII	*MPN*, II, 27—35	
XCIV, 1	*B St, p.* 84	See Matth. IV, 1 and Mark I, 13
XCIV, 2—13	*MPN*, III, 46—63	
XCV	*MPN*, IV, 14—57	
XCV, 6	*MPN*, IV, 25	John XIX, 28
XCV, 14—22	*MPN*, IV, 47—52	{ Matth. XXVII, 2 { Mark IX, 2
XCVI	*MPN*, V, 1—14, concerning Metteyya see *EH* s. v. *RbDB*, *pp.* 180, 200; *Old, G,p.* 153, etc.	John XIV, 26
XCVII	*MPN*, V, 52—69, and VI; *Fo, vv.* 2303—2310 . .	John VIII, 31
XCVII, 19—20 } XCVII, 23—24 }	*Mabātanhāsamkhaya-Sutta, Majjhima Nikāya*, vol. I, *p.* 263, quoted by *Old, G, p.* 349 *E, p.* 325	
XCVII, 22	*Suttavibhanga, Parājika* I, *pp.* 1, 4 quoted by *Old, G, p.* 349, *E, p.* 325 . .	I Cor. XV, 20
XCVIII	*EA*, embodying later traditions see *EH* and almost any other work on Buddhism	The Christian Trinity dogma
XCIX	*EA*	
C	*EA*, in imitation of a formula at present in use among Northern Buddhists	

ABBREVIATIONS IN THE TABLE OF REFERENCE.

AN.—Añguttara Nikāya in Warren's Buddhism in Translations.
Bf.—Burnouf, Introduction à l'histoire du Bouddhisme Indien, Paris 1844.
Bgt.—The Life or Legend of Gautama, by the R. Rev. P. Bigandet.

BL.—Buddhist Literature in China by Samuel Beal.

BP.—Buddhaghosha's Parables. Translated by T. Rogers, London, 1870.

BSt.—Buddhist Birth Stories or Jâtaka Tales. Translated by Rhys Davids.

C.—The Jātaka edited by Prof. E. B. Cowell, Cambridge.

CBS.—A Catena of Buddhist Scriptures from the Chinese by Samuel Beal. London, 1871.

ChD.—[Chinese Dhammapada.] Texts from the Buddhist Canon, commonly known as Dhammapada. Translated by S. Beal, London and Boston, 1878.

Dh.—The Dharma, or The Religion of Enlightenment by Paul Carus. 5th ed. Chicago, 1907.

DP.—The Dhammapada. Translated from Pāli by F. Max Müller, Vol. X, Part I, of the Sacred Books of the East. Oxford, 1881.

EA.—Explanatory Addition.

EH.—Handbook of Chinese Buddhism, by Ernest J. Eitel. London, 1888.

Fo.—The Fo-Sho-Hing-Tsan-King. A Life of Buddha by Asvaghosha, translated from Sanskrit into Chinese by Dharmarakhsha, A. D. 420, and from Chinese into English by Samuel Beal. Vol. XIX of the Sacred Books of the East. Oxford, 1883.

G.—Reden Gotamo's by Karl Eugen Neumann.

HF.—Hymns of the Faith (Dhammapada) transl. by Albert J. Edmunds.

HM.—A Manual of Buddhism, by R. Spence Hardy.

LKG.—Die Legende von Kisāgotamī, by Jakob H. Thiessen. Breslau, 1880.

LV.—Lalita Vistara, translated into German by Dr. S. Lefmann. Berlin, 1874.

MPN. The Mahāparinibbāna Suttanta. The Book of the Great Decease. Vol. XI of the Sacred Books of the East. Oxford 1881.

MV.—The Mahāvagga. I—IV in Vol. XIII; V—X in Vol. XVII of the Sacred Books of the East. Oxford, 1881—1882.

MY.—Outlines of the Mahāyāna as Taught by Buddha, by S. Kuroda. Tokyo, Japan, 1893.

OC.—The Open Court, a monthly magazine, published by the Open Court Publishing Company, Chicago.

Old G.—German Edition, Buddha, sein Leben, seine Lehre und seine Gemeinde, by H. Oldenberg. Second Edition. Berlin, 1890.

Old E.—English translation, Buddha, His Life, His Doctrine, and His Order by H. Oldenberg. London, 1882.

PT.—Pantschatantra, translated into German by Theodor Benfey. Two vols. Leipsic, 1859.

QKM.—The Questions of King Milinda, translated from Pāli by T. W. Rhys Davids, Vol. XXXV of the Sacred Books of the East. Oxford, 1890.

RB.—The Life of the Buddha from Thibetan Works, transl. by W. W. Rockhill. London, 1884.

rGya.—rGya Tchee Roll Pa, Histoire du Bouddha Sakya Mouni, by Foucaux. Paris, 1868.

RHB.—The Romantic History of Buddha from the Chinese Sanskrit, by S. Beal. London, 1875.

RhDB.—Buddhism, by T. W. Rhys Davids, in the Series of Non-Christian Religious Systems. London, 1890.

S42S.—Sutra of Forty-two Sections. Kyoto, Japan.

SB.—Sacred Books of the East.

SN.—Sutta Nipāta, translated from the Pāli by V. Fausböll. Part II, Vol. X of the Sacred Books of the East. Oxford, 1881.

SS.—A Brief Account of Shin-Shiu by R. Akamatsu. Kyoto, Japan, 1893.

SSP.—Sept Suttas Pālis by M. P. Grimblot. Paris, 1876.

TPN.—Buddhistische Anthologie. Texte aus dem Pâli-Kanon. By Dr. Karl Eugen Neumann. Leyden, 1892.

Ug.—Uttarādhyayana, translated by H. Jacobi. Vol. XLV of the Sacred Books of the East.

US.—The Udāna by Major General D. M. Strong.

V.—Visuddhi-Magga in Warren's Buddhism in Translations.

W.—Buddhism in Translations by Henry Clarke Warren.

The original Pāli texts are published in the Journal of the Pāli Text Society, London, Henry Frowde.

GLOSSARY OF NAMES AND TERMS.

[In the text of the present booklet all unnecessary terms have been avoided. Whenever a good English equivalent could be found, the foreign expression has been dropped. Nevertheless, the introduction not only of many foreign-sounding names, but also of some of the original terms, was unavoidable.

Now we have to state that the Eastern people, at least those of Hindu culture during the golden age of Buddhism in India, adopted the habit of translating not only terms but also names. A German whose name is Schmied is not called Smith in English, but Buddhists, when translating from Pāli into Sanskrit, change Siddhattha into Siddhārtha. The reason of this strange custom lies in the fact that Buddhists originally employed the popular speech and did not adopt the use of Sanskrit until about five hundred years after Buddha. Since the most important names and terms, such as Nirvāna, Karma and Dharma, have become familiar to us in their Sanskrit form, while their Pāli equivalents, Nibbāna, Kamma and Dhamma, are little used, *it appeared advisable to prefer for some terms the Sanskrit forms,* but there are instances in which the Pāli, for some reason or other, has been preferred by English authors [e. g. Krishā Gautamī is always called Kisāgotamī], we present here in the Glossary both the Sanskrit and the Pāli forms.

Names which have been Anglicised, such as "Brahmā, Brahman, Benares, Jain, and karma," have been preserved in their accepted form. If we adopt the rule of transferring Sanskrit and Pāli words in their stem-form, as we do in most cases (e. g. Nirvāna, ātman), we ought to call

Brahma "Brahman," and karma "karman." But *usus est tyrannus*. In a
popular book it is not wise to swim against the stream.

Following the common English usage of saying "Christ," not "the Christ,"
we say in the title "Buddha," not "the Buddha."]

Abhi'ññā, *p.*, Abhi'jñā, *skt.*, supernatural talent. There are six abhiññās
which Buddha acquired when attaining perfect enlightenment:—(1) the
celestial eye, or an intuitive insight of the nature of any object in any
universe; (2) the celestial ear, or the ability to understand any sound
produced in any universe; (3) the power of assuming any shape or form;
(4) knowledge of all forms of pre-existence of one's self and others;
(5) intuitive knowledge of the minds of all beings; and (6) knowledge
of the finality of the stream of life.—175, 176.

Acira'vatī, *p.* and *skt.*, a river.—96.

Agni, *p.* and *skt.*, a god of the Brahmans, the god of fire.—49.

Ajātasa'ttu, *p.*, Ajātaśa'tru, *skt.*, the son of king Bimbisāra and his successor to the throne of Magadha.—110—112, 219.

Alā'ra, *p.*, Ārā'da, *skt.*, a prominent Brahman philosopher. His full name
is Ālāra Kālāma.—29, 239.

Ambapā'lī, the courtesan, called "Lady Amra" in Fo-Sho-Hing-Tsan-King.
It is difficult for us to form a proper conception of the social position
of courtesans at Buddha's time in India. This much is sure, that they
were not common prostitutes, but ladies of wealth, possessing great
influence. Their education was similar to the hetairæ in Greece, where
Aspasia played so prominent a part. Their rank must sometimes have
been like that of Madame Pompadour in France at the court of
Louis XIV. They rose to prominence, not by birth, but by beauty,
education, refinement, and other purely personal accomplishments, and
many of them were installed by royal favor. The first paragraphs of
Khandhaka VIII of the Mahāvagga [*S. B.*, Vol. XVII, pp. 171—172] gives
a fair idea of the important rôle of courtesans in those days. They were
not necessarily venal daughters of lust, but, often women of distinction
and repute, worldly, but not disrespectable.—227, 228, 231, 232.

Amitā'bha, *p.* and *skt.*, endowed with boundless light, from *amita*, infinite,
immeasurable, and *ābhā*, ray of light, splendor, the bliss of enlightenment. It is a term of later Buddhism and has been personified as
Amitābha Buddha, or Amita. The invocation of the all-saving name
of Amitābha Buddha is a favorite tenet of the Lotus or Pure Land
sect, so popular in China and Japan. Their poetical conception of a
paradise in the West is referred to in Chapter LX. Southern Buddhism
knows nothing of a personified Amitābha, and the Chinese travellers

Fa-hien and Hiuen-tsang do not mention it. The oldest allusion to Amita is found in the *Amitāyus Sūtra*, translated A. D. 148—170. [See Eitel, *Handbook*, pp. 7—9.]—172, 173, 174, 175.

Āna'nda, *p.* and *skt.*, Buddha's cousin and his favorite disciple. The Buddhistic St. John (Johannes).—86, 87, 90, 92, 93, 120, 177, 190, 191, 196, 197, 219, 220, 225, 226, 233, 234, 235, 236, 238, 239, 240, 241, 245, 246, 247, 248, 249.

Anāthapi'ndika, *p.* and *skt.*, (also called Anāthapi'ndada in *skt.*) literally "One who gives alms *(pinda)* to the unprotected or needy *(anātha)*." Eitel's etymology "one who gives without keeping (anātha) a mouthful (pinda) for himself" is not tenable. A wealthy lay devotee famous for his liberality and donor of the Jetavana vihāra.—72, 75, 76, 77, 81, 168.

Annabhā'ra, *p.* and *skt.*, literally "he who brings food"; name of Sumana's slave.—189, 190.

Aññā'ta, *p.*, Ājñā'ta, *skt.*, literally "knowing", a cognomen of Kondañña, the first disciple of Buddha.—56.

Anuru'ddha, a prominent disciple of Buddha, known as the great master of Buddhist metaphysics. He was a cousin of Buddha, being the second son of Amritodana, a brother of Suddhodana.—86, 249, 253, 254.

A'rahat, *p.*, Ar'hant, *skt.*, a saint. (See also Saint in Index.)—97.

Arati, dislike, hatred. The opposite of *rati*. The name of one of Māra's daughters, *q. v.*—36.

A'sita, *p.* and *skt.*, a prophet.—9, 10.

A'ssaji, *p.*, Aśvajit, *skt.*, one of Buddha's disciples by whose dignified demeanor Sāriputta is converted.—70.

Ā'tman, *skt.*, Atta, *p.*, breath as the principle of life, the soul, self, the ego. To some of the old Brahman schools the âtman constitutes a metaphysical being in man, which is the thinker of his thoughts, the perceiver of his sensations, and the doer of his doings. Buddha denies the existence of an atman in this sense.—29, 30, 32, 33, 154, 158.

Balā'ni, or pañca-balāni, *p.* and *skt.*, (the singular is *bala*, power), the five moral powers (also called pañca-indriyāni), which are: Faith, energy, memory or recollection, meditation or contemplation, and wisdom or intuition.

Beluva, a village near Vesālī.—232.

Benares, the well-known city in India; Anglicised form of Vārānasī, *skt.*, and Bārānasī, *p.* (See Kāsī.)—47, 48, 49, 58, 61, 104—106, 215.

Bha'gavat, *p.*, Bha'gavant, *skt.*, the man of merit, worshipful, the Blessed One. A title of honor given to Buddha.—21, 170, 195.

Bha'llika, *p.* and *skt.*, a merchant.—42.

Bhāradvā'ja, *p.* and *skt.*, name of a Brahman.—139, 141, 194.

Bhā'vanā, *p.* and *skt.,* meditation. There are five principal meditations: metta-bhāvanā, on love; karunā-bhāvanā, on pity; muditā-bhāvanā, on joy; asubha-bhāvanā, on impurity; and upekhā-bhāvanā, on serenity. [See Rhys Davids's *Buddhism,* pp. 170–171.]—174, 175.

Bhi'kkhu, *p.,* bhi'kshu, *skt.*, mendicant, monk, friar; the five bhikkhus, 34, 35, 47, 49, 55, 56, 88, 90, 91, 93, 94, 95, 96, 97, 98, 99, 100, 101, 102, 103, 108, 120, 170, 171, 172, 177, 183, 209, 234; bhikkhus doffed their robes, 95; bhikkhus rebuked, 109; bhikkhus prospered, 221; the sick bhikkhu, 213.

Bhi'kkhunī, *p.*, bhi'kshunī, *skt.*, nun.—93, 95, 96.

Bimbisā'ra, *p.* and *skt.*, the king of Magadha; often honored with the cognomen "Sai'nya," *skt.*, or "Se'niya," *p.*, i. e. "the warlike or military."—25, 26, 65, 69, 90, 98, 110, 111, 219.

Bo'dhi, *p.* and *skt.*, knowledge, wisdom, enlightenment.—151.

Bodhi-a'nga or Bojjha'nga, or Sa'tta Bojjha'nga, *p.*, meditation on the seven kinds of wisdom, which are:—energy, recollection, contemplation, investigation of scripture, joy, repose, and serenity.—97.

Bodhisa'tta, *p.*, Bodhisa'ttva, *skt.*, he whose essence *(sattva)* is becoming enlightenment *(bodhi).* The term denotes (1) one who is about to become a Buddha, but has not as yet attained Nirvāna; (2) a class of saints who have only once more to be born again to enter into Nirvāna; (3) in later Buddhism any preacher or religious teacher.—9, 21, 25, 86, 118, 192, 194, 214–216; appearance of, 25; Bodhisattas, 130.

Bodhi-tree, the tree at Buddha-Gaya, species *ficus religiosa.*—36.

Bra'hmā, Anglicised form of *skt.* stem-form *Brahman* (nom. s. *Brahmā*). The chief God of Brahmanism, the world-soul. See also *Sahampati.*— 43, 44, 45, 87, 141; Brahmā, a union with, 139; Brahmā, face to face, 140; Brahmā's mind, 141.

Brahmada'tta, *p.* and *skt.*, (etym. given by Brahma) name of a mythical king of Kâshî, *skt.*, or Kāsī, *p.*—104–108, 192, 199, 200, 215.

Bra'hman, the priestly caste of the Indians. Anglicised form of *Brahmana* (*p.* and *skt.*). Priests were selected from the Brahman caste, but Brahmans were not necessarily priests; they were farmers, merchants, and often high officials in the service of kings. Brahmans, the two—139.

Buddha, *p.* and *skt.*, the Awakened One, the Enlightened One—. Buddha is also called Sakyamuni (the Sakya sage), Sakyasimha (the Sakya Lion), Sugata (the Happy One), Satthar, nom. Satthâ, *p.*; Shāstar, *skt.*, (the Teacher), Jina (the Conqueror), Bhagavat (the Blessed One), Lokanātha (the Lord of the World), Sarvajña (the Omniscient One), Dharmarāja (the King of Truth), Tathāgata, etc. [See Rh. Davids's B. p. 28.] B., faith in the, 226; B., I am not the first, 245; B. not Gotama, 160; B., refuge in the, 42, 60, 61, 68, 71, 150, 160, 168, 202, 206, 211, 247, 257; B. remains, Gotama is gone, 247; B. replies to the deva, 168; B., the sower, 194; B., the teacher, 177; B., the three personalities of, 252; B., the truth, 2, 161, 254; B., truly thou art, 45, 150; B. will arise, another, 245; B.'s birth, 8; B.'s death, 249; B.'s farewall address, 249; consolidation of B.'s religion, 89; Buddhas, the praise of all the, 258; Buddhas, the religion of all the, 68; Buddhas, the words of immutable, 20, 22.

Cha'nna, *p.* and *skt.*, prince Siddhattha's driver.—15, 25.

Chu'nda, *p.* and *skt.*, the smith of Pāvā.—237, 240, 241.

Dāgo'ba, modernised form of *skt.* Dhātu-ga'rbha, "relic shrine," (also called Stūpa in Northern Buddhism) a mausoleum, tower containing relics, a kenotaph.—250, 253.

Dā'namatī, *p.* and *skt.*, name of a village. The word means "having a mind to give."—152.

De'va, *p.* and *skt.*, any celestial spirit, a god especially of intermediate rank, angel.—Deva, questions of the, 168; Buddha replies to the deva, 168; Devas, 29, 55, 69, 92.

Devada'tta (etym. god-given) brother of Yasodharā and Buddha's brother-in-law. He tried to found a sect of his own with severer rules than those prescribed by Buddha. He is described undoubtedly with great injustice in the Buddhist canon and treated as a traitor. [About his sect see Rh. Davids's B. p. 181—182.]—86, 88, 110—112, 214.

Devapu'tta, *p.*, Devapu'tra, *skt.*, (etym. Son of a God) one of Buddha's disciples.—250.

Dhammapa'da, *p.*, Dharmapa'da, *skt.*—131.

Dha'rma, *skt.*, Dha'mma, *p.*, originally the natural condition of things or beings, the law of their existence, truth, then religious truth, the law, the ethical code of righteousness, the whole body of religious doctrines as a system, religion.—40, 41, 42, 44, 57, 61, 64, 68, 71,, 74, 84, 98—101, 138, 145, 146, 147, 150, 160, 168, 170, 171, 178, 179, 214, 246, 248, 250, 252, 253; let a man take pleasure in the dharma, 171; the goodness of the dharma, 134.

Dharmakā'ya, *skt.*, the body of the law.—254.

Dharmarā'ja, *skt.*, Dhammarā'ja, *p.*, the king of truth.—21, 78, 130.

Dīghā'vu, *p.*, Dīrghā'yu, *skt.*, the etymology of the word is "livelong." Name of a mythical prince, son of king Dīghīti.—104—108.

Dīghī'ti, *p.*, Dīrghe'ti, *skt.*, literally "suffer-long," Name of a mythical king, father of prince Dīghā'vu.—104—108.

Ganges, the well known river of India.—14, 21, 224.

Gava'mpati, *p.*, Gavā'mpati, *skt.*, literally "lord of cows," a friend of Yasa.—61.

Ga'yā Kassapa, brother of the great Kassapa of Uruvelā.—64.

Go'tama, *p.*, Gau'tama, *skt.*, Buddha's family name.—7, 48, 49, 62, 65, 71, 140, 141, 142, 144, 145, 151, 160, 195; Gotama denies the existence of the soul, 151; Gotama is gone, Buddha remains, 247; Buddha not Gotama, 160; Gotama the samana, 246; Gotama Siddhattha, 110, 165, 253.

Gotamī, name of any woman belonging to the Gotama family. Kisā Gotamī, 16, 209, 210, 211.

Hīnayā'na, *skt.*, the small vehicle, viz., of salvation. A name invented by Northern Buddhists, in contradistinction to Mahāyāna, to designate the spirit of Southern Buddhism. The term is not used among Southern Buddhists.—Pp. ix—x.

Hira'ññavatī, *p.*, Hiran'yavatī, *skt.*, a river.—241.

I'ddhi, *p.*, Ri'ddhi, *skt.*, defined by Eitel as "the dominion of spirit over matter." It is the adjusting power to one's purpose and the adaptation to conditions. In popular belief it implies exemption from the law of gravitation and the power of assuming any shape at will. (See Iddhipāda.)

Iddhipā'da, *p.*, Riddhipā'da, *skt.*, the mode of attaining the power of mind over matter, four steps being needed: (1) the will to acquire it, (2) the necessary exertion, (3) the indispensable preparation of the heart, and (4) a diligent investigation of the truth.—177.

Indra, one of the principal Brahman gods.—141, 198.

Indriyā'ni or panc'-indriyāni, the five organs of the spiritual sense. (See Balāni.)

I'si, *p.*, Ri'shi, *skt.*, a prophet or seer, an inspired poet, a hermit having acquired wisdom in saintly retirement, a recluse or anchorite.

Iś'vara, *skt.*, Ī'ssara, *p.*, (lit. independent existence) Lord, Creator, personal God, a title given to Shiva and other great deities. In Buddhistic scriptures as well as in Brahman the *skt.* Iśvara (not the *p.* Issara) means always a transcendent or extramundane God, a personal God, a deity distinct from, and independent of nature, who is supposed to have created the world out of nothing.—72, 73.

Jain, modernised form of *skt.* Jaina; an adherent of the Jain-sect which reveres Vardhamāna (Nātaputta) as Buddha. (See *Jainism.*)—48.

Jainism, a sect, founded by Vardhamāna, older than Buddhism and still extant in India. It is in many respects similar to Buddhism. Buddha's main objection to the Jains was the habit of their ascetics of going naked. The Jains lay great stress upon ascetic exercises and self-mortification which the Buddhists declare to be injurious.

Ja'mbu, *p.* and *skt.*, a tree.—19, 35.

Jambū'nada, *p.*, Jāmbū'nada, *skt.*, a town of unknown site. (Also the name of a mountain and of a lake.)—202.

Ja'tila, *p.*, "wearing matted hair." The Jatilas were Brahman ascetics. Buddha converted a tribe of them, and Kassapa, their chief, became one of his most prominent disciples.—62, 63, 64, 65.

Je'ta, the heir apparent to the kingdom of Sāvatthī.—76.

Je'tavana, a vihāra.—76, 77, 81, 168, 191, 195, 208, 215.

Jhā'na, *p.*, Dhyā'na, *skt.*, intuition, beatic vision, ecstasy, rapture, the result of samādhi. Buddha did not recommend trances as means of religious devotion, urging that deliverance can be obtained only by the recognition of the four noble truths and walking on the noble eightfold path, but he did not disturb those who took delight in ecstasies and beatific visions. Buddha's interpretation of the Dhyāna is not losing consciousness but a self-possessed and purposive eradication of egotism. There are four Dhyānas, the first being a state of joy and gladness born of seclusion full of investigation and reflexion; the second one, born of deep tranquillity without reflexion or investigation, the third one brings the destruction of passion, while the fourth one consists in pure equanimity, making an end of sorrow. [See Rhys Davids's B. pp. 175—176.] In the Fo-Sho-hing-tsang-king, the Dhyāna is mentioned twice only: first, III, 12, vv. 960—978, where Ārāda sets forth the doctrine of the four Dhyānas which is not approved of by Buddha, and secondly, at Buddha's death; when his mind is said to have passed through all the Dhyānas.—176, 249.

Ji'na, *p.* and *skt.*, the Conqueror, an honorary title of Buddha. The Jains use the term with preference as an appellative of Vardhamāna whom they revere as their Buddha.—48.

Ji'vaka, *p.* and *skt.*, physician to king Bimbisāra. According to tradition he was the son of king Bimbisāra and the courtesan Salavatī. We read in Mahāvagga VIII that after his birth he was exposed but saved; then he became a most famous physician and cured Buddha of a troublesome disease contracted by wearing cast off rags. He was an ardent disciple of Buddha and prevailed upon him to allow the Bhikkhus to wear lay robes.—89, 90, 91.

Jo'tikkha, *p.*, name of a householder, son of Subhadda.—119.

Kālā'ma, *p.* and *skt.*, (see Alāra).

Ka'nthaka, prince Siddhattha's horse.—25.

Kapilava'tthu, *p.*, Kapilava'stu, *skt.*, the capital of the Sakyas, the birthplace of Buddha.—7, 13, 77, 82, 86, 87.

Ka'rma, anglicised form of *skt.* stem-form *ka'rman* (nom. s. *karma*), the *p.* of which is *ka'mmam*. Action, work, the law of action, retribution, results of deeds previously done and the destiny resulting therefrom. Eitel defines karma as "that moral kernel [of any being] which alone survives death and continues in transmigration." Karma is a well-defined and scientifically exact term. Professor Huxley says, "In the theory of evolution, the tendency of a germ to develop according to a certain specific type, e. g., of the kidney bean seed to grow into a plant having all the characters of *Phaseolus vulgaris* is its 'karma.' It is 'the last inheritor and the last result' of all the conditions that have affected a line of ancestry which goes back for many millions of years to the time when life first appeared on earth." We read in the Anguttara Nikāya, Pancaka Nipāta: "My action (karma) is my possession, my action is my inheritance, my action is the womb which bears me, my action is the race to which I am akin [as the kidney-bean to its species], my action is my refuge." [See the article "Karma and Nirvāna" in *Buddhism and Its Christian Critics*, p. 131 ff.]—29, 31, 32, 33, 86, 110, 115, 117, 118, 157, 172, 223, 225, 240.

Kā'sī, *p.*, Kā'sī, *skt.*, the old and holy name of Benares.—104 et seq., 192.

Ka'ssapa, *p.*, Kā'syapa, *skt.* (the etymology "He who swallowed fire," is now rejected), a name of three brothers, chiefs of the Jatilas, called after their residences, Uruvelā, Nadī, and Gayā. The name Kassapa applies mainly to Kāssapa of Uruvelā, one of the great pillars of the Buddhistic brotherhood, who took at once, after his conversion, a most prominent rank among Buddha's disciples. [Kassapa of Uruvelā is frequently identified with Mahā-Kassapa, the same who was president of the council at Rājagaha, but H. Dharmapala states, on the authority of the Anguttara Nikāya, that the two were altogether different persons.]—62–65, 119, 120, 163, 164, 254.

Kha'ndha, *p.*, Ska'ndha, *skt.*, elements; attributes of being, which are form, sensation, perception, discrimination, and consciousness.—30.

Kile'sa, *p.*, Kle'sa, *skt.*, error.

Ki'sā Go'tamī, *p.*, Kri'shā Gau'tamī, *skt.*, the slim or thin Gotamī. Name (1) of a cousin of Buddha, mentioned in Chap. VI, p. 16, (2) of the heroine in the parable of the mustard seed.—209, 210, 211.

Ko'lī, a little kingdom in the neighborhood of Kapilavatthu, the home of Yasodharā.—13.

Kond'añña, *p.*, Kaundi'nya, *skt.*, name of Buddha's first disciple, afterwards called Ājñā'ta Kaundi'nya in *skt.* and Aññā'ta Konda'ñña in *p.*—55, 56.

Ko'sala, *p.* and *skt.*, name of a country.—75, 76, 77, 94, 104, 105, 139.

Kosa'mbī, *p.*, Kauśā'mbī, *skt.*, a city.—100, 103, 187.

Kusinā'rā, *p.*, Kuśina'gara, *skt.*, a town.—238, 239, 241, 249, 250.

Kūtada'nta, *p.* and *skt.*, a Brahman chief in the village Dānamatī, also called Khānumat; is mentioned in Sp. Hardy's *M. B.*, p. 289 and in *S. B. E.*, Vol. XIX., p. 242 [Fo, v. 1682].—152—160. Cf. Rhys Davids's *Dialogues*, pp. 173—179.

Li'cchavi, *p.* and *skt.*, the name of a princely family.—228, 231.

Lu'mbinī, *skt.*, a grove named after a princess, its owner.—8.

Ma'gadha, *p.* and *skt.*, name of a country.—65, 68, 70, 71, 90, 98, 111, 219, 223, 224.

Ma'gga, *p.*, Mā'rga, *skt.*, path; especially used in the Pāli phrase "Ariyo atthangiko maggo," the noble eightfold path, which consists of: right views, high aims, right speech, upright conduct, a harmless livelihood, perseverance in well-doing, intellectual activity, and earnest thought. [See *S. B. E.*, Vol. XI, pp. 63 and 147.]

Mahārā'ja, the great king.—78.

Mahāse'tu, the great bridge. A name invented by the author of the present book to designate the importance of Christianity compared to the Hīnayāna and Mahāyāna of Buddhism.—ix, x.

Mahāyā'na, the great vehicle, viz., of salvation. Name of the Northern conception of Buddhism, comparing religion to a great ship in which men can cross the stream of Samsāra to reach the shore of Nirvāna.—ix, x.

Ma'lla, *p.* and *skt.*, name of a tribe.—239, 241, 245, 246, 249, 250, 251.

Manasā'kata, *p.*, Manasā'krita, *skt.*, a village in Kosala.—139, 140, 142.

Mandā'ra, *p.* and *skt.*, a flower of great beauty.—9.

Mā'ra, *p.* and *skt.*, the Evil One, the tempter, the destroyer, the god of lust, sin, and death.—5, 9, 25, 34, 36, 39, 42, 43, 44, 79, 116, 117, 130, 131, 133, 172, 173, 205, 235.

Māra's daughters are always three in number but their names are variously given as Tanhā, Arati, Rati (Dh. 164), and Tanhā, Arati, Ragā (Ab. 44 etc.).—36, 258.

Mā'tali, *p.* and *skt.*, name of a demon in the retinue of Yama.—198.

Māta'nga, *p.* and *skt.*, literally, of low birth; the Mātanga caste comprises mongrels of the lowest with higher castes.—196, 197.

Mā'thurā, *p.* and *skt.*, name of a place.—200.

Mā'yā, *p.* and *skt.*, Buddha's mother. (See Māyā-devī.) The term "veil of Māyā," viz., the illusion of self, popularly known through Schopenhauer, does not refer to Buddha's mother, but to the Vedāntic conception of māyā. The word means "charm, magic enhancement."—7, 91. The similarity of sound in the names Māyā and Maria is curious.

Māyā-de'vī, also called Mahā-Māyā, or simply Māyā, *p.* and *skt.*, the wife of Suddhodana and mother of Buddha. She died in childbed, and Buddha ascends to heaven to preach to her the good law and the gospel of salvation.—7, 91.

Mette'yya, *p.*, Maitre'ya, *skt.*, etymology, "full of kindness"; the name of the Buddha to come.—241, 245.

Moggallā'na, *p.*, Maudgalyā'yana, *skt.*, one of the most prominent disciples of Buddha, a friend of Sāriputta.—70, 71, 85.

Mu'ni, *skt.* and *p.*, a thinker, a sage; especially a religious thinker. Sakyamu'ni, the sage of the Sakyas, is Buddha.—26, 62, 103, 170, 171, 172.

Nadī'-Ka'ssapa, *p.*, Nadī'-Kā'śyapa, *skt.*, brother of the great Kassapa of Uruvelā.—64.

Nā'dika, *p.* and *skt.*, name of a village.—225.

Nā'ga, *p.* and *skt.*, literally serpent. The serpent being regarded as a superior being, the word denotes a special kind of spiritual beings; a sage, a man of spiritual insight; any superior personality. Nāga kings, 9.

Nalagiri, name of an elephant.—111.

Nāla'ndā, *p.* and *skt.*, a village near Rājagaha.—221, 223.

Nanda, *p.*, Siddhattha's halfbrother, son of Pajāpatī.—86, 88.

Na'ndā, daughter of a chief of shepherds, also called Sujātā.—35.

Nātapu'tta, *Jain Prakrit*, Jñātapu'tra, *skt.*, the son of Jñāta. Patronym of Vardhamāna, the founder of Jainism.—145, 146.

Nera'ñjarā, *p.*, Naira'ñjanā, *skt.*, name of a river identified by some with the Nilajan, by others with the Phalgu.—35, 43, 235.

Nidā'na, *p.* and *skt.*, cause. The twelve nidānas, forming the chain of causation which brings about the misery in the world. [See Oldenberg, *Buddha*, Engl. tr., pp 224—252].—40.

Nigga'ntha, *p.*, Nirgra'ntha, *skt.*, literally "liberated from bonds"; a name adopted by the adherents of the Jaina sect.—145, 146; Nigganthas, give also to the, 150.

Nigro'dha, *p.*, Nyagro'dha, *skt.*, a tree, *ficus indica* well known for its air roots.—43, 235.

Nirmā'na Kā'ya, *skt.*, the body of transformation.—254.

Nirvā'na, *skt.*, Nibbā'na, *p.*, extinction, viz., the extinction of self; according to the Hīnayāna it is defined as "extinction of illusion," according to the Mayāyāna as "attainment of truth." Nirvāna means, according to the latter, enlightenment, the state of mind in which upādāna, kilesa, and tanhā are extinct, the happy condition of enlightenment, peace of mind, bliss, the glory of righteousness in this life and beyond, the eternal rest of Buddha after death. Buddha himself has refused to decide the problem whether or not Nirvāna is a final extinction of personality. When questioned, he indicated by his silence that the solution is not one of those subjects a knowledge of which is indispensable for salvation.—2, 4, 6, 16, 20, 41, 43, 44, 48, 50, 51, 55, 64, 65, 67, 70, 71, 74, 76, 81, 83, 91, 97, 118, 122, 123, 130, 143, 153, 154, 160, 164, 170, 171, 188, 195, 235, 236, 237, 245, 249, 250, 252, 253; where is Nirvāna? 154; Nirvāna not a locality, 154; the city of Nirvāna, 130; the harvest, Nirvāna, 195; he one aim, Nirvāna, 164; Samsāra and Nirvāna, 2, 6, 225.

Okkā'ka, *p.*, Ikshvā'ku, *skt.*, the name of a mythological family from which the chiefs of the Sakyas claim descent.—7.

Pabba'jjā, *p.*, pravra'jyā, *skt.*, the act of leaving the world for receiving admittance to the Order. The first step of the Buddhist ordination. (See Upasa'mpadā.)

Pajā'patī, *p.*, Prajā'patī or Mahā-Prajā'patī, *skt.*, the sister of Māyā-devī, second wife of Suddhodana, aunt and fostermother of Buddha. She is also called by her husband's family name Gotamī (feminine form of Gotama).—10, 13, 86, 92, 93, 103.

Pajjo'ta, *p.*, Pradyo'ta, *skt.*, name of a king of Ujjenī.—90, 91.

(Pakati, *p.*) Pra'kriti, *skt.*, name of a girl of low caste.—196, 197.

Paramitā', *p.* and *skt.*, perfection, or virtue. The six pāramitās are: almsgiving, morality, patience, zeal or energy, meditation, and wisdom.

Paribbā'jaka, *p.*, Parlvrā'jaka, *skt.*, a sect belonging to the Tîrthika school.—98.

Pase'nadi, *p.*, (Prase'najit, *skt.*, also called Pasenit) king of Kosala, residing at Sāvatthī.—75, 77.

Pātalipu'tra, *skt.*, Pātalipu'tta, *p.*, also called Pātaligāma, a city on the Ganges north of Rājagaha and belonging to the kingdom of Magadha, the frontier station against the Vriji (Vajji), the present Patna. Buddha is reported to have predicted the future greatness of the place, which is an important passage for determining the time in which the account of Buddha's sojourn in Pātaliputra was written. It is still uncertain, however, when Patna became the important centre which it is now. It was the capital of the country when Megasthenes, the ambassador of Seleucus Nicator, at the end of the third century B. C., visited India. He gave in his book a detailed description of the city.—223, 224; Pātaliputra, three dangers hang over, 224.

Pātimo'kkha, *p.*, Pratimo'ksha, *skt.*, (usually spelt Prātimoksha in Buddhistic Sanskrit,) literally "disburdenment." It is the Buddhist confession. Rhys Davids says "that it almost certainly dates from the fifth century B. C. Since that time—during a period that is of nearly two thousand and three hundred years—it has been regularly repeated, twice in each month, in formal meetings of the stricter members of the Order. It occupies, therefore, a unique position in the literary history of the world; and no rules for moral conduct have been for so long a time as these in constant practical use, except only those laid down in the Old Testament and in the works of Confucius" (p. 163).—98, 99.

Pā'vā, *p.* and *skt.*, a village where Buddha took his last meal.—237, 239.

Pokkharasā'ti, *p.*, Paushkarasā'ti, *skt.*, a Brahman philosopher.—139.

Pubbārā'ma, *p.*, Pūrvārā'ma, *skt.*, the Eastern garden.—94.

Pu'kkusa, *p.*, Pu'kkasha or Pu'kkasa, *skt.*, name of a low caste.—239.

Puññ'aji, *p.*, Pu'nyajit, *skt.*, a friend of Yasa.—61.

Ragā, pleasure, desire or lust; a synonym of *rati*. The name of one of Māra's daughters, *q. v.*—36.

Rā'hula, *p.* and *skt.*, the son of Buddha, was admitted to the fraternity while still a boy. Buddha gave him a lesson in truthfulness [see Chapter LVI]. He is always named among the prominent disciples of Buddha and is revered as the patron saint of novices.—14, 85, 86, 87, 88, 165, 166, 167.

Rainy season (see Vassa).—58, 232.

Rā'jā, *p.* and *skt.*, nominative form of the stem rājan, a king (in composition rāja).

Rājaga'ha, *p.*, Rājagri'ha, *skt.*, the capital of Magadha and residence of king Bimbisāra.—26, 65, 69, 71, 72, 80, 91, 98, 110, 119, 144, 219, 220, 255.

Ra'tana, *p.*, ra'tna, *skt.*, "jewel."

Rati, love, liking; a synonym of *ragā*. The name of one of Māra's daughters, *q. v.*—36.

Saha'mpati, occurs only in the phrase "Brahmā Sahampati," a name frequently used in Buddhist scriptures the meaning of which is obscure.

Burnouf renders it *Seigneur des êtres patients*; Eitel, Lord of the inhabitable parts of all universes; H. Kern [in *S. B.*, XXI, p. 5] maintains that it is synonymous with Sikhin, which is a common term for Agni.

Sa'kka, *p.*, Sa'kra, *skt.*, Lord; a cognomen of Indra.—69.

Sa'kya, *p.*, Śā'kya, *skt.*, the name of a royal race in the northern frontiers of Magadha.—7, 14, 26.

Sakyamu'ni, *p.*, Śākyamu'ni, *skt.*, the Sākya sage; a cognomen of Buddha.—27, 28, 33, 34, 36, 62, 63, 64, 65, 71, 83, 120, 121, 142, 144, 178, 196, 198, 210, 254.

Sā'la, *p.*, Śā'la, *skt.*, a tree, *vatica robusta*; sāla-grove, 241, 245; sāla-trees, 241.

Samā'dhi, *p.* and *skt.*, trance, abstraction, self-control. Rhys Davids says (*B.* p. 177): "Buddhism has not been able to escape from the natural results of the wonder with which abnormal nervous states have always been regarded during the infancy of science. . . . But it must be added, to its credit, that the most ancient Buddhism despises dreams and visions; and that the doctrine of Samādhi is of small practical importance compared with the doctrine of the noble eightfold Path." Eitel says (*Handbook*, p. 140): "The term Samādhi is sometimes used ethically, when it designates moral self-deliverance from passion and vice."

Sa'mana, *p.*, Śrā'mana, *skt.*, an ascetic; one who lives under the vow, 26, 36, 42, 59, 70, 87, 93, 119, 152, 165, 188, 189, 194, 195, 207, 223; the Samana Gotama, 151, the vision of a samana, 20.

Sambho'ga-Kā'ya, *skt.*, the body of Bliss.— 254.

Sammappadhā'na, *p.*, Samyakpradhā'na, *skt.*, right effort, exertion, struggle. There are four great efforts to overcome sin, which are: (1) Mastery over the passions so as to prevent bad qualities from rising; (2) suppression of sinful thoughts to put away bad qualities which have arisen; (3) meditation on the seven kinds of wisdom (Bojjhaṅga) in order to produce goodness not previously existing, and (4) fixed attention or the exertion of preventing the mind from wandering, so as to increase the goodness which exists. [See the Mahāpadhāna-Sutta in the *Dīgha-Nikāya*. Compare *B. B. St.*, p. 89, and Rh. Davids's *Buddhism*, pp. 172—173.]

Samsā'ra, *p.* and *skt.*, the ocean of birth and death, transiency, worldliness, the restlessness of a worldly life, the agitation of selfishness, the vanity fair of life.—2, 5, 172, 225.

Sa'ngha, *p.* and *skt.*, the brotherhood of Buddha's disciples, the Buddhist church. An assembly of at least four has the power to hear confession, to grant absolution, to admit persons to the priesthood, etc. The sangha forms the third constituent of the Tiratana or three jewels in which refuge is taken (the *S. B. of the E.* spell Sa*m*gha).—56, 61, 64, 68, 69, 71, 86, 92, 95, 96, 98, 99, 100, 102, 103, 104, 108, 145, 150, 168, 178, 250, 253, 254; sangha may be expected to prosper, 221.

Sa'ñjaya, *p.* and *skt.*, a wandering ascetic and chief of that sect to which Sāriputta and Moggallāna belonged before their conversion.—70.

Sankhā'ra, *p.*, Samskā'ra, *skt.*, confection, conformation, disposition. It is the formative element in the karma as it has taken shape in bodily existence.—155, 157, 158.

Sāripu'tta, *p.*, Sāripu'tra, *skt.*, one of the principal disciples of Buddha; the Buddhistic St. Peter.—70, 71, 76, 77, 85, 87, 103, 112, 120, 212, 213, 222; Sāriputta's faith, 213, 221.

Sā'vaka, *p.*, Srā'vaka, *skt.*, he who has heard the voice (viz. of Buddha), a pupil, a beginner. The name is used to designate (1) all personal disciples of Buddha, the foremost among whom are called Mahā-sā-vakas, and (2) an elementary degree of saintship. A sāvaka is he who is superficial yet in practice and comprehension, being compared to a hare crossing the stream of Samsāra by swimming on the surface. [See Eitel *Handbook*, p. 157.]—172, 173, 174.

Sati-patthā'na, *p.*, Smrityupasthā'na, *skt.*, meditation; explained as "fixing the attention." The four objects of earnest meditation are: (1) the impurity of the body, (2) the evils arising from sensation, (3) ideas or the impermanence of existence, and (4) reason and character, or the permanency of the dharma. (Rh. D. B., p. 172.) The term is different from "bhāvanā," although translated by the same English word. (*S. B. of the E.* XI, p. 62.—211).

Sāva'tthi, *p.*, Srāva'stī, *skt.*, capital of Northern Kosala. It has been identified by General Cunningham with the ruins of Sāhet-Māhet in Oudh and was situated on the river Rapti, northwest of Magadha.— 75, 77, 81, 94, 96, 97, 103, 188, 195, 212, 215.

Se'niya, *p.*, Sai'nya, *skt.*, military, warlike, an honorary title given to Bimbisāra the king of Magadha.—65, 69, 90, 98.

Siddha'ttha, *p.*, Siddhā'rtha, *skt.*, Buddha's proper name. Etymology, "He who has reached his goal."—10—26, 48, 82—86, 88, 110, 165.

Sigā'la, *p.*, Srigā'la, *skt.*, literally, "jackal"; name of a Brahman converted by Buddha.—144, 145.

Si'mha, *skt.*, Sī'ha, *p.*, literally, "lion." Name of a general, an adherent of the Niggantha sect, converted by Buddha, 145—151; Simha, a soldier, 147; Simha's question concerning annihilation, 146.

So'ma, *p.* and *skt.*, derived from the root *su*, to press in a winepress; not as, according to Eitel, Chinese scholars propose from "exhilarate (*su*) and mind (*mana*)." Name of a plant and of its juice, which is intoxicating and is used at Brahmanical festivals; the Soma drink is identified with the moon and personified as a deity.—141.

Subā'hu, *p*. and *skt*., a friend of Yasa.—61.

Subha'dda, *p*., Subha'dra, *skt*., name of a samana. Subha'dda, Buddha's last convert, must not be confounded with another man of the same name who caused dissension soon after Buddha's death.—119, 246, 247.

Suddho'dana, *p*., Śuddho'dana, *skt*., Buddha's father. The word means "possessing pure rice." Buddhists always represent him as a king, but Oldenberg declares that this does not appear in the oldest records, and speaks of him as "a great and wealthy land-owner." (See his *Buddha*, English version, pp. 99 and 416—417).—7, 8, 13, 14, 25, 82, 83, 85, 91.

Su'mana, *p*. and *skt*., name of a householder.—189, 190.

Suprabuddha, father of Devadatta.—110.

Su'tta, *p*., Sū'tra, *skt*., literally" thread," any essay, or guide of a religious character.

Tanhā, *p*., Tr'ishnā, *skt*., thirst; the word denotes generally all intense desire, cleaving and clinging with passion. The name of one of Māra's daughters, *q. v.*—36, 138.

Tapu'ssa, *p*. and *skt*., a merchant.—42.

Tāru'kkha, *p*., Tāru'kshya, *skt*., name of a Brahman philosopher.—139.

Tathā'gata, *p*. and *skt*., generally explained as "the Perfect One." The highest attribute of Buddha, 21, 32, 34, 44, 49, 50, 55, 58, 59, 63, 65, 68, 69, 71, 73, 74, 80, 82, 85, 86, 87, 90, 92, 93, 95, 96, 111, 121, 124, 127, 128, 129, 130, 138, 142, 143, 144, 147, 148, 150, 151, 152, 154, 156, 157, 158, 163, 164, 165, 171, 172, 174, 175, 176, 177, 181, 188, 195, 197, 198, 199, 201, 202, 213, 214, 217, 225, 233, 234, 235, 236, 237, 239, 240, 242, 246, 247, 248, 249, 253; robe of the Tathāgata, 127; soldiers of the Tathāgata, 130; the law the body of the Tathagata, 253; Tathāgatas are only preachers, 131.

Tiratana, *p*., Trira'tna, *skt*., the three jewels or the holy trinity of the Buddha, the Dharma, and the Sangha, a doctrine peculiar to Northern Buddhism. (See Trikāya.)

Ti'tthiya,*p*., Tī'rthika, *skt*., a religious school of India in Buddha's time.—98.

Trikā'ya, the three bodies or personalities of Buddha, the Dharmakāya, the Sambhoga-kāya, and the Nirmāna-kāya.—254.

Uddaka, *p*., U'draka, *skt*., a Brahman philosopher.—29, 31.

Ujje'nī, *p*., Ujja'yinī, *skt*., name of a city.—90.

Upādā'na, *p.* and *skt.*, desire, a grasping state of mind. One of the nidānas.

(Upagutta, *p.*), Upagu'pta, *skt.*, name of a Buddhist monk.—200, 201.

U'paka, *p.* and *skt.*, name of a man, a Jain, who met Buddha, but was
not converted by him.—47, 48.

Upā'li, *p.* and *skt.*, a prominent disciple of Buddha. Before his conversion
he was, according to the Buddhistic tradition, court-barber to the king
of the Sakyas.—86, 104, 252.

Upasa'mpadā, *p.* and *skt.*, admittance to the Buddhist brotherhood, ordination. (See Pabbajjā.)

Upava'ttana, *p.*, Upava'rtana, *skt.*, a grove in Kusinagara. The word
means a rambling-place, a gymnasium.—241, 245.

Upo'satha, *p.*, Upava'satha, *skt.*, the Buddhist sabbath. Rhys Davids says
(pp. 140—141): "The Uposatha days are the four days in the lunar
month when the moon is full, or new, or half way between the two.
It is the fourteenth day from the new moon (in short months) and
the fifteenth day from the full moon (in the long months), and the
eighth day from each of these. The corresponding Sanskrit word is
Upavasatha, the fast-day previous to the offering of the intoxicating
sôma, connected with the worship of the moon. Instead of worshipping the moon, the Buddhists were to keep the fast-day by special
observance of the moral precepts; one of many instances in which
Gotama spiritualised existing words and customs."—98, 99, 101, 102;
observe the Uposatha or Sabbath, 99.

Uruve'lā, *p.*, Urubi'lvā, *skt.*, a place south of Patna on the banks of the
Neranjarā river, now Buddha Gayā. The residence of Kassapa, the
chief of the Jatilas.—34, 62, 64, 65, 206.

Va'jji, *p.*, Vri'ji, *skt.*, name of a people living in the neighborhood of
Magadha, 120, 219, 220; assemblies of the Vajji, 220.

Va'rana, *p.* and *skt.*, a tree; *Crataeva Roxburghii.*—184, 185.

Vardhamā'na, *skt.*, Vaddhamā'na, *Jaina Prākrit*, proper name of the founder
of Jainism. Also called Jñātapu'tra in *skt.* and Nātapu'tta in *Jaina
Prākrit.*

Va'runa, *p.* and *skt.*, a Brahman deity, the god of heaven and regent of
the sea; one of the guardians of the world.—141.

Vāsavada'ttā, *p.* and *skt.*, a courtesan of Mathurā.—200, 201, 202.

Vāse'ttha, *p.*, Vāsi'shtha, *skt.*, name of a Brahman.—139, 142.

Va'ssa, *p.*, Va'rsha, *skt.*, rain, rainy season. During the rainy season of
Northern India, which falls in the months from June to October, the
samanas could not wander about, but had to stay in one place. It

was the time in which the disciples gathered round their master, listening to his instructions. Thus it became the festive time of the year. In Ceylon, where these same months are the fairest season of the year, Buddhists come together and live in temporary huts, holding religious meetings in the open air, reading the Pitakas and enjoying the Jātakas, legends, and parables of Buddhism. [See Rhys Davids's *B.*, p. 57.]

Vassakāra, *p.*, Varshakā′ra, *skt.*, lit. "rain-maker." Name of a Brahman, the prime minister of the king of Magadha.—219, 220.

Ve′das, 50, 140, 141, 187; I know all the Vedas, 159.

Veluva′na, *p.*, Veṇuva′na, *skt.*, a bamboo-grove at Rājagaha, 70, 80; Veluvana vihāra, 110.

Vesā′lī, *p.*, Vaiśā′lī, *skt.*, a great city of India, north of Patna.—150, 220, 227, 228, 232, 236.

Vihā′ra, *p.* and *skt.*, residence of Buddhist monks or priests; a Buddhist convent or monastery; a Buddhist temple.—67, 75, 76, 95, 99, 110, 111, 165, 213, 214, 242.

Vi′mala, *p.* and *skt.* (etym., the spotless), name of a friend of Yasa.—61.

Vi′naya, 57.

Visā′khā, *p.*, Viśā′khā, *skt.*, a wealthy matron of Sāvatthi, one of Buddha's most distinguished woman lay-disciples. Says Oldenberg, *Buddha*, English translation, p. 167: "Every one invites Visākhā to sacrificial ceremonies and banquets, and has the dishes offered to her first; a guest like her brings luck to the house."—94, 95, 96, 97; eight boons of Visākhā, 95; gladness of Visākhā, 97.

Ya′ma, *p.* and *skt.*, also called Yama-rā′ja, death, the god of death.—206, 207.

Ya′sa, *p.*, Ya′śas, *skt.*, the noble youth of Benares, son of a wealthy man and one of Buddha's earliest converts.—58—61.

Yaso′dharā, *p.*, Ya′śodharā, *skt.*, wife of Prince Gotama Siddhattha before he became Buddha. She became one of the first of Buddhist nuns. [See Jātaka, 87—90; Commentary on Dhammapada, vv. 168, 169: Bigandet, 156—168; Spence Hardy's *Manual*, 198—204; Beal, pp. 360—364: *B. Birth Stories*, 127.]—13, 84—87, 92, 110, 165.

INDEX.

Novices, precepts for the, 124.
Now is the time to seek religion, 21.
Now my lot to help, 214.

Obedience to the laws of righteousness, 152.
Obey the truth, let us, 254.
Object and senses, contact of, 66.
Observe the Uposatha or Sabbath, 98.
Ocean, 226; rivers in the ocean, 214; my doctrine is like the great ocean, 177.
Offering, four kinds of, 186.
Omens abolished, 173.
Omens of Buddhahood, 10.
One hemp-grain each day, 34.
One in essence, 259.
One, the truth is but, 138, 164, 257.
One thing that is needed, the, 153.
Oneself, purity and impurity belong to, 131.
Order, rules for the, 233.
Order, the, (sangha) the sowing-ground of merit, 226.
Ordination, 58, 59, 88, [see also Pabbajjā and Upasampadā in the Glossary].
Others art thou thyself, 157.
Others, the faults of, 134, 137.
Our water is all gone, 193.
Outcast, the, 195; by deeds one becomes an outcast, 196; who is an outcast? 195.
Outcome of evil, pain is the, 133.
Outcome of good, happines is the, 133.
Outwitted, 184.
Overcome anger by love, 137.

Overcome evil by good, 137.
Overcome grief, 234.
Ox led to slaughter, 211.

Pain is the outcome of evil, 133.
Parable, 165, 179 &c.
Parable of the hungry dog, 198.
Paradise in the West, the, 173; living in paradise, 207; the paradise of the pure land, 173.
Parties, listen to both, 103.
Party in search of a thief, a, 206.
Pass away, about to, 242; people pass away, 212; the truth will never pass away, 152.
Passed away according to his deeds, 194.
Passion, rain and, 132.
Past, thou wilt reap the harvest sown in the, 159.
Path of transmigration, weary, 237; sign of the right, 143; the eight-fold, 41; the immortal path, 76; the noble eightfold path, 143, 237, 258; mortification not the path, 35; walk in the noble path, 160; a pathless jungle, 142; are all paths saving? 139. [See also Maggo in the Glossary.]
Peace on earth, 9.
Peacemaker, the, 197.
People dissatisfied, the, 71; people pass away, 212; wise people falter not, 133; wise people fashion themselves, 133.
Perception of truth, the refreshing drink, 118.
Perishable, the *I*, 66.
Personalities of Buddha, the three, 232.
Pestilence, 121.

Physician, 20, 181, 210; the best physician, 169; without beholding the physician, 246.

Pit, treasure laid up in a deep, 171.

Pity me not, 28.

Plantain-tree, 39.

Pleasure, he who lives for, 133; let a man take pleasure in the dharma, 171.

Pleasures destroy the foolish, 134; pleasures of self in heaven, 153; why do we give up the pleasures of the world, 172; religious wisdom lifts above pleasures, 209.

Potter, 163; potter, vessels made by the, 211.

Power, incantations have no, 33; magic power, 119.

Powerful elephant, 166.

Powerful king, 130.

Powers, moral, 97.

Practise the truth, 160.

Praise of all the Buddhas, the, 258.

Prayers, 141; prayers vain repetitions, 33.

Preach the doctrine, glorious in the beginning, middle, and end, 58; preach to all beings, 129.

Preacher's mission, the, 127; the preacher's sole aim, 128.

Preachers, Tathāgatas are only, 131.

Precepts, 247; precepts for the novices, 124; ten precepts, 124. walk according to the precepts, 241.

Precious crown jewel, 130.

Precious jewel, a, 252.

Priceless, the lives of men are, 198.

Priest and layman alike, 74.

Prince, test of the, 13.

Problem of the soul, the, 29.

Profitless, mortification, 49.

Prohibitions, 120.

Promoted him higher, he, 182.

Propound the truth, 127.

Prosper, sangha may be expected to 221.

Prospered, bhikkhus, 120.

Punishment of the criminal, 147.

Punishment, the fruit of the criminal's act, 148.

Puppets on a string, 123.

Pure land, the paradise of the, 173.

Purity and impurity belong to oneself, 131.

Purpose of being, the, 255.

Purpose, speak to the, 126.

Qualities, cloud of good, 129; eight wonderful qualities, 178.

Quality, the thing and its, 30.

Quarrels, 100.

Quarters, the four, 143; the six quarters, 144.

Question concerning annihilation, 145.

Questioned, the sages, 13.

Questions of the deva, 168.

Rabbit rescued from the serpent, 27.

Rags, cast-off, 89, 91, 110.

Rāhula, lessons given to, 165.

Rain and passion, 132.

Rain fell, 94.

Rain, good works are, 195.

Rare in the world, 228.

Reap the harvest sown in the past, thou wilt, 159.

Reap what we sow, we, 153, 200.

Reason, as the helpmate of self, 256.

Sacrifices, 33; sacrifices cannot save 159.

Sages questioned, the, 13.

Saint, a sinner can become a, 172.

Salvation alone in the truth 234; assured of final, 248; salvation the extinction of self, 4; work out your salvation, 237, 249.

Sameness and continuity, 157.

Sandy desert, a, 192.

Save, faith alone can, 213.

Saving paths? Are all paths, 139.

Saving power, incantations have no, 33.

Saviour of others, a, 163.

Saviour appeared, the, 256.

Saviour, truth the, 5.

Scepticism, 126.

Schism, the, 100.

Search of a thief, a party in, 206.

Season, flowers out of, 241.

Season, rainy, 58, 232.

Sect of Devadatta, 110.

Seed, faith is the, 195.

Seeing the highest religion, 138.

Seek thou the life that is of the mind, 153.

Self, 72; self an error, 67; self an illusion, 41, 67; self and the cause of troubles, 67; self and truth, 4, 41, 148; self begets selfishness, 5; cleaving to self, 158; complete surrender of self, 148; eradication of self, 147; self-extinction, 152; identity of self, 158; illusion of self, 67; pleasures of self in heaven, 153; self is change, 158; self is death, 153, 160; self-mortification, 89; my self has become the truth, 163; reason as the helpmate of self,

256; rebirth without the transmigration of self, 33, 153; sacrifice of self, 152; the conquest of self, 149; the extinction of self, salvation, 4; the idea of self, 242; self, the maker, 73; the nature of self, 65; self, the veil of Māyā, 6; truth and self, 153; truth guards him who guards his self, 132; thou clingest to self, 122; where is the identity of my self, 155; compounds lack a self, 158.

Selfhood, the cause of, found, 40.

Selfhood, thirst for existence and, 39.

Selfish is my grief, 210.

Selfishness, self begets, 5.

Selfishness, surrender, 67.

Sense, moral, 97.

Senses and object, contact of, 66.

Sentiency, truth vibrated through, 255.

Separation, combination subject to, 31.

Sermon on abuse, the, 167; the sermon on charity, 75; sermon on fire, 64.

Serpent, rabbit rescued from the, 27.

Seven kinds of wisdom, 97.

Sevenfold higher wisdom, 222.

Shaveling, 195.

Shedding of blood, 33.

Shine forth, let your light, 109.

Shines by night, the moon, 139.

Sick bhikkhu, the, 213.

Sickness fell upon him, 232, 237.

Sight, blind received, 8.

Sign of the right path, 143.

Signs forbidden, astrology and fore-

Supplications have no effect, 172.
Suprabuddha, 110.
Surrender, 148.
Surrender selfishness, 67.
Surrender to evil powers, no, 148.
Swear not, 126.
Sweet, wrong, appears, 133.
Swooned, the Blessed One, 35.
Sword, sorrow compared with, 19

Tailor, the greedy, 184.
Talents. [See Abhiññâ in the Glossary.]
Talk, foolish, 140.
Tastes not the flavor of the soup, a spoon, 191.
Teach the same truth, 258.
Teacher, the, 131; teacher of gods and men, 226; the teacher unknown, 177; we have no teacher more, 247.
Temporary, many laws are, 253.
Ten commandments, the, 126.
Ten great calamities, 215.
Ten precepts, 124.
Terms of the world, such are the, 211.
Test of the prince, 13.
That it be well grounded, 222.
There is mind, 151.
They knew me not, 178.
Thief, a party in search of a, 206.
Thinkers are bright, 139.
Thing and its quality, the, 30.
Things as they are, 67.
Thirst for existence and selfhood, 39.
Thirst, the extinction of, 138.
Thirsty, I am, 238; water for the thirsty, 1.
This is done by me, 132.

Thorn in the flesh, 138.
Thou art the Buddha, 150; thou canst not escape the fruit of evil actions, 159; thou clingest to self, 122; thou tearest down religion, 152; thou wilt reap what thou sowest, 159.
Thought, helmet of right, 93; the thought of I, 31.
Thoughtlessness the path of death, 132.
Thoughts continue, 154; made up of thoughts, 131, thoughts of love, 143; thoughts will endure, 132.
Three dangers hang over Pātaliputta, 224.
Three personalities of Buddha, the, 252.
Three vows, 56.
Three woes, the, 14.
Thyself, others art thou, 157.
Tidings, glad, 1; good tidings, 21.
Tie all souls together, bonds that, 259.
Time of grace, the, 183, 192.
Time to seek religion, now is the, 21.
Times, hard, teach a lesson, 122.
To-day, reform, 123.
Together, bonds that tie all souls, 259.
Traditions, revere the, 254.
Transiency, immortality in, 3.
Transmigration, eddies of, 166; rebirth without the transmigration of self, 33; weary path of transmigration, 237.
Transmission of the soul and the I, 32.
Treacherous, charms are, 202.

[Names and terms must be looked up in the Glossary, where references to pages of the present book are separated by a dash from the explanation.]

O·KORETZKY

REMARKS ON THE ILLUSTRATIONS
OF THE GOSPEL OF BUDDHA.

UPON the task of illustrating *The Gospel of Buddha,* I have spent three years, the first of which was entirely devoted to preparation. By the kind assistance of Dr. Hans Schnorr von Carolsfeld, Director of the Royal Court and State Library at Munich, I was enabled to make very extensive use of the treasures of this institution, and I am under great obligations to him for the courtesies extended to me. Above all I endeavored to obtain a solid foundation for my work by acquiring a clear conception of the personality of the Buddha from religious, historical and artistic standpoints and by familiarizing myself with all the Buddhist dogmas, symbols and religious observances.

Detailed studies of Indian costume, armor, decoration, architecture and the arrangement of dwellings and gardens, as well as the fauna and flora of the country, were likewise indispensable. Not only modern documents, explorers' reports and photographs of ancient ruins provided me with available material, but also some old Dutch works of the seventeenth century.

The two main sources of our knowledge of ancient Buddhist art will always remain the monuments of Gandhāra, and the cave dwellings of Buddhist monks in Ajantā and other places. The former bear witness to the extraordinary influence of Greek art on Buddhism; and the latter are rich in wonderful fresco paintings of the classical period of Buddhist art. A description of all the caves as well as a selection of the best mural paintings in colored pictures are to be found in Griffith's elegant work *The Paintings in the Buddhist Cave Temples of Ajanta*[1] and some reproductions from it have been made further accessible in Dr. Carus's *Portfolio of Buddhist Art*.[2] The two great expositions in Munich, "Japan and Eastern Asia in Art" and "Expositions of the Masterpieces of Mohammedan Art," 1910, were very instructive to me from the point of view of art history, containing invaluable material conveniently arranged from the great museums, royal treasures and private collections from London, Paris, Berlin, Vienna, St. Petersburg, Moscow, and Cairo. In the former the great wave of the marvelous Buddhist faith which had been flowing towards China for two millenniums and which had brought new life from China to Japan was evidenced in many rare pieces. Yet almost more fruitful for my purpose was the exposition of Mohammedan art. It displayed wonderful Persian and Indian book-making and lacquer work, tapestries, ceramics, fabrics, armor and metal work. To be sure these were exclusively of Mohammedan manufacture, but many large museums and institutions (native and foreign), collectors

---

[1] Two volumes, 1896, Published by order of the Secretary of State for India in Council.

[2] Chicago, Open Court Publishing Company.

During the time of printing "The Gospel of Buddha" the following valuable works on Indian art have come under my notice:

Ananda K. Coomaraswamy: The Arts and Crafts of India and Ceylon.

E. B. Havell: The Ideals of Indian Art; Indian Sculpture and Painting.

Dr. Curt Glaser: Die Kunst Ost-Asiens (Leipzig, Insel-Verlag).

and explorers had sent also chests of Buddhist works, which, not falling within its compass, had been excluded from the exhibition, but were placed at my disposal in the so-called Library Department reserved for students.

Indian art has been greatly neglected by archeologists and connoisseurs at the expense of the so-called classic style, and explorers seem to be more interested in the geographical and political conditions of the country, or even look down with contempt and lack of understanding on the early artistic monuments of India, although they have enriched our European middle ages. Thus there are great gaps in the history of Indian art which I was obliged to fill up for myself, and certainly a very different kind of study was needed to illustrate a Gospel of Buddha than for a pictorial construction of the life of a Plato or a Jesus.

Fräulein Emily von Kerckhoff, an artistic and highly cultured lady of Laren in Northern Holland, sailed on November 9, 1909, to join her family in Java where she remained for some time. Her journey occurring just at this time was of great help to me, for she complied with all my wishes in the most accommodating manner and filled up many gaps in my knowledge of India.

In Colombo she became acquainted with the Dias Bandaranaike and other refined Singhalese families, who were very friendly in answering my questions. Further she met Sister Sudham Machari of Upasikarama, Peradeniya Road, Kandy, a prominent Singhalese nun, who with the assistance of Lady Blake, the wife of a former governor, had founded the first modern Buddhist nunnery in Ceylon where she now lives as lady superior. She is well posted on Buddhism, for she has studied Pāli, Sanskrit, and Burmese for nine years in Burma, and has received ordination. Through her, Fräulein von Kerckhoff had an opportunity to visit the temple in Kandy where the strange relic of the "Sacred

Tooth of Buddha" is perserved, and on this occasion was able to obtain some leaves from the sacred Bodhi tree which I wished to possess. She also became acquainted in Kandy with Dr. Kobekaduwe Tikiri Banda, a Singhalese physician who belonged to a Buddhist family and is the son of a Kandian chief. He had studied in England for a long time and possesses a remarkable knowledge of the country and people of India and Ceylon, by which I thus had an opportunity to profit.

Fräulein von Kerckhoff gathered further material for my purposes in Gampola, a place in the mountains about an hour's ride from Kandy, on the occasion of a visit to the family of the district judge, Mr. De Livera, and by the acquaintance with Mr. J. B. Yatawara Rata-Mahatmaya, Governor of the District and a zealous Buddhist, who has translated into English part of the Jātakas (stories of the various rebirths of Buddha) in collaboration with the late Prof. Max Müller, of Oxford.

Later, in December, 1910, she sent me leaves from the Bodhi tree at Anuradhapura, the sacred city of the Buddhists, where there are ruins of ancient palaces and temples, and where stands that Bodhi tree which Mahinda, the first Buddhist apostle in Ceylon, is said to have planted from a branch of the sacred Bodhi tree in Buddhagaya under which Buddha attained enlightenment.

With regard to customs, habits and usages at princely courts I received information, though to be sure referring mainly to Java, through Prince Paku Alam, his uncle Prince Noto, his sisters and other relatives, all of whom talked Dutch fluently with Fräulein von Kerckhoff. She was also kind enough to send me all the interesting photographs she could find of famous Indian temples and ruins, views of native life, types and landscapes, pictures of the newly excavated temple ruins of Sarnath, where Buddha first preached after attaining enlightenment, and particularly also of the splendid temple of Boro-Budur. (She also went to Japan in search of traces of Buddhism for me).

By means of the Hagenbeck Indian ethnological exposition (Oct. 1911, in Munich) I was able to study types of the different Indian races and castes from nature, and this in addition to a personal observation of the features of Indians in the harbors of Genoa and Venice enabled me to draw my figures according to nature from genuine Indian models.

However, all these studies slightly influenced the externalities only of the whole series of pictures, for the knowledge obtained by detailed study had been covered to a remarkable extent at the beginning when I made my first sketches on the first inspiration. Still they have proved of great value to me since they gave me the assurance that historical fidelity has been preserved in my work.

MUNICH, BAVARIA.   OLGA KOPETZKY.